Exploring Nationalism

Other titles by Andrew Sangster in print with Pen & Sword Books

'Pug' – Churchill's Chief of Staff (2023)

How Hitler Evolved the Traditional Army Establishment
(with Pier Paolo Battistelli) (2024)

Hitler's New Command Structure and the Road to Defeat
(with Pier Paolo Battistelli) (2024)

Major Blunders of the Second World War (2024)

'Make Germany Great Again' (2024)

From Stalingrad to Italy – Von Senger's War (2025)

Why Appeasement Failed (2025)

Exploring Nationalism

Identifying its forms, particularly those which lead to War and Mayhem

Andrew Sangster

Pen & Sword
MILITARY

First published in Great Britain in 2025 by
Pen & Sword Military
An imprint of Pen & Sword Books Limited
Yorkshire – Philadelphia

Copyright © Pen & Sword Books Limited 2025

ISBN 978 1 03613 091 6

The right of Andrew Sangster to be identified as
Author of this Work has been asserted by him in accordance
with the Copyright, Designs and Patents Act 1988.

A CIP catalogue record for this book is
available from the British Library.

All rights reserved. No part of this book may be reproduced, transmitted, downloaded, decompiled or reverse engineered in any form or by any means, electronic or mechanical including photocopying, recording or by any information storage and retrieval system, without permission from the Publisher in writing. NO AI TRAINING: Without in any way limiting the Author's and Publisher's exclusive rights under copyright, any use of this publication to "train" generative artificial intelligence (AI) technologies to generate text is expressly prohibited. The Author and Publisher reserve all rights to license uses of this work for generative AI training and development of machine learning language models.

Typeset by Mac Style
Printed in the UK by CPI Group (UK) Ltd, Croydon, CR0 4YY.

MIX
Paper | Supporting
responsible forestry
FSC® C013604

The Publisher's authorised representative in the EU for product safety is Authorised Rep Compliance Ltd., Ground Floor, 71 Lower Baggot Street, Dublin D02 P593, Ireland.
www.arccompliance.com

For a complete list of Pen & Sword titles please contact

PEN & SWORD BOOKS LIMITED
47 Church Street, Barnsley, South Yorkshire, S70 2AS, England
E-mail: enquiries@pen-and-sword.co.uk
Website: www.pen-and-sword.co.uk
or
PEN AND SWORD BOOKS
1950 Lawrence Road, Havertown, PA 19083, USA
E-mail: uspen-and-sword@casematepublishers.com
Website: www.penandswordbooks.com

Contents

Acknowledgements	vii
Preface	viii
Foreword	ix
Brief Introduction	xi

Chapter 1	**Nature of Nationalism**	1
Nationalism or Patriotism		1
Concept of a Nation		4
Influence of Language		6
Ethnic Problems		9
Anti-Semitism in Europe		11
Influence of Religious Faith and Cultures		14
Greed for Territory, Wealth, and Power		17
Chapter 2	**From Caves to Nations**	20
From Cavemen Onwards		20
Tribes		22
Developing Power Centres		28
The Dark Ages		31
The Developing Nation		33
More Nationalistic Ingredients		36
Chapter 3	**Europe Takes Shape**	43
Features of Fourteenth to Seventeenth Centuries		43
The Renaissance		49
The Reformation involving Nationalism		50
Eighteenth Century and Beginning of Colonialism		53
A Brief Overview of Europe		54
Europe and its Expansion in Colonies		60
A Cross-Slice of European Aggressive Nationalism		62
The Time of Revolution		66

Chapter 4	The Nineteenth Century	74
Introduction		74
Colonialism Continues		78
State of Europe		80
Political Changes		83
Nationalism into the Modern Era		85
Survey of European Nations		87

Chapter 5	The Twentieth Century	100
Introduction		100
The First World War and Consequences		101
Interbellum Years		105
Nationalism during Interbellum Years		113
The Second World War		119
Immediate Postwar Years		129
After the Second World War		130

Chapter 6	The Modern Era	136
Survey of European Postwar Politics		136
A Unified Europe		138
Eastern Europe		140
The Cold War		144
1989–91 Significant Change in Soviet Russia		146
Unresolved Aggressive Nationalism		148
Holding the Peace		151

Chapter 7	Observations on Recent Years	156

Final Thoughts	177
Notes	182
Bibliography	187
Index	189

Acknowledgements

Over the years I have been very grateful to those who work and administer the various archives, and for the work of fellow historians with their various insights and perceptions.

However, I am exceptionally grateful to my wife, Carol Ann, for her incredible patience as I disappear into archives and rarely emerge from my study. I am also grateful for the support and encouragement of my friend and colleague the Revd Dr Canon Peter Doll, Vice-Dean of Norwich Cathedral.

The Revd Dr Andrew Sangster

Preface

As a lifetime student of European history and having written some twenty plus books on various aspects on this subject, it dawned on the writer that most of our history always involves friction leading to conflict and war. There were always several reasons for each and every conflict, but one major thread remained constant, namely the nature of aggressive Nationalism and its constant role in bringing mayhem and destruction between different communities. The Jewish historian Zimmermann stated in an interview that history is more than telling a story, because a historian needs to infer from the past about the present. Aggressive nationalism is a major characteristic of our history as a human race, and the trouble is that we ignore the lessons of history and the nature of human conduct.

Its primary seeds may be traced back to the earliest of times because it is part of humankind's nature. To make this case-study it was necessary to make a broad sweep with the historical brush of European history, using Norman Davies's *Europe a History* as the guide in seeking the earliest signs of nationalism to the twentieth century. The next step was to move from the historical focus to the current day when Europe's significant role became less significant with the rise of the superpowers. It will undoubtedly be the case that this study will be challenged and seen as contentious, not least by an historian stepping from historical research into current day issues, always bearing in mind our failure to learn from history.

Foreword

By The Revd Canon Dr Peter Doll

Andrew Sangster is a prolific historian, and in recent works like *Blind Obedience and Denial* and *From Plato to Putin* he has struck a rich vein of reflection on the place of morality in human events and history. In this book, which he begins with an exploration of the earliest evidence of human instincts and motivations, he rightly challenges the common historiographic assumption that nationalism emerged only in the wake of the French Revolution. What became known as nationalism has expressed itself throughout history in many forms, from the benign desire to avoid cultural homogenisation to the murderous determination to eliminate those who are 'other' than ourselves, but it has consistently been expressed through language, culture, religion, ethnicity, power, and territoriality.

In explicitly finding the origin of nationalism in the behaviour of 'cavemen' and primitive tribalism, Dr Sangster pulls no punches. When it comes to the expression of nationalism there is little evidence of 'progress' in history or even of the suppression of humankind's most brutal instincts. In the twenty-first century governments may sometimes justify military action on the basis of humanitarian protection of the weak and the vulnerable (as in the war against Iraq in 2003), but more often than not such claims are only a mask for more self-interested motivations.

It is not to say that humankind's moral and ethical structures have failed to recognise the dangers inherent in our nationalist instincts. The tenth of the Ten Commandments (from some time in the mid-second millennium BC), 'Thou shalt not covet', recognised that the human desire for what belongs to another is destructive of a peaceful and just society. It is symptomatic of the paradoxes of human nature that the same religious instincts that provided the desire to mitigate our malign behaviours have also encouraged some of the most destructive expressions of nationalism, as in the current support of the Russian Orthodox Church for the war on Ukraine.

The second half of the twentieth century was marked by an international determination to avert and neutralise the European nationalism which had brought so much death and destruction to the world. The nations had to learn the lessons of the terrible world wars. The United Nations and the institutions which came to form the European Union would prevent the re-emergence of virulent national hatreds and rivalries. To some extent they succeeded. The fall of the Iron Curtain in 1989 and the re-unification of Germany marked a high point of optimism and hope for the future. That potential was squandered, however, and our own day is marked by the resurgence of right-wing nationalism all across Europe; we can only guess where such developments may lead.

The same period also marked the high point of the recognition of 'human rights' as a foundational principle of the global community. Recent historians, including Tom Holland, have however pointed out that notions of 'human rights' are by no means common to all times and cultures but have emerged specifically from the Jewish and Christian teaching that every human being is created by God in his own image and likeness. It is only in this light that humans can make any claim to equality with one another, to an equal dignity and right of respect, but it is fundamentally this equality that aggressive nationalism denies in favour of the superiority of 'my tribe' and 'my leader'. At a time when the Christian tradition is losing its hold on the imagination and loyalty of Europeans, it is no coincidence that the bonds of international and community cohesion should also be fracturing in the face of resurgent nationalism. Dr Sangster's book is a clarion reminder of what human beings do to one another when we fail to heed what President Lincoln called 'the better angels of our nature'.

Brief Introduction

This book is a study of 'Nationalism' which has many shades of meaning depending on the adjectives attempting to give it a more precise definition within different historical contexts. The book begins with the critical understanding that patriotism and nationalism are often confused as the same concept when they represent different aspects of human emotions and conduct.

Some aspects of nationalism are more acceptable or understandable than others, and these differences need to be monitored. The most dangerous form of nationalism is known as aggressive, and often linked with expansive nationalism. Aggressive nationalism is when one country invades another either for its resources, territory, or power, often based on some perceived or alleged excuse. The terms aggressive and expansionist in the context of nationalism are often interchangeable. Linked to this is irredentist nationalism (sometimes referred to as revanchism) when a country fights to reclaim land which it once owned, and which can invoke some sympathy, explaining to a degree how Hitler at the Munich conference managed to take back the Sudetenland without bloodshed as the world wanted peace. Other powers had recognised some justification in Hitler's claims, not realising they were dealing with a man obsessed with aggressive nationalism. There is isolationist nationalism when a country cuts itself off not wanting much to do with its neighbours, which tends to be more negative than positive, and the book will indicate this happening in the USA during the 1918–39 interbellum years, reflected again during President Trump's time in office, and also in Britain following the Brexit debate. It also reflects countries which are well-known for attempting to stay neutral, most notably Switzerland and Sweden. One form of nationalism which many find the more acceptable is secessionist nationalism in which a nation attempts to free itself of domination or occupation by another.

Some refer to revisionist nationalism linked closely with revisionist history where the past is examined closely for aspects of lost tradition, and culture and language are pushed to the fore to re-establish a national identity, which was recognisable in the Slavic drive to establish themselves as an identifiable entity. There was also a form of cultural nationalism, mainly studied by intellectuals who were trying to define their nation's culture, sometimes described as romantic nationalism, which seemed safe enough, but was often close to revisionist nationalism as a country tried to find its identity in order to free itself from another's domination. This has possible links to unification nationalism, which is bringing regions together, some by healing wounds from the past, claiming a common culture, but others using a degree of threat and force. At the lower end of the selected spectrum is banal nationalism which is difficult to define with accuracy. For this writer it finds the best description as patriotism taken to extremes when supporters of a national sports team lead to stupid confrontations between the fans, often seen in football hooliganism.

Later a form of what is best described as internal political nationalism emerged when the ruling elite held their own views of how its nation should develop, and the growing number of the masses, the working population, held other views. It was often based on traditions maintained from the past clashing with the demand for a change in the social, economic, and political structures of the country. The ruling elite of the day wanted to tighten their grip while others demanded changes which resulted or verged on revolution leading to the right and left-wing divide.

There are almost too many conjectured adjectives which can be applied, but this study focuses on some of the above as they occur, and it concentrates on aggressive and expansionist nationalism and the unfortunate ingredients which emerge when nationalism is deployed. These ingredients vary but often include ethnic and language bigotry, abuse of religious beliefs, a clashing of traditions, culture, and greed for more territory, wealth, and power. This study proposes that although most observers see nationalism as a modern phenomenon its seeds and ingredients can be found in humankind the moment that they left the sanctuary of their caves. A few historians have seen the early forms of nationalism, describing it as a prototype or archetype, but this study sees it as a human problem with its roots going back to the beginning of man as it is almost part of his genetic makeup. Humankind appeared at the start of known history as nomadic, seeking better pastures, with family and immediate neighbours becoming tribes of various shapes and sizes dependent upon warrior type leaders.

From this era the concept of the home country appeared, and the nation state soon followed. This study takes a broad sweep of the history of Europe from East to West, working through the centuries and various countries, the growth of empires and dynasties, looking at the way aggressive and expansionist nationalism played a major role, gathering more force as the larger states tried to extend their domination over others. As early as the fourteenth century Europe spilt across its borders with colonisation of distant lands, an aggressive expansionist form of nationalistic conflict across the oceans. It has often been argued that nationalism made its modern appearance in Napoleonic times, but it had always been a part of humankind's makeup. In the modern era, with its scientific and technological development leading to the twentieth century, came indications that aggressive nationalism with its hostile components led to devastating consequences of a global conflict for most of that century's duration.

This book's final chapters are a mixture of historical survey and current affairs as a survey across Europe, and the global superpowers. This study clearly indicates that although the era of peace had been anticipated following the self-destruction of the Soviet Union in 1989–90, neither Europe nor the world are free from nationalistic aggression, and perhaps with more dire consequences than any major medieval war. This book has no answers but tries to highlight the common causes of conflict in the aggressive elements of nationalism with the ongoing plea that we never learn from history.

Chapter One

Nature of Nationalism

Nationalism or Patriotism

There is a high degree of confusion between the words patriotism and nationalism, many people regarding them as words with identical meanings. George Orwell wrote that 'by patriotism I mean devotion to a particular place and a particular way of life, which one believes to be the best place in the world but has no wish to force it upon other people', [whereas]... 'nationalism, on the other hand is inseparable from the desire for power'.[1]

The confusion of these two words is not assisted by various dictionaries. Patriotism tends to be more associated with love of one's home country, or a form of empathy for the place where one was born and brought up. In supporting a national sports team this should be the epitome for the word patriotism, but there should be no demand that patriotism means one must be prepared to die for their country. However, the word is often exploited to this expectancy in many countries to this day, associating the word patriot with the need to fight for one's country. In the USA a patriot is often linked with veteran, the person has fought and prepared to fight again. In some dictionaries the same implication can arise, stating that it is love for one's country which demands vigorous support. This debate continues to this day, as nationalism and patriotism both involve love of one's homeland. It has also been argued that patriotism tends to be more emotional and passive whereas nationalism demands more. Patriots may see values in their homeland, in its geography, its culture, even in its political basis, but may agree that other countries are better, and their own homeland is not necessarily the paradise of existence, or that their country is always right.

The patriotic assumptions are sharpened by the word nationalism. For some nationalism is regarded as a good concept, for many it appears to open the gates of potential disaster. In an international football match the patriot might say on losing the game that the other side were better, or they played that game well. A nationalist might blame the referee claiming he was bribed or demand the home coach is instantly sacked. The subtle nuances between the two words becomes much more critical beyond the sports gates, when it involves the possibility of disagreement between two countries with the possibility of war. Lord Acton famously wrote that 'nationalism was both a modern development and a retrograde step in history, the spread of which would be marked with material as well as moral ruin'.[2] George Orwell, who wrote extensively on nationalism stated that 'by nationalism I mean first of all the habit of assuming that human beings can be classified like insects, and that whole blocks of millions or tens of millions of people can be confidently labelled good or bad. But secondly, and this is much more important, I mean the habit of identifying oneself with a single nation or other unit, placing it beyond good and evil and recognising no other duty than that of advancing its interest'. He wrote this indictment in 1945 after firsthand experiences in the Spanish Civil War and the Second World War. Returning to the confusion of dictionaries which have more recently identified nationalism with the sense of importance in the national consciousness as against other nations, and most interestingly the synonyms for patriotism are the same, but for nationalism the associated words of xenophobia and chauvinism have made an appearance. Patriotism tends to focus on affection and nationalism on a sense of national superiority, and its consequential entanglement often creating resentment. When one nation sees its neighbours as sub-human and itself as the master race this is nationalism in the extreme. This has led to many wars in the history of mankind, both in the distant past and to this day. When this book was being written the memories of the Great War, the Second World War are still recalled, and the problems today in the Ukraine and Middle East can be seen in the various shades of extreme nationalism. Nationalism is often on the lips of a country's leaders as they call for war to claim their country's rights which can be seen as a general tendency to regard 'nationalism as a kind of political disease'.[3]

On the other hand, it has been argued that nationalism should be regarded as 'a vivifying and inspiring force. It makes for national unity when it is genuine, and not merely a cloak for national ambitions'.[4] This is an idealistic viewpoint based more on the meaning of patriotism than nationalism and seems to ignore the lessons of the past. In any outline history of Europe, it can be interpreted that 'National States are themselves 'imagined communities:' they are built on powerful myths and on the political rewriting of history'.[5] Such a view may have some credibility, and it too often encourages a sense of extreme nationalism. Nationalism and patriotism may have much in common, but history tends to see nationalism as more negative because it thrives on antipathy. This source of nationalistic feeling involves many issues ranging from racism, religious faith, language, culture, thereby creating the element of 'them and us' and producing a perceived common enemy.

Nationalism and patriotism have much in common and considerable contention over their definition. Even Orwell looked at positive and negative nationalism and what he called transferred nationalism, which to use Orwell's language can be both positive and highly negative.[6] Unifying nationalism can bring regions and principalities into an identifiable state, which can involve secessionist nationalism, when it is deemed necessary for a nation to extricate itself from a powerful empire. In using the description of 'secessionist nationalism' Orwell underlines that there is a variety of different forms or types of nationalism, including secessionist, revisionist, irredentist, isolationist, aggressive, expansionist, banal. Many of them overlap and more will come to light. Hitler used many of them, the most acceptable for even some of his critics was irredentist nationalism which was the recovery of lost lands to a previous victor. He also deployed aggressive and expansionist nationalism thereby creating a major global war; had he stopped after reclaiming Germany's lost territories there may possibly have not been a global disaster. Perhaps the strangest form is isolationist nationalism when a neighbour decides to isolate itself, wanting nothing to do with their neighbours. President Trump in his first and now second presidency has always asserted nationalistic isolationism, and now in his current presidency (2025) there are distinct signs of aggressive nationalism. In the Paris Agreement of 2015, he withdrew American agreement on grounds of nationalist isolationism, making the problems of climate change even more dangerous. The USA had been isolationist after the First World War until the next war drove them into the conflict. Britain on leaving the European Union was declaring an isolationist policy. Isolationists frequently are often associated with the right-wing elements who 'tend to care far less about things like pollution and endangered species than left-wing progressives'.[7] These forms of nationalism are like the various and many shades of one colour. If, for example, secessionist nationalism releases a country from the clutches of a powerful neighbour this would be seen in a more favourable light than the aggressive and expansionist versions. To try and understand the ways these forms of nationalism emerged with some having dangerous consequences for the community of nations, it will be necessary to take a broad view of historical events and incidents in European history. Nationalism does not have a starting point, though some have pointed to the Napoleonic era, but its origins may be traced further back. The Jewish writer Harari wrote that 'nationalism too upholds a linear story' and is correct so far that roots go deep into human history.[8] Nationalism describes an attitude or political stance taken by people which reflects a propensity built into many human beings from the start of recorded history if not beyond.

Nationalism is not the product of one country nor of one continent and is now a global issue, but this book will focus on European history relating to other areas of the globe when necessary, and more so later with the appearance of the superpower era. However, Europe is significant because of the huge number of small and large nations living in a complex jigsaw pattern. It has been argued that 'the emergence of the European nation state is commonly seen to depend on three connected processes of centralisation: the emergence of supralocal identities and cultures (the nation), the rise of powerful and authoritative institutions within the public domain (the State); and the development of particular ways of organising production and consumption (the economy)'.[9] It has also been noted that because Europe is a conglomeration of close neighbouring nations, it must be recalled that 'Europe cannot be seen as a model of future developments in the world, but rather as a historical instance of global processes that affect the entire world'.[10]

Concept of a Nation

The word nationalism by its very nature is descriptive of an entity called a nation and is associated with attitudes and policies prevalent in any one country. However, it is the contention of this study that the impulses, the motivations, and intentions behind the various shades of nationalism have deeper roots in history than most historians allow. It could be argued that nations evolved from tribes into what may be called pre-states or pre-nations all in a picture of a forming embryo and at various times. Nationalism had its embryonic roots deep in humankind's distant past, almost part of his genetic makeup, with its 'seeds and ingredients'. This is detectable in man's nature as early as the suspicious caveman seeing strangers in his assumed territory, or preferring their valley, followed by forming tribes to capture the new territory thereby starting the process of creating their own country, then onto nation status.

In European history, even by the middle of the thirteenth century, there was no clear sense of nationhood in terms of the modern pattern. There were provinces, cities, as for example in Spain there were kingdoms and dynasties but no singular unified Spain. Italy and the modern Germany were very much in the same mould. England did exist, but it had greater connections with the European mainland in places such as Gascony and Aquitaine, than it did with its immediate neighbours the Welsh, Irish, and Scots. The sense of associating an area of territory or assuming ownership of a parcel of land was a mental attitude like animals having their sense of territory. This holding or ownership of a portion of land under its given name signalled the early growth of nation development. This emerged because people identified themselves with their territory in which they were bred and raised and became their home. It was usually the result of nomadic tribal invasions adopting the original inhabitants who had to adapt themselves to the newcomers, often with some initial friction. This created the sense of belonging which took on both political and emotional feelings which were the growing seeds and ingredients of both patriotism and nationalism, not that this would have been recognised at the time.

Frequently a newly forming stronghold or nation was controlled by the dominant military leaders who became the powerful and rich, and for whom it was their province, territory, or lands, and not a country in the modern understanding of the word. However, it could be argued that it was becoming recognisable as a country, or at least a precursor of the modern concept. For example, Portugal controlled the western coast of the Iberian Peninsula and had been independent since 1179, and it could be recognised as a forming nation. It was during the late fifteenth century that Pope Alexander VI agreed to Spanish and Portuguese insistence that he formally delineated the border between the two countries, and at this juncture it could be assumed there was a growing sense of nationhood. There was no discernible pattern, but similar developments occurred. When the Netherlands had isolated itself from Spanish domination with its determined sense of secessionist nationalism it became a formidable maritime power, developing its own governance and could claim to be taking the form of a modern state.

From the vexed year of '1848 onwards, nationalism was a major driving force in European politics', with a gathering organisation of political parties and single-issue groups, with mass communication possibilities becoming a characteristic of this period.[11] As such, by the mid-nineteenth century the map of Europe was dominated by polyglot dynastic states of the Habsburgs, Romanovs, Hohenzollerns and Ottoman structures. During this period nationalism was a matter of attempting to unify regions and fragments of territory into a single nation, a period which has been described as unification nationalism.

There were other factors important in determining a country, not least a common law for a region or nation, as in Spain which tried to codify its laws, and notably Henry II of England who created the common law much of which later spread worldwide. The Roman Empire had been able to thrive with its sense of law over huge swathes of territory, and the Emperor Justinian (527–65), was widely known for the codification of Roman law, and thereby tried to re-assert his control over the West. Commerce and trade were also critical features, but the main impulse for nationhood came from the dynastic ruling houses through inter-marriage, complex diplomacy, and war.

From well before the seventeenth century there were many definable nations even if despots ran them, benevolent or otherwise, and in taking their populations to war, it was frequently done under the banner of nationalism. This aggressive nationalism dictated by the leaders, proposed to those who were fighting for the cause the reasons they should be prepared to make the final sacrifice, namely for their kith and kin, and loyalty to their leader who represented their nation.

The defining of a nation from regions and cities took a long time, with major countries such as Germany and Italy being late on the scene of nationhood.

The formation of larger groups for reasons of safety and survival, led to those generations who were competing for trade and resources. Aristotle had once 'observed that humans were animals because of their biological drive to reproduce and preserve themselves'.[12] This ancient philosopher also noted that humans had brains and minds which can foresee a future. These impulses revolved around the inbuilt natural need for survival which was stronger in some than others. It has been claimed by the historian O'Brien that when there is a war it is 'essentially one of self-determination by a Darwinian process of armed conflict'.[13] The reference to Darwinism is sometimes used to explain why humanity behaves in such ways, implying it is ingrained in their nature and their evolution, though many religious and philosophical thinkers might disagree. The binding influences came not just from the rulers of the time and the need for survival, but many other factors including the language they spoke.

Influence of Language

The individual can claim his neighbour speaks a different language, looks different, was born elsewhere, has different gods, and like me he is a member of humanity and if he does not harm me all is well. Another person will be suspicious of a person who speaks in another language, looks different, was born in another land, and believes another person's religion is wrong. The human tendency is often to see the other as a distinct threat against his territory and decide attack is the best form of defence. Language can be a significant barrier between people because it seems that the strangers are speaking in their own code, creating a sense of suspicion. Language can be used as a tool, as when Joseph Stalin would talk to his henchman from Georgia his head of the NKVD (KGB), Lavrenty Beria so other comrades could not follow, thereby creating a 'them and us' situation even within the same grouping.

The bond of language went back to the beginning of known history, and it has been noted that 'the tribal map is, therefore, essentially a linguistic map', which has left its mark on modern thinking.[14] It has also been argued that 'the old idea that language is necessarily linked to race has been discredited. Languages can be easily transferred from one racial group to another'.[15] There is validity in this argument, but the fact remains that language and the ignorance of what is being said creates a barrier by raising mutual suspicion. The use of a common language is believed to bind people together, and as Bede in his *Ecclesiastical History of the English People* (c.730) wrote 'tribes and stock are held together' by their ethnic bonds, and language is frequently one of the critical determinants in the question of ethnicity.

Nor is language merely a tribal feature but surfaced throughout history into the twentieth century during the 1912 Balkan War and remained an issue in the same area eighty years later. Chadwick observed language breeds a sense of kinship, and although a nation does not mean one language, it is often true that 'the sense that nationality is determined by language'.[16] In the proposed survey of Europe's history in this study, the sense of Pan-Slavism will be mentioned as it helped identify a grouping of peoples. The Slovaks as they considered their future started to demand that their language should be used as a sign of their nationalistic intent, and some Czech intellectuals during the latter part of the eighteenth century felt the same way. The nature of language was never far from the surface, especially when it was deemed essential to ease the spread of Germanic or Russian influence.

As the migratory tribes settled, taking control of their assumed personal territories, and safely sheltered within their borders, frequently delineated by geographical barriers of water and mountains, their language took on its own features. It was never an easy process as the language of the new occupier was not always welcome. In Wales they never let go of their original language and it survives today, and the same attitude of keeping their original language can be found in both Scotland and Ireland, and for these peoples it is more than an intellectual or cultural exercise but for many a political statement of their nationhood. Linguistic experts delight in finding the commonality of all languages which over the generations have changed so much, but another person's language remains another race's code. It is part of the human dilemma that language differences create the inclination to regard another language as belonging to an alien people and therefore a potential enemy. Even within the same country dialect can often be used to detect social classes which can also be responsible for a sense of alienation. The various languages of the world are seen by many as shrouded in mystery and in 1866 the Linguistic Society of Paris decided to ban future debates because it was so hopeless. The aetiological Old Testament story of the Tower of Babel was the earliest attempt to explain it as a form of God's punishment and the problem has puzzled humanity for thousands of years.[17] There is no doubt that language can prove to be a barrier between people because of the fear they are in code-mode, often causing serious alienation.

In Europe there were forty to fifty languages spoken, some differing only slightly, and some evaporating. In terms of distinct languages, it is now not less than forty. The historian Munro Chadwick in 1945 drew a map of Europe indicating the influences of seven major families of languages. These included the Altaic (or Turco-Tataric) family, the Baltic group, Celtic, Finnic (or Urgo-Finnic family), Romance grouping (Latin), the Slavonic and finally the Teutonic group. It is a complex study but still sadly true that language creates barriers, even though 'the old idea that language is necessarily linked to race has been discredited'.[18] Language changes with a generation, new idioms, new words and dictionaries always have to be updated, but language causes suspicion and distrust to this day.

The English language belongs to the *Teutonic* family which has three categories. At one stage the Frisian dialects may have been understood by the early English speakers. The second strand was Dutch and German, both with dialectic lines, the most well-known was what was called Low and High German. Chadwick noted that the 'growth of the feeling for nationality in Germany was due in the first place to the current of thought, and then, more especially, to the disturbance caused by the French wars of aggression', this national movement was bound up with High German.[19] Language is a binding element within different groups and areas whether they were tribes or the nations of today. In some countries there are two languages, in Wales this is the case, and in Belgium both French and Flemish speakers have the equal rights as citizens, and it is the same in Switzerland. Nevertheless, there are undeniable tensions in Belgium. The third element of the Teutonic groups within the north-eastern part of Europe are the Swedish, Norwegian, and Icelandic strands.

Strangely, the Basque language appears quite isolated from other family groupings with no obvious connection to other languages. Chadwick suggested that it may well have been connected to the original Iberian language, but it has, like the Basque area, played little part in European history.[20] As a matter of historical curiosity, it has also been indicated that Basque DNA has its own distinctive traits. Some of the European languages are just as old, and their origin lost to human memory. In terms of European history, the three groups of Latin (Romance), Teutonic and Slavonic languages are the important strands, and it is the Latin element which carries the most available information.

Language has proved a formidable barrier creating moments of alienation, even to this day as modern immigrants settle into their adopted countries. Many of the established host communities resent hearing another language, and there have been governmental demands that the nation's language should become a citizen's test. It is a widely held belief that a person's nationality is determined by language.

Where different countries have languages which are either in common or closely linked, it creates a sense of kinship. This is certainly the case in the Scandinavian countries, amongst the Slavs of Eastern Europe, and helps Britain with the USA link. The expert in this field, Chadwick, suggested there was a

Pan-Latinism, and this was used for political motivation. Mussolini and others looked to Rome and Italy as the rightful powerhouse of the Mediterranean scene. The medieval writer Dante 'had already discussed the possibility of a standard written language' but it was the time of printing which gave this dream any chance of realisation.[21] Regional language was often regarded as impure, whereas standardised languages appeared to be prestigious. This emerged in places as a linguistic pride, and much later even to linguistic xenophobia leading to 'Franglais' with the French complaining of too many English words in their language. In Britain, Oxford or BBC English was seen as the norm for many years. Dialects divide people by raising suspicion, and during the Irish problems of the late twentieth century border control guards were adept at listening to dialect to detect if the speaker were Southern or Northern Irish, and thereby possibly Protestant or Catholic. It has been noted that 'Whether or not a written vernacular is necessary to the development of a nation, there can be little doubt that it stimulates national pride and helps form a national identity'.[22] However, it can be used as a means of stirring up suspicion between neighbours in the same country, and other countries. It is entirely irrational, but the fact continues that for many people language can be barrier building producing the 'them and us' attitude. It is one of the major factors which surfaces in the understanding of nationalism, as it can be used to stir up suspicion and hatred against perceived enemies.

Ethnic Problems

It was not just language which defined groups, but traditions, customs, ways of life and ethnicity, even the colour of one's skin, hair, and eyes. The most aggressive side of nationalism originated from this issue, still asserting itself with the Nazi belief in Aryan superiority. It was purported by Nazi theories that a true Aryan had fair hair and blue eyes, none of which the Nazi political leaders could claim. After a time when various tribes settled there was a mixing of peoples with intermarriage becoming common, and it needs a DNA test to find the truth of any individual's background. These tests have recently become open to the public, and one of this writer's friends who always considered himself in Tony Hancock's words as 'Anglo-Saxon with a dash of Viking' has discovered he is a mixed variety of Nordic, Saxon/Celtic, Latin, Asian and African DNA.

A pseudo-scientific racialism emerged which tried to provide theories for believing in a caste system of races ranked in superiority, but modern science has announced that racial differentials have no genetic significance. As early as 1758 the Swedish botanist Carolus Linnaeus tried to subdivide the human species into biological based races. In 1869 the English Francis Galton devised a sixteen-point scale of racial intelligence. As noted by one academic, 'In its most extreme forms, hostility to racial anarchy produced discrimination, segregation, persecution, expulsion, and, ultimately, attempted annihilation', especially in recent human history.[23] This racial attitude was not just a German trait as is often claimed based on Nazi behaviour, but globally widespread. Feeling superior because of racial background is characteristic of humankind. Some Germans believed the French were inferior and the Austro-Hungarians developed similar attitudes towards the Slavs, while the English often saw themselves as superior to anyone else. In the 1720s a Swiss visitor, César de Saussure, noted this bigoted chauvinism claiming, 'I do not think there is a people more prejudiced in its own favour than the British people'.[24] Europe has always been made up of significant ethnic minorities many of whom suffer simply because of who and what they are. During the interbellum years of 1918–1939 the Czech and Polish issue focused on whether ethnic minorities were allowed to play any part in the governmental structure, causing a serious degree of animosity. To this day skin colour has remained a significant issue with apartheid of one sort or another in many parts of the world. In Britain colour prejudice was epitomised by the influx of families from the West Indies post Second World War, which led to unimaginable friction between next door neighbours.

When for political or historical reasons reference is made to the Slavs, Teutons, Jutes, Latins, and Anglo-Saxons there is always a distinct link with the tribal background of humankind. This was the warning sign of an aggressive form of nationalism which would have disastrous effects upon humanity, in which the colour of nationalism became ugly, and it emerged in its various hues across Europe, the ingrained problem of ethnicity.

It is now believed that humanity is just one strain and not different breeds, and genetical differences are extremely limited with racial differences being no more than a matter of climate. Nevertheless, humans have this ongoing propensity to attach importance to these minor differences. The ancient map of Europe reveals a patchwork of ethnic groupings, some large enough to form their own nation states. Before the Great War there had been controlled population movements, most especially in the Balkans with Turks, Greeks, Serbs, and Bulgarians, where 'such exchanges were designed to transform regions of ethnically mixed settlement into the homogenous societies that so appealed to the nationalist imagination'.[25] As a consequence of these political adjustments the Greek population of Western Thrace fell by 89 per cent, and the Muslim population of Eastern Thrace rose by a third. The implications were 'distinctly ominous for the many multi-ethnic communities elsewhere in Europe'.[26] After the First World War 'in the new Czechoslovakia, for example, 51 per cent of the population were Czechs, 16 per cent Slovaks, twenty-two per cent German, 5 per cent Hungarians, and 4 per cent Ukrainians'.[27] This was a common feature across Central and Eastern Europe, and because of human nature it led to conflict.

The concept of belief in the new modern state is still tarnished by humankind's inclination to want to be of one race, no longer a tribal instinct, but often amounting to racism which is dangerously contagious. Human divisiveness has been present throughout the history of Europe and remains a 'pressing anthropological and philosophical puzzle as to why humans often organise themselves divisively into various forms of kinship, of which the nation is one example'.[28] The French diplomat Arthur de Gobineau (1816–82) argued that mankind was divided by races and thereby culture, and claimed he saw a decline of civilisation by this inclination. He was undeniably correct in his views, but for many people the word 'civilisation' related to fine art, architecture, music, luxury, laws, and polite social behaviour. For de Gobineau civilisation was more than this, implying moral attitudes, respect, and dignity. It remains a feature of life to this day, and this writer recalls the shocking news of the politician Enoch Powell's talk in 1968 dubbed the *Rivers of Blood* speech, not because Powell was a politician from whom such behaviour often originates, but because Powell was regarded as something of a Christian New Testament scholar. There was an ingrained bigotry against people with different skin colours which still persists in many places.

Anti-Semitism in Europe

In Europe a major form of racism was anti-Semitism which has a history going back over a thousand years and more (even blaming them for the Black Death) and it has erupted to one level of barbarity or another in every European nation. Anti-Semitism has ranged from excluding Jews from golf clubs, officer ranks, to national exclusion and finally extermination. The long vicious Russian pogroms against Jews was the main driving force for the Jewish move westwards. These racial attacks were constant and vicious, but anti-Semitism reached its lowest depths during the Holocaust.

There have been constant debates as to whether the Russian pogrom was Tsarist inspired or state controlled, but studies indicate it was generally a popularist movement which gained impetus following the assassination of Tsar Alexander II in 1881. In today's corporate mind it is more often associated with Hitler's obsession against Jews because he took it to the lowest possible depths, but in reality, he exploited what was already in existence. There was the well-known Jewish diaspora and most of them eked out a living as ethnic minorities wherever they lived, many using their skills and education to join the professions, and they appeared astute and gifted in financial circles causing unwarranted jealousy.

The French writer Alphonse Toussenel (1840s) who leaned towards the left-wing described Jewish financiers as the new form of feudalism, but this criticism rapidly descended to calling them parasites. In Germany, an Otto Böckel referred to them as the 'Kings of Our Time' (1886) but attacking their financial acumen. By the turn of the century, it was not just their economic ability which was causing resentment and jealously, but because they were becoming phenomenally successful in most of the professions. Their wealth was resented, and it is 'noteworthy that 31 per cent of the richest families in Germany were Jewish and 22 per cent of all Prussian millionaires'.[29] This along with their dominance in the professions caused a degree of resentment amongst many who had not achieved such status. This economic and professional jealousy prompted a German Catholic magazine called *Germania* to issue the warning 'don't buy from Jews' (1876), and in the late 1870s an anti-Semitic priest called Adolf Stoecker demanded Jews should be excluded from the teaching and legal professions.

As noted, anti-Semitism was not invented by Hitler, but for centuries had criss-crossed Europe. The Nazis exploited this immoral attitude by defining the Jew in pseudo-science, measuring skulls, shapes of noses and any other configuration, which they believed would give credence to their propaganda that Jews were sub-human. This was the infamous Nazi racial policy which deeply scarred European history. The Nazi attitude of racism was not confined to the Jewish race but extended to Slavs. In so doing it created its own form of aggressive and brutal nationalism, by making the claim that as sub-humans they were not part of humanity, namely 'not one of us'.

The Nazis produced an organised effort of total annihilation of European Jewry which will never be forgotten. Curiously, there were in fact few European countries in the world where ethnic minorities were less of a problem than in Germany after the First World War. There were fewer than 503,000 Jews in Germany in 1933, a tiny 0.76 per cent of population, and the number had been falling steadily since the war as a result of a striking decline in the Jewish birthrate to roughly half that of the rest of the population.[30] This did not mean that all Germans were anti-Semitic, albeit widespread because of Joseph Goebbels's propaganda, but the Nazis turned it into a powerful weapon by sheer barbarity.

This Nazi policy also turned against the Sinti and Roma, having first initiated *Aktion T-4* to eliminate the mentally handicapped, to ensure through a eugenic policy the Aryan race was pure. It was observed by Sebastian Haffner in 1940 (a liberal journalist) that none of this was new, but 'was an attempt to deny humans the solidarity of every species that enable it to survive; to turn human predatory instincts, that are normally directed against animals, against members of their own species, and to make a whole nation into a pack of hunting hounds'.[31]

It proved a difficult task for the persecuted German Jew to find refuge in other countries, the USA having introduced immigration quotas during the 1920s, which was followed by British Commonwealth countries such as South Africa, Canada, Australia, and New Zealand. 'Racial prejudice also played a key role in identifying Jews (along with Southern Italians) as immigrants inferior to previous generations from the British Isles, Germany or Scandinavia'.[32] These prejudices were primitive in the history of humanity but emerged with a vengeance again in the twentieth century, all part of the ingredients which stirred up aggressive nationalism and a hatred for other human beings.

This Nazi racial programme soon became known to the wider world, and the evil is encapsulated in the one word 'Holocaust'. It was the systematic campaign of racial annihilation focusing on Jews, and what the Nazis considered as other sub-human elements (*untermenschen*). This included Russian PoWS and Slavs who showed any opposition. The Nazis must have known how other nations would have viewed their policy, and it was deliberately subdued during the 1936 Berlin Olympics trying to keep this barbarity below the surface. It was the same concern of poor publicity they feared from their euthanasia plan to eliminate people with disabilities, but it was so shocking it took little time to be known internationally, but like the Holocaust was so shocking many people refused to believe the rumours. The Holocaust was a policy of total annihilation systematically and efficiently carried out in extermination camps plus thousands of massacres such as Babi Yar near Kiev. Names such as Eichmann, Himmler, Auschwitz, Chelmno, Sobibór, Zyklon-B gas and the Final Solution are familiar to this day because of the sheer unimaginable sense of terror. It was so evil that postwar it was almost put to one side, and it was not until the 1960s that the Holocaust was studied leading to widespread reading. It has been proposed that the initial plan to exterminate the European Jews may have been 65 per cent achieved, with new legal expressions such as genocide and crimes against humanity being devised and which is now common linguistic currency. Even Europe's most historical barbaric leaders would have been shocked by this behaviour in the twentieth century. Poland had once been a refuge for Jews, albeit with its own anti-Semitic tendencies, and many had fled to that country only to be exterminated under the German policy. The reasons and causes have long been studied, because it raises questions of man's inhumanity and depravity, with its racial and ethnic bigotry persisting to this day. This major criminal and immoral scenario raises fundamental questions about the lack of morality regarding extreme or racial nationalism. The well-known Italian survivor Primo Levi (1919–1987) despite his suffering and lifetime thinking on this issue said he could not think of a single reason for this barbarity. In this he was correct, and despite volumes of studies Primo Levi's comment remains firm with the reasons for this barbarity still elusive.

On 2 February 2019 the headlines in France were about demonstrations against anti-Semitism in that country where a Jewish graveyard had been desecrated; in Germany during late May of the same year, the Minister of Justice informed the public that hate crimes and personal aggression against Jews was rising; and in Britain the Labour Party was losing MPs in a breakaway group on the same issue. Today as this work is being written (2024) the state of Israel is fighting in Gaza and anti-Semitism is reaching new heights again. The problem is that in what should be a protest about war or the behaviour of a particular state, Jewish people are being attacked making it anti-Semitism despite the warnings of the past. Racism of any kind has always been a major tool used by aggressive nationalism to stir up action.

Influence of Religious Faith and Cultures

During the eighteenth and nineteenth centuries nations further defined their territories, nearly always bound up with their language and race thereby creating divisions with neighbouring countries. There were many other factors such as religious beliefs and overall culture. Each and every ethnic group from the earliest of times had its own customs and a different way of living daily lives. The homes they built, their clothes, the way they cooked, their attitude towards their elderly were often different. Archaeologists often use their burial traditions to trace ancient movements, and today tourists travel to see how 'the others live'. The response is sometimes one of awe and at other times disdainful. The 'them and us' can still influence a person's attitude towards others, even in exploring other people's living habits and customs.

However, even more contentious is the issue of religion, and nationalism has all too often recruited religious belief to provide a justification for crusades and converting others, and usually for reasons of wealth and territory, indicating aggressive and expansionist nationalism. Most European countries have a history of using religion as a tool for national identity and for aggression against others.

In Russia the focal point tended to be the Church and the Tsar (Russia was often called Holy Russia) with their early conflicts tending to be against Catholics and Muslims. The continuous struggle between the emerging nations was consistent and frequently used religion for stirring up feelings and for justification. It was sadly the case that language and religious faith became entwined as essential components for rallying one side against another. The conflict of language and religion was epitomised recently in the onetime nation of

Yugoslavia during the 1990s. Chadwick in 1945 wrote that 'no nation in Europe has encountered greater difficulties in attaining to its unification than that of the Yugoslavs', and fifty years after he wrote this, there ensued a bitter conflict in that country as the tensions spilt over using language, race, and religious belief as an impetus (1990–2001). This Balkan war came as a shock at the end of the twentieth century, but in many ways, it had started with the first Balkan war in 1912, and language and religious differences remained a problem.

Nationalism is often regarded as relating to nations which took time to form, but such roots as religious faith and racial issues are ancient and from the earliest of times the ingredients typical of nationalism can be identified within tribal structures, and they were used throughout the medieval period for the excuse of nationalistic-type expansionism. It has been argued that a modern national society is defined in secular terms and is dependent on the marginalisation of religion, namely secularisation. During the twentieth century there is evidence of the 'unchurching' of Europe, yet Christian Democratic parties are still important. However, it may be argued 'that both nationalism and religion are modern transformations of pre-modern traditions and identities…but deeper than proto-nationalism that precedes nationalism, there are ancient understandings of linguistic, religious, and ethnic unity, coupled with notions of territorial sovereignty, that can be found amongst the ancient Hebrews, Greeks, Indians and Chinese'.[33] Religion is a sensitive and complex subject, and is best regarded as influencing nationalism as a 'modern force that shapes and is shaped by important available symbolic traditions, be they religious, ethnic or regional', but from a distant past.[34]

In the Old Testament the Yahweh of Israel and the Chemosh of Moab were worshipped as territorial gods, thereby unifying their people. For the Jewish people Yahweh was the monotheistic God who justified the occupation of their land, calling themselves the Chosen People in the land flowing with milk and honey. In projecting this view of the divine they set themselves apart from their neighbours as a superior country. This special association with a deity has been a characteristic to modern times, be it the Catholic support in Poland, Tsarist Russia calling itself Holy Russia, or the recent proclamation (2019) that the Ukrainian Orthodox Church is independent of the Russian variation. The Deity was often regarded as the power of the people and their nation. This produced many traditions, as for example in the Orthodox Church, claiming the Virgin Mary fought against the Persians in their attack on Constantinople, in the same way as the Poles claimed a similar miraculous incident when they were under attack from the Swedes. Divine protection and sympathy can be quite recent as the appearance of the Angel of Mons indicated in the Great War.

Nations in a state of war have frequently made the claim that God was on their side, choosing their patron saints to represent their claims. The phrase

Gott mit uns (God with us) was used in Prussia since 1701 and appeared on German belt-buckles between 1871–1918, later used by the Nazi regime (1933–1945) and in West Germany from 1949 to 1962. There was nothing new in this assumption, Roman Emperors had deified themselves, supporters of the English King Charles I regarded him as a martyr, and the history of Europe is packed tight with claims that God was on their side. It remains an issue to this day, the Christian Church has often condemned war unless for defensive reasons but is still turned to for national thanksgiving and identification. The Americans claim that they are under God, and thereby special to God. In the study of nation and nationalism the question of religion cannot be ignored.

Religion often became a weapon against itself. Religious belief has been used in the past by the English distrust of Papists, especially the Irish variety, and the Protestant leaders of the Dutch revolt against Spanish domination using the same propaganda. The religious wars at the end of the sixteenth century stretched into the next century before it calmed down (1648). It raised many puzzling questions such as if it were possible for an Englishman to be Catholic, or a Polish citizen to be Protestant.

In the current century seeking the support of religion has become less significant in a secular type of society. However, the use of religious faith persists in nationalistic terms with the emergence of a militant/terrorist form of Islam, which too often tends to vilify ordinary peace-living Muslims. Today most Western nations tend to avoid using religion as a justification for conflict, as the Church leaders tend to argue against using war, and it is becoming rare for a person's religious faith to be raised at the political level. America is one Western country which still pays considerable attention to its Christian heritage, with the growing right-wing tendency looking for support from what is termed the evangelical Christians, the so-called Bible belt. In the past nations have often defined themselves by their chosen religious faith, and although Lenin and Stalin denounced the church, today's President Putin claims to be a strong Russian Orthodox adherent, which remains an inbuilt form of nationalism.

Religion has played a key role in world history and especially in Europe, where Christianity and Islam have often dominated various countries, despite the fact that each religion has its own sub-divisions or denominations. Nor can it be claimed that religious faith is without its own form of corruption. There is, for example, no question that historically Christian leaders in time past have sought power, wealth, and territory despite Christ's message of 'love your neighbour'. In the study of medieval times, the Papacy was absorbed with territorial gains, and extending its power with methods which fell far short of Christ's message. This has not just been a characteristic of the Roman Catholic Church, because when the political machinations of the Church of England's past are explored there are similarities. Much of Catholic and Protestant histories include Christians torturing and killing one another in the most brutal fashion. Overall, the Jewish faith played the smallest role, but many of its gifted individuals were involved in nation building and nationalism. However, as these words are being written, there is the conflict of Israel's attack on Gaza under the claim of defence and retaliation, which has been done with such ferocity that it may invoke a major war in the Middle East. In the early stages of European history Islam made incursions retaining small footholds. It has been proposed that it was more comfortable for the individual citizen of another faith to live under Muslim rule than under Christian patronage. Today a few small sections of extreme Muslims have rekindled the religious element, in a para-militaristic fashion, which does not reflect the inner core of Islamic belief. These three monotheistic faiths have their sub-divisions, but Christianity divided and sub-divided not only between East and West, but after the Reformation in a complex and bewildering fashion. The lives of Martin Luther, Ulrich Zwingli, John Knox, and John Calvin are just a few of the names mentioned in the text who intentionally or otherwise, produced a variety of Christian denominations. The irony is that the three faiths are monotheistic, so the cynic, used in terms of meaning the realist, might claim they worship the same God in their diverse ways.

However, Christianity has been the major religious faith of Europe from as early as the fourth and fifth centuries in a dominant role. It has been an activator and servant of nationalism in all countries, as well as at recent times a critic. Religion was often used to help a nation maintain its sense of identity, and the Muslim control over Greece had allowed their church to survive, and this helped Greece maintain its sense of nationhood during a time of Islamic subjugation. However, the clash of extreme Islamic movements persists to this day.

There are no patterns or typical features which can be outlined. One historical event follows the next with no discernible guidelines, each country or event is virtually always on a stand-alone basis. What they do have in common is the role of religion playing a part. As in the study of history much depends on objectivity, which can be elusive or obscure depending on the writer's own religious leanings.

Greed for Territory, Wealth, and Power

From the earliest tribal times the distinctive human tendency was to see the neighbour's land or wealth as something worth acquiring, even if it meant conflict. It is humankind's weakness of coveting what the neighbour has, making people suspicious of others. The European history briefly sketched in the following chapters demonstrates war after war, border disputes, marriage alliances, diplomatic wrangling, threats and seeking alternative ways for countries to expand their territory and power. It is not a straightforward traceable development, but the common denominators are the human need for wealth and power.

The major problems exposed in history revolve around the issues of power, which results from the desire to dominate others, often a consequence of some perverse ideology or a tyrant. As Solzhenitsyn wrote, 'unlimited power in the hands of limited people always leads to cruelty'.[35] It is a form of atavistic tribalism which becomes known in aggressive nationalism using racism amongst its persuasive ingredients, which all too often leads to war and crimes against humanity. To this day borders are still in flux and dispute, as is access to sea routes or guarding them. The Netherlands was of interest to others because of its coastline, Russia has always sought access to the oceans, and the British and Spanish issue over Gibraltar are just a few examples of this singular question. Today it is a concern over China and the Nine Dash line which will be mentioned in the main text. The need for natural resources makes oil-rich countries of international interest, but all too often aggressive nationalism is used for power and influence by some individual leaders. The question of power, wealth and territory has remained the fixation of humanity on a global scale.

It was this search for wealth and power which propelled colonialism when the first Portuguese explorers travelled down the African coastline, which later expanded at an exponential rate. This conquest of territories overseas expanded with Spain and Portugal making deep inroads into South America, and cross-ocean trade became important and naturally a cause of friction. The Dutch founded colonies in Guyana and Curaçao and the Russians moved eastwards even claiming Alaska, and the French and British with their wider sea access created their vast and individual empires. The colonial development took some of the friction out of Europe but placed it overseas. It amounted to the grabbing of land with anticipated wealth and global dominance. It was nothing short of a scramble for more land however valuable or poor in resources the new territory might be, and the indigenous populations were irrelevant and too often treated as sub-human. In the last quarter of the nineteenth century alone, half a dozen European countries gobbled up nearly a quarter of the planet's surface area. It was driven by the quest for power, economics, and often an imposition of culture often utilising Christianity. The British with their maritime power took the most, and power, wealth, territory, and influence persist as typical of human conduct.

A major portion of European history has been the barbaric wars between nations, led by despotic rulers, ideologies, and even elected governments have fought their neighbours to be the major influence in Europe. It reached the rock bottom of self-destruction during the first half of the twentieth century when men like Hitler, Mussolini, Stalin and even Franco used their various political ideologies as a justification, trying to accumulate land and wealth from others. Hitler was well-known to believe Germany had a right or could control the whole of Europe if not beyond, and Stalin, as Lenin before him, wished the whole world to be communist, which in Stalin's case was similar with that of Hitler's passion, expanding territory and dominance. The history of this form of gross nationalism did not stop in 1945, there have been wars in many parts of the globe since, and at the time of writing (2024) Russia is attempting to occupy Ukraine, and Israel under the pretence of self-defence appear to have as their aim the occupation of the Gaza strip.

Chapter Two

From Caves to Nations

From Cavemen Onwards

Perhaps one of humanity's earliest propensities was the need for security by binding with others of the same disposition. This must have started, quite understandably, at the tribal stage if only for survival purposes. It must be recalled that about four-fifths of humanity's time in Europe was based on the tribal structure, which tended to see others as a potential threat. One of the contentions of this exploration has been to consider that tribalism has never left humanity, even though it has changed in shape and form.

It may be speculated that when a caveman emerged from his rock to survey the valley below, he may have called his neighbours out if he spotted strangers in the area, seeing the valley as their hunting ground and their property. The same cavemen when pursuing the possible immigrants out of their land, they may have seen that beyond their valley were more fertile green lands which they considered worth occupying. To do this they needed to be stronger than their neighbours and somehow saw occupying another's territory as their natural rights. Even in the twentieth century there were Neo-Darwinists who claimed that humans are virtually programmed towards the belief that only the strong can survive and must do so by expanding. This was not nationalism in the modern sense, but the critical ingredients can be detected. The necessary determinants include territorial demands, seeking wealth power and influence, and treating neighbours as somewhat alien and constantly under suspicion. This human propensity appears to be part of human nature, forming the basic recipe for nationalism which took long to emerge during our history. In his *History of Europe* H. A. L. Fisher in his preface mentioned the difficulty of finding patterns or rhythms, writing 'I can only see one emergency following upon another... and there can be no generalisations'.[1] Despite this warning it is possible to be a historical detective and identify the early clues of nationalism.

For nationalism to take a recognisable shape there must be a nation, and the two words which cause problems are 'nation and country', not just in their precise linguistic meaning, but the way they are understood by most people. According to the Oxford dictionary a *country* is 'a nation with its own government, occupying a particular territory', and a *nation* is defined as 'a large body of people united by common descent, history, culture or language, inhabiting a particular state or territory'. They are both defined as inhabited territories, but some regard a country as a self-governing political entity, whereas a nation is more about a group of people who share a culture, language, and history. By the term nationality a person may be German by nationality, but by living permanently in Britain he or she is also British. Most countries today are multi-cultural, the original residents of the USA are the smallest of minorities, and very few if any residents in Britain can claim a DNA ancestry dating back to the original inhabitants. This provides a mixture of problems: when war was declared in 1939 a British person born in Germany was often interned in a sense of panic, as were many Japanese in America following Pearl Harbor. Much of a nation's self-belief is built on a kaleidoscope of oral tradition based on myths and legends. Today's Jewish people hold to their perceived right of domination in their area of the Middle East. The story of King Alfred burning cakes was undoubtedly legendary, and Joan of Arc portrayed as the saviour of France are all similar in a nation's makeup, and these and many other examples were all part of the necessary tradition for the early development of most countries. Some of the stories may have a factual background, other accounts less so, but this national package assists the collective consciousness necessary for justifying the existence of a nation. This along with the commonality of language and culture tends to bind even those who were originally strangers.

There can be factors which cause disruption and even disorder such as the arrival of immigrants or refugees, and the emergence of significant minority groups. This has led to definitions of citizenship being frequently changed, and governmental forms may ask one's colour, place of birth and first language. In various countries national membership is wide open to change, but it inevitably varies from country to country. It is true that kinship and tradition are critical, yet they remain mobile and open to new interpretations. In a fluctuating society of newcomers other methods apart from a shared language and culture are often required.

One major factor which bound a nation as an identifiable unit was its legal structure, the law. Even in medieval times the written law became prolific and stabilising, namely 'the law of the land'. In the early regional areas of Italy and Germany they had local codified laws, but they had no unifying centres, whereas in thirteenth century France there was a strong monarchy and royal court with the *Parlement of Paris* acting as a binding influence. The English feudal system had the ultimate authority of the monarch. King Henry II (1133–1189) helped develop the legal system, with judges, local courts, the start of the jury system and above all the Common Law, which meant it was to treat all people the same in all regions of the nation, a system which has spread widely around the world.

It was a unifying process for the nation, which was demonstrated in English history during the Plantagenet era.

In the time of Henry II the Assize of Arms demanded both the rich and poor should supply a national army, which helped bind the classes as a single nation. Henry's son King John was obliged to sign the 1215 Magna Carta to appease the barons, which much later helped prompt the concept of a legislating parliament. The parliamentary concept was far from the minds of the Barons of that day and age, despite the myths attached to Magna Carta. However, these decisions helped with the emergence of a national community where even the king was supposedly bound by the law. There were similar developments in other countries, but it was more pronounced in England, giving rise to the myth that England was the source of a parliamentary type of democracy. The commonality of law helped bring a nation into being, with one historian noting in his history of eighteenth century England, that 'even the discontented and oppressed often felt passionate loyalty to their place in the order of things… inheritance of stations in life reinforced jealously guarded territoriality'.[2] The coming together of a country or nation was often built on wide-ranging myths, be it the Jewish concept of the God given land 'flowing with milk and honey' or that King John started the democratic process when obliged to sign the Magna Carta.

In a broad sweeping statement, it could be speculatively claimed that when the caveman had spotted strangers this was followed by the growth of tribes which became migratory as they sought better territory. Their new lands became their homes under various forms of leadership and reinforced through law as an identifiable territory.

When the vast tribal migrations across Europe and nations started to take a shape, they had much in common but much more to divide them from one another. Language development, their varying myths and legends, their religious beliefs, and even physical features covered by the term race. When the cavemen and neighbours came together the origin of tribes started, each seeking better territories and often feeling superior when victorious, and it could be proposed that in these earliest of times the ingredients used by future nationalism may be found.

Tribes

It is generally accepted that the origin of humankind was probably somewhere deep in Africa, and probably elsewhere on the great continents, living the life of hunter-gatherers in small groups, dependent on one another for survival. Family groups merging for mutual support was no different from a pack of wolves. This joining of families or tribes may have evolved simply because of the sheer necessity of survival, and the need for protection against other groups.

As the groups enlarged and became identifiable many tribes became nomadic in their search for better climes, while others remained static. Some scholars have seen this in the ancient Biblical texts of Cain and Abel, the tiller of the soil and the hunter gatherer or shepherd seeking new climes, which can be interpreted as explaining why one brother hated another. The word tribe may be defined in many ways, but it usually infers a group of numerous families taking in others to increase their strength. The word is used today to describe people who hold the same interests, usually in a derisory fashion. The Oxford dictionary defines tribe as 'a group of persons forming a community and claiming descent from a common ancestor', although the 'common ancestor' may well just be a myth. 'In some cases, the tribe can hardly be otherwise described than as the group of men subject to one chieftain'.[3] Samuel Johnson labelled a tribe as a 'distinct body of the people as divided by family or fortune or any other characteristic', and a nation as 'people distinguished from other people'.[4] The word tribe may be described in many ways dependent on changing times. From the beginning of man's emergence was the demand for survival which rapidly raised the problem of treating other people as a risk, which indicates this was part of our so-called biochemistry or genetics. It was humanity's sense of security and the need for binding together with others sharing the same views.

Chadwick pointed out from a study of early Indo-European languages that tribes and their languages 'implied great movements of population from very early times, perhaps from the third millennium BC'.[5] Undoubtedly Chadwick was correct, and it is generally accepted that for 3–4,000 years about four-fifths of humanity's time in Europe was based on the tribal structure, and many of them on the move. A few, in the best places, would have stayed in their area tilling the soil, as they were living in 'milk and honey'. Their area would naturally be of interest to the more nomadic tribes living in more unstable or difficult geographical regions. 'The great advantages which the nomads possessed against settled communities were those of speed and mobility. Military organisation too is more easily carried out by them', and nomadic tribes tended to be the major issue of human existence.[6] The tribe in the overall view of human history dominated the world's stage for the longest period, and in some global regions still exists. In some ways it could be argued that it is part of our psychological if not physical inheritance, and one of the early seeds of nationalism as humans was the perceived need to expand and dominate their area of control.

In geological and dinosauric terms humankind has not roamed this planet for long, but some experts have noted that there are cave figures and paintings which date back to 30,000 years, and China had some form of writing approximately for some 8,000 years. The early dynastic period of Egypt dates from 3,500 BC and was followed by the Sumerians of Mesopotamia. Before and during this time humankind left their caves in enlarging tribal groups to survive or seek a better way of life. Unquestionably there were exceptions, but historical studies suggest the leader or chieftain tended to be male, not for his wisdom, but for his physical aptitude: they tended to be the alpha-component as in a wolfpack. This leadership of the alpha-male was to remain a characteristic of human development to this day. The current Russian President Vladimir Putin had his photographs of himself playing ice-hockey and riding with his shirt off on a horse in a background of rocky terrain, and he is not the only national leader trying to present himself as a tough single-minded leader. The contest for kingships and dynastic struggles is well documented in man's earliest writings and continues to this day, and again is one of the seeds of nationalism.

In the ancient scriptures of the Old Testament, a book shared by Christians, Muslims and Jews, the number of tribes mentioned is vast. The Philistines are still well-known because they have entered the English language with 'Philistine acts', the Amalekites, the Jebusites, and others are less well-known. Names occur such as King Toi of Hamath, a place in modern Syria and only mentioned twice in the books of Samuel and Chronicles. In the Old Testament the words nation and country are mentioned, but it was the tribes who were at the core of these growing larger units.

The Jewish nation had twelve tribes, in two countries called Israel and Judah, and an early contest for power was described as between the House of Saul and the House of David. It was the House of David which conquered: 'all the nations he subdued, from Edom, Moab, the Ammonites, the Philistines, Amalek, and the spoil of King Hadadezer son of Rehob of Zobah'.[7] It reflected a barbaric era, Saul informing David that the only dowry he required was 'a hundred foreskins of the Philistines to take vengeance on the king's enemies'.[8] War has been a human characteristic to this day and they are, when racial, the most vicious, and the religious input was already self-evident in these ancient texts. After their early defeats the Jewish tribes called for the monarch type leader to ensure victory, a centralised figurehead. These warlords brought in the word kingdom as their territory grew.

This was not unique to the Middle East, but with similarities across the globe. They also sought the justification of their gods for their plans of growth. Thor was a warrior god defeating all opponents and who was associated with thunder, lightning, storms, and oak trees, all representing super-human strength. He had other names, but his Germanic and Norse background meant he was significant in northern European tradition. It is not surprising that to this day that Thursday is named after Thor, and Wednesday after Woden an Anglo-Saxon god, Friday associated with the gods Frigg and Freyja. The studied accounts of these ancient tribes which became developing powers, indicate that humanity's behaviour has not changed, as it demonstrates man's passion for power, dominance, territory, wealth, and usually under the leadership of a powerful personality.

Tribes became nations and soon many became empires as the greed to dominate neighbours intensified and started to emerge over 2,000 years ago. The Old Testament is a work which reflects this development in the Middle East. There was the ancient Egyptian colossus with its dramatic pyramids, the Syrian and Assyrian Empires, the Babylonian, the Persian, the Greek followed by the dominance of the Roman Empire. They did not reflect a federation of nations but conquered and occupied territory, but the tribes, especially in Germania continued to challenge Rome, which by its overwhelming power, almost brought a sense of peace to the area for nearly two centuries (*Pax Romana*). The Roman and Greek Empires in many ways influenced the future of Europe and parts of the yet undiscovered areas by early Europeans. The Greeks made headway to India, and Rome crossed what is now called the English Channel to Britain with inhabitants ranging from Iberians and Celts and other tribes.

As Rome crumbled under the weight of its own decadence and tribal assaults the British Isles were invaded and occupied by a variety of tribes. In Bede's history of the Anglo-Saxon invasions, he noted that 'they came from three very powerful nations of the Germans; that is, from the Saxones, Angli, and Iutae. Of the stock of the Iutae are the Cantuarii and Uictuarii; that is, the race which holds the Isle of Wight, and the race in the country of the West Saxons which is still called Iutarum natio, [Jute Nation] established over against the Isle of Wight'.[9] Bede used the term nation, which seems far from the modern sense of the word, and his use of stock and race felt more appropriate. However, the word nation stems from *natio*, which was a Middle-English word from the old French Latin, based on *nat* (born) derived from the verb *nasci*, the place of origin. Bede's use of the words stock and race indicate that the tribe was bound by ethnic bonds. The anthropologist Kroeber stated that the word nation had a double meaning: 'First, nation denotes a people organised under one government, a body politic. Second, a nation is a people of common origin, tradition, and language...now the latter is just what a nationality is, by universal consent; and it would be fine if everyone would always use the word nationality when that was the meaning, and if nation on the contrary were restricted to denoting politically organised people'.[10] This points to the obvious conclusion that, for example, there is German nationality and a German State. Nevertheless, the word nation remains contentious, and according to Harris 'the notion of nation is rooted in false and dangerous ideas of race…the wedding between racism and struggle was fierce…the fiction of common descent enshrined in the metaphor of fatherland and motherland…', but it certainly was a major ingredient of nationalism.[11]

In terms of the new tribal Britain following the collapse of Rome, the historian Professor Frank Stenton provides various maps in his Oxford history of Anglo-Saxon England, which reveal a confusing picture of minor kingdoms and territories, mainly ruled by Angles, Saxons and Jutes, all mentioned by the Roman Tacitus.[12] The county of Kent stood apart as its own form of nation, but there was the confederacy of the southern English, there was Mercia, Wessex, a Kingdom of Lindsay. Today in Britain there is political talk of the north-south political economic divide, and it also existed in the early centuries.

The British Isles were simply a few islands off the west coast of Europe dominated by various tribes, with some original settlers still lurking in the mountainous regions of Scotland and Wales. Because Britain consisted of islands surrounded by seas it was not easy to invade. However, it had its mountainous area which 'impeded the first rush of Saxon immigrants' and Ireland was only reached in the twelfth century under the feudal banner of Strongbow.[13] Geography and its terrain was always a major factor in occupying some countries and in defining borders, and mountains and coasts in those days proved to be strong defences.

When areas had eventually been occupied and under control, the tribe remained 'the manifestation of over-riding group loyalties by members of a culturally affiliated society to locally based interests which involve tradition, land, and opportunities for survival and growth'.[14] There was undoubtedly interbreeding but the tribal system remained 'a social group speaking a distinctive language or dialect and possessing a distinctive culture that marked it off from other tribes'.[15] The importance of language as mentioned earlier remained a critical key. This was not only true of the British Islands but the whole of Europe where 'the tribal map is therefore, essentially a linguistic map', and it left its marks on modern thinking, and as noted became one of the seeds of nationalism.[16] This was one of the issues which made borders important, and 'enemies tend to be adjacent, sharing larger resource areas, not separated by natural boundaries such as rivers or hill crests'.[17] The tribe was a political entity as clans or tribes became villages, but it has been argued that tribes were not so territorial, but 'the use of the concept of tribe as a way-station in the evolution of the state violates ethnographic knowledge'.[18] The study of tribalism is a kaleidoscope of many opinions, but it seems apparent they were the opening phase of developing localities, then regions and countries, and the reasons they grew and changed, or developed, carried the seeds of future nationalism.

Later when the Vikings (Norsemen) started their invasion of the British coast having gained some mastery of the seas, an area of Danelaw was established with their well-known dynamism. Although the internal tribal fighting continued for a time, interbreeding and cooperation started once they became less nomadic and more sedentary, thereby becoming part of an identifiable landscape. This period of British/English history was as tribally prolific as the Middle East and other areas, but the barriers of settled countries was taking shape. Tribal bias remained a hallmark but in places could be regarded as forming a recognised country in some places of Europe.

There are some historical observers who claim that the tribal instincts remain to this day which can be discerned in dialects and words specific to areas as well as deep traditions. It has been utilised by some politicians, and as is well-known, the Nazi regime recently appealed to the mythical Aryan as the superior race, but generally the word tribe is seen as an almost derogatory word. Nevertheless, even in the twentieth century the notion of the original tribe was exploited. The 'term Germanic was too vague and ill-defined; and Teuton appears the best description, but it served to bring out the antiquity of the German nation and to impress upon Germans of the present day [written in 1945] that they were the descendants and heirs of the Germani who fought successfully against the Romans more than eighteen centuries before…[and]… it served to arouse a quite legitimate feeling of national pride in a nation which at the time had no political unity'.[19] This deep tribal instinct which has often pervaded even in the modern period still emerges especially in international sport. This is a form of what has been described as 'banal' nationalism and is often demonstrated in international football (soccer) games when the fans turn to violence and throw racial abuse at one another, basing their claims of superiority not on ball-skills but ethnicity. It may be argued that the old seeds of tribal superiority are still emerging and reflecting the barbarity of the tribal period which still simmers within some human conduct. As the Second World War was ending the famous historian Chadwick reflecting on this disaster, wrote in 1945 that 'we must learn to respect their characteristics and traditions, their national feelings and ideologies, even when they differ from our own'.[20] This sense of nationalistic seeds or ingredients which were embedded in the tribal development was therefore ingrained in our earliest history, and tribalism has since been exploited, having distinctive roots in humanity's nature and often comes to the surface during times of crisis.

Developing Power Centres

While these massive tribal movements were battling their ways to better territory other developments were happening which offered some hope for man's future in forging intellectual progress. In Greece men such as Plato, Socrates and Aristotle, still carefully studied today, were placing the foundation stones for the intellectual world. The philosophical thoughts of Socrates were encapsulated by his pupil Plato in his book *The Republic* as to how men should govern themselves.[21] Aristotle wrote his remarkable *Nicomachean Ethics* around 350 BC, a book debated and used to this day.[22] Given the remarkable contribution these ancient thinkers gave to their own generation, let alone today's world, it is astonishing what they achieved, and raises the question of how this happened in such early and fraught times. It is far too easy to forget what was happening in places like Greece and Egypt, because most of our European ancestry was busy fighting tribal wars from the Eurasian Steppe and the northeastern climes to the Atlantic islands of Britain.

The Greek intellectuals ahead of their times were simply phenomenal. The Greek city-states stood in stark contrast to the tribes on the Steppe and the surrounding mountains, both those near and far. They had their problems of city state fighting city state and the attacks of outside tribes whom the Greeks referred to as barbarians. Hellenistic influence would permeate the centuries ahead, but even in this area of Utopian intellectualism, the seeds of nationalism were evident as one city sought to dominate another, and men like Alexander the Great rose to power seeking to dominate Western Asia, creating an empire from Greece to near the borders of modern-day India, the ingredients of nationalism were already evident.

As Greek power lessened, Rome emerged as a dominating monolithic structure of immense proportions, with a unified political structure, a strong military, based on immense organisational skills. Greece had developed city-states, but Rome's origin was wider. Historians have varying views on these two ancient powers, some regarding Rome as the natural successor, others that Greece had style but Rome money. However, the Romans had their own genius in matters of law, engineering, organisation, and they produced their own literary and art works. Rome had its Romulus and Remus legends with its seven hills, which commanded a dominating view of the important River Tiber. Rome began as a republic starting as early as 509 BC, nearly destroyed by the Cisalpine Gauls' incursion in 390 BC, but they recovered to fight more wars against Pyrrhus and the well-known Carthage conflicts.

The greed for power and dominance were features of the Roman Empire. There were bitter civil wars and in BC 48 Julius Caesar declared himself *Imperator* having rid himself of the opposition. Once Julius Caesar had crossed the Rubicon River it had spelt the end of the republic and absolute power soon dwelt with one man. The need for power and domination eventually brought Egypt into the growing Empire. However, Rome was once again preoccupied with defending its territories against alien tribes, ranging from Hadrian's Wall for keeping out the Picts and Scots, keeping them at bay and deploying its defences as far as the Danube Delta. Such was the nature of their religion they had a similar pattern to the Greeks with their belief in the gods of Mount Olympus, but the Roman leaders deified themselves to avoid any religious problems, an idea which would reoccur with modern fascist leaders. As mentioned above the issue of a legal system helped bind their empire for centuries, a law which applied to everyone, succeeded in this deployment but was always centred on the demands of the Roman rulers.

Later, the British would claim that their empire and imperial policies would civilise or Christianise barbaric parts of the world, and the Romans held the same attitude about their own values. 'Cicero asserted that only under Roman rule could civilisation flourish', and from Wales to Syria the wealthy emulated the Romans in dress and life-codes.[23] Stephen Howe in his study of *Empire* wrote: 'Some historians think that we should not refer to nationalism in any relation to any period before the past two hundred years or so. But we can surely, without gross anachronism, speak of Rome's empire as a multi-ethnic or multi-cultural one, but also one where what a later age would call cultural assimilation was vigorously practised and widely accepted'.[24] On appearance this appears as a reasonable assertion, but the cynic might note that the politically clever Romans eschewed this as a means of holding their territorial empire together.

In time the Romans came under the influence of the Christian faith, at earlier times they had persecuted its adherents. The appeal for the Christian message was the hope of life after death, and during the early persecutions in their arenas this had become clear. Christianity had spread through much of Europe because of the *Pax Romana* which had allowed St Paul and others to travel, without too much hinderance. It was under Emperor Constantine in 325 that Christian problems with the various heresies were resolved (for a time) and Christianity became the state religion, though Constantine may not have been as Christian as the Church portrays him in its hagiographies. It was possibly from this time on that the Church became involved with politics to its detriment as a spiritual faith, and it has been proposed that Theodosius I in 392 was probably the first Christian Roman Emperor.

The Roman Empire was by any standard of measurement a remarkable matter, but it continually faced tribal attacks, which in some cases could be described as an early form of secessionist nationalism, trying to unyoke the dominant power of an occupier, at time aggressive nationalism as the boundaries of the Roman Empire were breached to gain their territory. It was not nationalism in the modern sense of the meaning, but indicative of the ingredients, the early identifiable seeds. The Chinese had destroyed the Hunnic Empire around 35 BC and the Huns were now nomadic, moving west towards the northern end of the Caspian Sea and towards what we now call the Ukraine. However, they did not attack the Roman Empire until 441 making a late appearance, settling in the area now called Hungary. It amounted to an upheaval of the peoples who would one day give Europe some shape of definition. The majority of these tribal movements were again looking for a place where they could establish themselves, as had many of the sea-raider Vikings, seeking better climes for their new home.

The expansion of the Teutonic tribes 'had begun before they came into contact with the Romans'.[25] The academic study of place names, burial methods, and language factors, indicated that they had conquered nearly all of what today would be west and southern Germany, as they conquered the earlier Celtic arrivals. When in 59 BC the Romans began the conquest of Gaul the Teutonic tribes had reached the Rhine. During the Roman period these Germanic movements were the most prominent. It was like a major Germanic diaspora, when as late as the upheavals of the twentieth century, enclaves of Germanic settlers became a point of contention.

Even before this movement of the Germanic elements the Cimbri and Teutons had swept one wave through to the south of Europe, but it was not until the third century there was a permanent conquest of Roman territory which was Romania (Dacia). It was during the fifth and sixth centuries that Teutonic expansion took on significant dimensions. The Rhine frontier was broken by the Vandals in 406 who moved into Gaul and Spain and then crossed to North Africa. They were followed by the Visigoths who invaded Italy and captured Rome in 410. Between 440–3 the Burgundians arrived from the middle Rhine area and took eastern Gaul, and during 431–486 the Salic Franks (sometimes regarded as the ancestors of the modern Dutch) took the rest.

Tribes moved at will while others were forced to move by others making incursions. Europe would have appeared like a great lake with ripples of water flowing in different directions causing clashing waves and whirlpools. There were pressure points from tribes such as the Huns, the Sclavenoi (Sclvinoi, Sclavi), the Avars, Bulgans, Sorabi, Iranians, Franks, and countless others. Unlike Rome, the Teutons had no empire and were independently minded. There were occasional references to alliances which did not last, even of some hegemonies or suzerainties which were of a short duration.[26] The Teutonic tribes never made a single authority or functioned as a single body being very individualistic. Their objectives were simply plundering for wealth, food, drink, and for some leaders personal power, and it was all distinctly tribal. They could at this juncture be described as 'pre-state' tribes. There has been considerable debate over years by historians of this era, some seeing tribes as connected by family and culture, some led by chieftains, but no classification seems possible, as there was no recognisable pattern, and as is typical of historical development there were a variety of differences, meaning the evidence is limited to inference and common-sense speculation. However, archaeology has been able to identify some certain facts in some areas, and anthropology can understand what may have happened in general terms, but the tribal incursions into Europe remain a mystery. There is no question that, as in all tribes they were led by warrior type leaders who would from time to time be challenged. This is typical human conduct whether it be seeking a new warrior leader or prime minister, the contest for leadership is a characteristic of humanity.

As the various tribes settled within a given territory, they remained distinct for a time with their language, culture, types of leadership, religion, social habits, rituals, and many other ways of life giving them a sense of commonality. In places they merged by interbreeding and survival necessities, the larger tribes tending to dominate the smaller units. It was a developing characteristic of humankind to claim rights of territory, bind it under their form or rule, with the widely held concept that ownership was theirs by right, and other people were therefore aliens and potential enemies. The elements of their language, religious belief, culture, laws were factors which often set them apart from their neighbours, and although most historians view nationalism as a phenomenon belonging to the time of nation-states, the ingredients were more than evident even in this early history.

The Dark Ages

During the tribal incursions, the Roman Empire fought on avoiding total destruction, surviving for many years. Emperor Justinian (527–65), widely known for the codification of Roman law, tried to re-assert Roman control but faced the problem of the Slavs making an appearance on the Adriatic coast, as well as the Persians re-asserting themselves. Justinian was successful in destroying the Vandal kingdom and taking on the arrival of the Ostrogoths in Sicily and Italy. However, the Huns reached the walls of Constantinople in 476, the general Slavic attack appeared, and Byzantine civilisation was regarded as the final remnants of the old Roman powerhouse but was unprepared to meet the Rise of Islam (622–778). Religious belief was a major factor in this period. The old Olympian gods had lost any following with the arrival of Christianity, but now

Islam was claiming to be the universal religion, turning a united Arabia into a springboard for a theocratic empire. The successors of the Prophet known as the caliphs took Kabul in the East, Carthage, and Tangier in the West, and in 711 the place now known as Gibraltar placed Islam inside Europe. Within a hundred years of the Prophet's death, they were within reach of Paris. The Battle of Poitiers (sometimes referred to as the Battle of Tours) was won by the Franks, and the Muslim onslaught was stemmed, most probably because the Islamic army had over-extended its resources, and the Pyrenees became the holding barrier against this new form of incursion. Despite the curious theme that Judaism, Christianity and Islam held monotheistic beliefs and had much in common, it was a history of continued belligerence regarding one another as the 'infidel'. It was a hallmark of humankind's behaviour with the three religions of Europe, Christianity, Islam, and Judaism, each with their own internal divisions. Christianity and Islam were the religious powerhouses which at times created their own conflicts. Islam soon divided into factions, and Christianity became a kaleidoscope of petty divisions. In the Eastern and Western branches of the Christian faith, now separated by the Muslim incursions, there were continuous and often heated debates. Doctrinal divergences were a characteristic of this period and remain so to this day, hopefully with less belligerence, but still significant.

Christianity was the dominant religion for much of Europe, and the centre for the West was becoming Rome again, with the Vatican growing widespread significance. The starting time of Papal authority is difficult to ascertain, although it was Gregory I (540–604) who is often regarded as the first of the future Papal powerholders. It was Gregory I, who with his evangelical zeal sent St Augustine to convert the English. The conversion of the pagans was no easy matter, and the church frequently accepted some pagan culture into its structure in order to achieve success. No one can be certain as to the precise birthdate of Christ, and there have been many suggestions, the most common ascribes it to Sextus Julius Africanus in 221 which undoubtedly appeased various mid-winter pagan traditions (Sextus Julius Africanus was a Christian historian and was the first to offer a universal chronology giving a date for the birth of Christ). The Germanic tribes held out the longest, but they were eventually converted by St Boniface of Crediton in England. These major efforts at conversions rarely reflected the Christian message of love, the Franks forced conversion through the fear of the sword, most notably in Saxony between 722 and 785. In all this conveyancing of religious belief, Christianity and Islam not only had internal frictions and fractions, but there were the crusades and bitter rivalry and wars involving the religious faiths are still happening to this day.

There is no clear definition for the closure of the so-called Dark Ages because barbarian eruption continued up to the Mongol raids finishing, arguably, in

1287, and Christian conversion, often by obligation, continued until the early fifteenth century. However, it indicated that religious belief was used as a factor in the question of political and territorial domination, and to this day remains a major ingredient of nationalism, as religious belief seems to indicate an unwanted stranger. Europe's current fear of immigrants, Britain's Brexit campaign focused on unwelcome visitors, today debates over whether sending them to Rwanda, President Trump's Mexican Wall and blocking Muslim migration are just a few examples of a continuing global problem, which was all too apparent during this early period of the so-called Dark Ages. Language, religion, and ethnicity persistently remain highly divisive in the modern world as it did during the Dark Ages. Man's propensity for this type of serious conflict has its roots early in history.

The Developing Nation

The linguistic, religious, and cultural backgrounds of the tribes separated some while amalgamating others, but all obsessed with increasing their territories, usually coming under a martial form of leadership with a designated name. The situation remained nebulous, but a vague pattern started to take shape, always dictated by a variety of factors. At this stage Poland did not exist as an obvious independent country, not least because their languages were diverse, and it could be argued from the available historical indicators that a common language was necessary for a potential nation. It was easier in Latin areas but more complex with the Slavic and Teutonic regions. The language issue apart it was also necessary to have some form of common culture, tradition, and religion.

The emerging states of north Europe were smaller, but it was from their amalgamations, conquests, and expansion that the modern map started to take shape. In these areas the smaller countries tended to be dominated by a family or a figurehead. There are examples where the ruling family shared leadership, and where succession by inheritance took place. Amongst the Franks in 511 Clovis was succeeded by his four sons, and fifty years later the last of these four sons, Hlothhari was succeeded by his four sons. It was mainly through oral tradition that these rules of hereditary were embedded into their tradition. In places, such as Russia, the family might share the responsibility of rule. In 1170 the head of the Russian leadership was based in Kiev and others of the family elsewhere bore the titles of kings, or princes. As the Roman power evaporated the word 'king' made its major appearance, as it had in the ancient Old Testament, probably first amongst the Goth family and the earliest example was probably Pippin (the father of Charlemagne) who was proclaimed king in 752. In England, the same route was seen in Northumbria and Mercia, and for England it became a vaguely identifiable territory in 1066 with King Harold II rapidly followed by the Norman William the Conqueror.

Under the leadership of one man or family in these emerging countries, it was soon clear that the help of families and officials was needed because of the growing size of the territory. This was especially true of the wide Frankish lands, where dukes and counts appeared, who also became hereditary for periods of time. As recorded history has clearly shown these supporters often became powerful, sometimes becoming overly independent and challenging the right of the king. The religion of the country followed suit, often becoming a political force with high-ranking ecclesiasts holding considerable powers and land. The country's religion often helped in their support of the king or queen by introducing the concept of the Divine Right of the monarchy. This concept was short, and dukedoms and similar offices of state frequently held their own principalities. Powerful families emerged, and some held control for a long time. The word Emperor appeared again, and in 1437 when the Luxemburg line came to an end, the famous Habsburg family survived. They acquired the thrones of Hungary and Bohemia in 1526, and in 1806 the imperial title was changed to Emperor of Austria.

As with the Russian empire the Habsburgs started to take shape in the Sixteenth Century. One of the main features of the Habsburg Empire was the immense number of different ethnic groups and languages it encompassed. At times efforts were made in this pluralistic background to accept this multicultural nature, and some have suggested the Habsburg efforts were akin to the ideals of the European Union of today, but that feels like a step too far. The undeniable feature of these times was that nationality was becoming associated with a name demanding personal allegiance, using the influence of the Church in supporting this process. The growing feudal system often added to this sense of nationality, and they offered subservience to the ruling dynasty, often for reasons of personal security. In some of the border regions where the sense of the smaller tribe persisted, that feeling of tribal nationality could be detected. As the powerful families consolidated and expanded their power, the masses simply worked and complied in order to eke out a living and survive. This did not mean that in a time of crisis the nobles could not stir up a sense of nationalism in defence or expansion, appealing to the masses for armed support of the nation and loyalty to their leaders. The seeds of nationalism detectable in the tribal era were now becoming identifiable ingredients in the developing nations.

As nations formed it was no longer a matter of tribal influence, but the political machinations between the developing leaders and royal houses with their various means of influence. Chadwick rightly claimed that a factor overlooked by some historians was the bartering done through marriage alliances.[27] Heirs and heiresses were a means of bringing about alliances, hegemonies, and a wider influence. This happened throughout the developing European scene. The final unification of Spain had to wait until 1469 and was mainly accomplished with the marriage of Isabel of Castile with Fernando of Aragon in 1469, with their daughter Joana becoming Queen of all Spain after the Moors (Islam) were conquered in 1492. Succession through marriage became a leadership means to an end, as Europe reshuffled its territories between the fourteenth and sixteenth centuries. Even until recently royal marriages have been intended as a means of alliance or at least better international relationships, it did not of course always work. A significant marriage was that of John Sigismund who in 1608 became the Elector of Brandenburg and who married Anne, daughter and heiress of Albert Frederic, Duke of Prussia. He became King of Prussia which was separated by a part of Poland. In England, the marriage of James IV with Margaret, daughter of Henry VII (1502) led to the union of English and Scottish crowns a century later. To this day there are shapes to some country configurations which were the result of arranged marriages. Later, as is well known, Queen Victoria's many children were married across the continental scene during her long reign.

The hereditary principle worked but was often challenged. Sometimes one family dynasty would supersede another for various reasons, but often with family links as with the Houses of Plantagenet, Tudors, and the Stuarts in England. Occasionally kings were elected who had no family or hereditary claims, as with the Danes electing King Christian I who was unrelated to the previous dynasty. In Russia there was considerable strife until 1613 when a National Assembly offered the throne to Michael Romanov, a name associated with that country until the death of Tsar Nicholas II in 1917. Elections in Western Europe were rare, although a case could be argued for the British Kings Charles II and George I, although it was a long distance from the current day notion of an election, as it was better expressed as an agreement within the leading nobility

These royal marriage machinations based on connecting powers or even who was the monarch had negligible effect upon national feeling, which was only apparent if an 'anti-foreigner' context was prevalent. National feeling was more aroused when the home country was under attack by a neighbouring enemy, or the country's leader was demanding expansion into another country by some presumed right of heritage. As in the tribal system, the belief that the foreigner was a threat was often utilised by various leaders, appealing to the basic impulses of the tribal instincts, which still happens to this day in the various forms of aggressive nationalism.

As these various machinations developed it became necessary to keep an eye on the masses of the population, especially the minor nobles, resulting in the creation of bodies such as Parliaments, Diets, Cortes, and Estates. They were far from the democratic institutions of today, with their members mainly representative of the powerful families of the land, senior ecclesiastical clerics, and occasionally influential people from the towns and cities. They were used to justify raising money through taxes for a standing army and other military necessities. This inventive system by the country's leaders to pretend the country was being consulted, later developed in strength so these bodies could question the ruling monarch usually over the need for money.

As the tribal instincts which bound a nation together as a loyal cohesive body disappeared, it became apparent that somehow the national leaders of the emerging nations needed to stimulate the old tribal values of loyalty to the leader, especially amongst the masses and the minor nobles who fought the battles. It belonged to the upper echelons of society, and it was not until the reign of James I that Acts of Parliament were published in the English language. The country's language, culture, and religion were major factors to arouse a sense of national feeling, and older features of writing parliamentary laws or regulations in French or Latin needed changing. Later the emerging conflict in Christendom between the Catholic and Reforming (Protestant) Churches could confuse the balance in national feelings. This need by the country's leaders to enthuse the masses with a national sense of total loyalty, was undoubtedly based on the need to enlist their enthusiastic support in times of war, be it defence or attack.

These aspects of the emerging nation are strongly linked to the concept of nationalism and were becoming part of the human genetic system. The nationalist ingredients during these centuries came from the ruling elite to garner the support of their workers, by making them into soldiers, when in effect they were being used as a means of upholding the ruling dynasty of the time. The national leaders when asking for armed support from the masses, with the likelihood of death, appealed to the sense of loyalty to their nation and leaders as the reason, even when coercion was used. It would have had more appeal to ask the serf or peasant to be prepared to fight for their land and homes rather than for 'your leader', who was probably responsible for any war in the first place.

More Nationalistic Ingredients

Before the advent of the fourteenth century as the early nations started to develop into recognisable shapes, often dictated by geographical borders such as the English Channel, and the mountains in places like Italy and Spain, it was an era characterised by the feudalistic society, church power, emerging individual leaders constantly seeking power and prestige.

It was the time of the metal-clad knight, the serfs or peasants ploughing the land and trying to survive under the patronage of their local lords. Christianity would soon be bitterly divided (as was Islam between the Sunnis and Shias) but it was a power base organised almost in the old Roman tradition, leading Hobbes to write that 'The Papacy is no other than the Ghost of the deceased Roman Empire sitting crowned upon the grave thereof'.[28] The Church was rapidly emerging as an influential political entity, both in the West and East of Europe. Growing Church power and influence was reflected during the establishment by Emperor Charlemagne of his empire (800) and fortified from 962 with the title of Holy Roman Empire.

Despite the emergence of nations, the tribal incursions had continued and from 866 Danelaw had been established from East Anglia northwards, and at the same time there was a similar movement in Normandy, albeit of a different hue. The settlements were wide-ranging and Knute (Canute) the Dane held an empire together from Denmark to England. In the East, the Magyars were to colonise the place named Hungaria (Hungary) which by the eleventh century was a regional power. They were not the last insurgents because the Mongols (or Tartars) controlled the large nomadic empires, and they impinged on the West with Genghis Khan conquering huge swathes of land from the Pacific to the Black Sea.

The Middle-Ages were beginning to appear, not with a specific timeline as it varied across the whole of Europe. This was the era when feudalism started to become the accepted norm, but it was not a uniform system even within the same country. This was the time of castle building in defensive positions, (especially in the ninth and tenth centuries), the knight, vassalage, and enfeoffment. The development of the stirrup meant men could fight from horses with lances, and the knight became important in military terms and gained social status. Feudalism implied the worker, who was dependent on the local lord, indicated a peasant or serf, namely a form of vassalage. Land was granted in return for taxes, and an expectancy that military service should be provided when demanded. From the serf in the field, to the knight, to the landowner, there was always an unwritten feudal contract producing a social hierarchy. The lines of military and social structure were becoming defined, especially for those in the upper echelons. Each and every area had different systems, but the overall realities remained the same, with the rich and powerful at the top; with the masses working hard and usually in extreme poverty, it was almost a caste system. The church was deeply involved in the structure, which clashed with the teachings of its founder Jesus Christ. Many Bishops held high baronial positions as officers of the state. This feudalistic system has left its mark even on modern society in terms of property (freehold, leasehold, rent, tithe, etc), law, manners, education, and speech. Many historians claim that Spain remained feudalistic into the twentieth century, and the infamous social classes of English society with its knighthoods, and exclusive clubs can be seen by cynics (or realists) as a hangover of this exclusive society.

The developing feudal system worked in different ways across Europe, but always in favour of those at the pinnacle of society. The German princes were forced to unite because of the Magyars entering Bavaria in 955, who were halted by Otto of Saxony near Augsburg. This brought Otto I of Saxony to high prominence (c.936–73; his father was Henry the Fowler), and he was formally crowned Emperor in Rome in 962. Otto needed Rome to enhance his elevation, but to him the Church was a mere means to an end, and he treated Rome with a degree of contempt. Meanwhile in 987 the last Carolingian king died, and the heir was Hugh Capet who founded a dynasty which would last for some 400 years. This started to form the shape of a country which was to be what the historian Norman Davies called 'the launch pad' for modern day France.

In the East the Byzantine Empire under the Macedonian dynasty grew commercially and was not troubled by the conflicts in the West, though they were the bulwark against Islam, and they had to deal with the growing appearance of the Bulgars. This was resolved in 1014 after a Byzantine victory at Serres in Macedonia, when Basil II blinded some 14,000 Bulgarian prisoners of war. Despite this barbarity the church was used to subjugate by conversion the pagan tribes, giving shape to Moravia, Bulgaria, Poland, and Hungary the East West division continued with the Latin and Greek churches trying to carry the major influence. This was not Christian morality, but power politics. The emerging nations found themselves caught between these two ecclesiastical powerhouses. In the north paganism continued, but in Poland the established Piast dynasty transformed Poland into a stronghold for Catholicism which remains as such to this day. Christianity was used as a means to an end by the emerging dynastic households.

Less than a thousand years ago Europe continued in a complex turmoil, incursions from outside, developing factions, but a slow formation of recognisable countries was taking place. In the East there was further external havoc when the Seljuk Turks and Mongols appeared. It was during this period that the Eastern Empire started its final decline when the infamous crusades took place. In the Byzantium Empire there were ecclesiastical and political infights while it faced outside challenges. The Seljuks had crossed the Oxus in 1031 gaining the upper hand over Persia, and in 1071 a minor battle with the Byzantine power transpired to be a significant victory for the intruders. The Eastern Empire never recovered and were reduced to defending their capital, as well as contesting the influence of the Latins which was also growing within the East. By 1204 the Eastern Empire no longer appeared to be a political entity. The year 1146 is often pinpointed as the date for the settlement of Moscow on the River Moskva, and Novgorod had become an independent region from 1126. The Byzantium collapse had many ramifications even beyond its original borders, and this led to changes in Transcaucasia, which was submerged by the Seljuks, although Georgia later broke free.

Defence along borders rapidly grew, and across Europe fortified castles appeared which tended to be constructed around ports and river crossings; many of them today are popular tourist spots. The Italian city ports are probably the most famous as growing commercial ports such as Venice and Pisa, but other regions flourished elsewhere in Lombardy, the Rhineland and Flanders, each with its own type of feudalism. There was a distinct sense of planning for a future in their selected area; with the nomadic tribal days finished, came the growth of institutions indicating a hopeful anticipation of durability.

The German royal households were continually trying to unite the different duchies and overcome all the complex dynastic patterns. Emperor Barbarossa (1159–90) was a powerful personality and for a time accomplished a degree of unity, but they rarely stayed the test of time, because contention and dynastic claims were the order of the day. In the meantime, the French were building up their power. The Capetian Kings of France ruled Paris and its environs, but from the time of Louis VI (1108–37) a series of monarchs increased their borders immensely. Louis VII (1137–80) was able to lead the Second Crusade and leave France at peace. He divorced his wife, the well-known Eleanor of Aquitaine who married Henry II of England. Henry II was the great law maker and his household, the Plantagenets, was not initiated by the start of Ireland's loss of independence (led by Richard Strongbow), but by English and French affairs having become intertwined. The French continued to gather strength under Philippe Auguste (1180–1223), who managed to block King John's claims on France, but then annexed Normandy, Anjou, Touraine, and Poitou. As France expanded England went through a baronial war with a revolt led by Simon de Montfort who was eventually killed at the Battle of Evesham 1265. These years reflected not only the past but to a degree the near future, in so far that it was a tussle for power between dynasties, powerful baronial houses and prominent figures seeking power.

Even the Church was re-organising itself when Pope Nicholas II in 1059 demanded that the College of Cardinals elect their Popes. This was an attempt to eradicate political intrusion. He even made relations smoother with his one-time opponents the Normans in the south of Italy, who had crossed the Messina Straits and taken Sicily from the Saracens. Expansion and the greed for territory was as rampant as the old tribes. However, it could be argued the tribes were seeking better homes, but this had evolved into seeking more power, possible wealth, and prestige. The Norman, Duke William, crossed the Channel to defeat Harold, and introduced the Norman variation of the feudal system into England. Nevertheless, the Church was trying to be the king on the chessboard rather than the bishop, and there was continuous wrestling with the knights and other would-be kings, when at times the Papacy was best described as a pawn. During the time of Pope Gregory VII (better known as Hildebrand) there emerged further Papal demands leading to serious clashes, exercising the feared weapon of excommunication, with the emperor intervening which led to two Popes at the same time. It was not until the Concordat of Worms in 1122 that there was some form of truce. However, this type of political wrangling between the Catholic Church and the political powers was to become an enduring problem.

There was at this stage no question of a national identity in the modern sense, but territorial acquisition and power were the dominant features of these centuries. The ruling classes in all countries had more in common with one another than with the masses of their people. The rulers often spoke their own language and not the vernacular, and the leading few lived very different lives, manipulating their followers and the impoverished populace. It was the grasping for power and territory when they needed armies raising the nationalistic claims that the enemy held their land or were planning an attack.

The Church had more in common with the rulers and power-politics than it did with the people, and church leaders were out of touch with the ordinary men and women who provided the food and joined the battle ranks when required. There were many aspects of the Church which were unrelated to the Christian message of love, a body seeking authority which could become ruthless. This had shown itself in the Crusades, especially in what was called the Albigensian Crusade (1209–29), in which Pope Innocent III had initiated this barbarity claiming their so-called heresy was treason against God. On these dubious grounds Pope Innocent III declared a crusade with the promised rewards of the remission of sins with the reward of loot. The Cathars, at the centre of this heresy found themselves having to choose between death or obedience to the Catholic belief. It also led to territorial gains for France who acquired the area of the Languedoc. In addition to this grasping for power, the conversion to the Catholic faith was threatened by the sword and had continued in the northern regions with German military monks. The Teutonic knights were of the same category, who saw their behaviour as an act of redemption, 'thus did civilisation advance'.[29] The nobles, ruling houses and the Church all sought power, wealth, and territory, which clearly indicated the necessary nationalistic ingredients.

The issue of Islam remained a problem for so-called Christian rulers, and in Spain in 1085 Alfonso VI of Castile-Leon captured the Muslim city of Toledo, and over the next 100 years forced much of Spain to become Christian. It was in 1095 that Pope Urban II called for the War of the Cross, namely the crusades to deliver Jerusalem from Muslim hands. These crusades would continue for some 200 years ending in failure. In the Fourth Crusade the Doge of Venice captured Constantinople, plundered it, and murdered the citizens. The brutality of the crusades stretched even the sensibilities of the day in cruelty, internal strife and achieved nothing.

It was apparent during this era of emerging nations that humankind's propensity for violence (despite the spread of Christianity) was led by a variety of power-mongers, who had shown few signs of progress to a more civilised and peaceful lifestyle. Despite this somewhat cynical view there was in Western Europe some development in towns and agriculture as the population eked out a life of survival, which also meant the population started to expand. The Mongols continued to unsettle the East but there was development in the west which led to different levels of progress. Even at these early times the Dutch were learning to control the Rhine's massive delta by dams and sluices reclaiming land from the sea.

By the middle of the thirteenth century there was no sense of nationhood as understood today. There were small provinces, cities, but no area with an identifiable singular unified nation. Insular England, because it was surrounded by sea, existed but with greater connections with the European mainland in places such as Gascony and Aquitaine than it did with its Celtic land-neighbours the Welsh and Scots. Scotland was still contesting its borders with the Norwegians, and at this time of transition the German Empire appeared to have evaporated. Some small countries like England, Portugal, Denmark had segregated themselves with the help of nature and were showing signs of national growth, and Serbia and Bulgaria were moving in this direction, signified by installing their own Orthodox Church and Patriarch as a step towards national identity. This use of a nation's own Church as an identity-aid was becoming a constant theme, and as recently as 2019 the Ukrainians demanded a national Church distinct from Moscow, and who a few years later, as this exploration is being written, are now at war with Russia.

When a parcel of territory was claimed and settled, as was happening, it was the beginning of what may be called nationhood, as they identified their existence with the stretch of land they occupied, especially the generation born and raised in that area, as it became 'home' and became more than just local soil. However, although there was a growing feeling of being bound together by the soil, local traditions were more abundant than any sense of one nationhood, an attitude often detectable to this day. As Europe struggled through this development and violence of the early Middle Ages, only 700 years ago, adherence to the smaller community was of greater importance than a nation. Humankind tends to associate itself with a specified area based on security and a sense of ownership.

Aggressive nationalism is often a matter of expansionism, fortifying borders for territorial control. This was a major feature of these years exercised by the overall rulers. Grasping land, power, and possible wealth constitutes our make-up, and as with tribalism, this propensity for expansion was already an embedded human characteristic. This is not to make the assertion that nationalism was a feature of this period, but the ingredients were there as part of human existence.

Chapter Three

Europe Takes Shape

Features of Fourteenth to Seventeenth Centuries

In fourteenth-century Europe, the ruling elite lived in their form of luxury in fortified homes and castles, with foods, self-perceived rights, while for most people, it was a case of day-to-day survival. Criminality increased in the lower social regions because of poverty, while their leaders were always plotting for territorial gain with the preparational intrigue. Superstition, plagues, and ignorance characterised most of the population, and not helped by the knowledge that the Church had the same problems. The Church leadership was far from reflecting the Gospels, which had portrayed the love of Christ. The Church had become part of the power-struggle, and in the west the Papacy was wrestling with kings and emperors, and often subjected to the developing powerful dynasties.

The Eastern Byzantium Church was little more than a church holding on in Constantinople. The Eastern parts of Europe were beset with the appearance of the Osmanli, (Osman I, 1281–1326) generally known as the Ottomans, who assaulted the fringes of the old Byzantine Empire. They established the major and permanent bridgehead of the Dardanelles, and the leader was called the Sultan, who surrounded and held siege to Constantinople. The once powerful Greece became one in a series of provinces, and Bulgaria moved away from Byzantine influence. Serbia suffered the same, and the only serious opposition appeared to come from the north-east in the shape of the Grand Duchies of Moscow and Lithuania. They had managed to survive the Mongolian hordes by paying tributes, and they had started to call their state or province by the Greek *Rossiya*, namely Russia. It was their variant of Eastern Slav which provided the basis for the Russian language. Lithuania remained pagan the longest, having retained a sense of independence in their difficult terrain from the Mongols and the Teutonic knights. They had leaders of some stature, especially Jogaila (1377–1434) who formed a union with Poland. Their (nationalistic) expansion through military activity was not halted until 1399 when defeated by the Tartars deep in the south on the river Vorksla. It was a period of territorial fighting for land and thereby power, and because of the incursion of the Mongols and Turks the first sense of what might be called modern nationhood started to be seen amongst the Serbs, Bulgars and Romanians. Eastern Europe was always in a state of flux and subject to outside efforts of domination power seekers, another ingredient of nationalism.

In western Europe, the main thrust of developing events was between the Empire, the Papacy, and the growing power of France. The Germans were absorbed in their own internal friction, and the Papacy was caught between powers, taking refuge in the Midi, and soon becoming divided over the turmoil of the great schism (the break-up of East and West between Catholic and Orthodox). France was suffering from the Hundred Years War with England, which was a two-way effort of gaining territory and enhancing power, a form of aggressive nationalism. By the year 1410 there were three emperors, three Popes and two kings of France until the fifteenth century which was marked by turbulence.

As noted above the fall of the House of Hohenstaufen led to minor princedoms weakening the Empire. Their politics tended to vacillate between leading dynasties, namely the Wittelsbachs based in Bavaria, the Luxemburgs, the Wettins in Saxony, and the Habsburgs of Austria. It was not until the fifteenth century with a series of Habsburg successions that the Empire could be said to have adapted to a form of hereditary monarchy. In Italy the power tended to revolve around Milan, Florence, and Venice, and it was a time of poets, poisoners, and Machiavellian machinations. It has been proposed that it was here that the rise of capitalism could first be detected. Florence produced the florin, and this standard currency spread beyond its own boundaries. During the fourteenth century Italy had its violent blood-feuds and produced the first merchant bankers who often benefitted from the conflicts, as does today's capitalism.

Meanwhile, the Papacy under Pope Boniface VIII (1294–1303) asserted its authority, but its political machinations and inhouse corruption caused such major ramifications it ended with the exile of the Popes to Avignon, which lasted until 1377. The French grasped the opportunity, and the next seven Popes were all French. The Church had become corrupted by high power politics. There were protests by men such as John Wycliffe (c.1330–84), Jan Hus (1372–1415) a Czech reformer, who were subject to political and ecclesiastical attacks. The Church failed to be a civilising influence and these times were noted not just for their brutality but the appetites for wealth and power.

Europe was always facing the issue of dynasties against dynasties trying to increase their territories by subduing their neighbours. France with its vast population by the standards of that day appeared to be the rising power. Under Philippe le Bel (grandson of St Louis) he took the city of Lyons (1312) thereby clashing with the Papacy. He was a tyrant, and his views became the country's law as with later modern tyrants such as Hitler and Stalin. However, he left a pattern of rule until the revolution of 1789. His Royal Council governed the kingdom, and the *parlement* controlled justice by registering the royal edicts, but it was not a parliament in today's understanding. However, during this century Philippe le Bel's three sons had no male heir between them, and the introduction of the Salic Law (excluding females) meant that in 1328 the throne passed to a new line with Philippe de Valois who founded his throne, rapidly contested by the English because of the Salic Law focused on by Shakespeare in his play *Henry V*.

In England under the Plantagenet King Edwards I-III, there was internal division, greedy nobles, and many foreign wars. It was the hope of King Edward I to create English domination over the British Isles. Shakespeare later made more of nationhood for political reasons during his life under the Tudors. King Edward I managed to hold down the Welsh, who never lost their sense of nationhood, and Scotland fought back with famous named figures such as Robert the Bruce and William Wallace and 'Scotland emerged as a nation-state much sooner than England did'.[1] It was not dissimilar in Ireland where the English gained a tenuous grasp, but Ireland persisted over the centuries to claim nationhood in its own right.

In the middle of the fourteenth century the quarrels and dynastic clashes took second place to the more frightening Black Death. The cause of this pandemic is uncertain, but it is generally accepted that 'it was fuelled by a devastating brew of three related diseases – bubonic plague, septicaemia-type plague, and pneumonic or pulmonary plague'.[2] The public reaction was curious, it ranged from sudden religious devotion and prayer, to fortitude, to 'eat, drink and be merry' because tomorrow we die. There was the fear that this was God's punishment, far different from today when the Covid pandemic was blamed on another nation, though in several places the Jews and lepers were blamed for the Black Death. The plague had many ramifications in Europe, and economic historians have indicated that amongst the impacts was the appearance of a labour shortage, demands for higher wages, and a more mobile population. It also gave rise to economic uncertainty and led to a series of revolts by the working classes from places such as Florence, Ghent, to England with the Peasants' Revolt in 1381, led by men such as Wat Tyler, Jack Straw and John Ball, a rebel priest.

The ingredients and seeds of aggressive and expansionist nationalism can be seen in these centuries with clarity. The forming nations of England and France were constantly in conflict in the so-called Hundred Years War (1337–1454) producing famous names and battles, and still continued long after with English claims on French territory through its so-called royal connections. This was the time of France's Joan of Arc as a prime figure of nationhood, and the English gloried in such battles as Crécy, Poitiers, and Agincourt, later used to stir up national fervour; the conflict possibly gave the English a sense of nationhood later exaggerated by Shakespeare. France was the more powerful, but England had its enduring benefit of the sea and naval fleet, a major strength until the late twentieth century.

England as governed by the Plantagenet dynasty had whipped up a sense of nationhood in its attacks on the French mainland, but it was somewhat dampened from the mid-fifteenth century onwards by its own dynastic struggles between the royal houses of Lancaster and York. They fought a civil war, not finishing until Henry VII the first Tudor rose to power, culminating at the battle of Bosworth (1485) with the death of King Richard III, whose body was recently discovered beneath a municipal carpark.

Similar machinations were occurring on mainland Europe with the rise of Burgundy as a would-be state, but in the late 1470s, when King Louis IX recovered what he considered his part of the original Burgundy, with the French increasing their dominance, East-Central Europe was a place of moving boundaries as the powerful dynasties vied with one another for control; the four main houses were the Habsburgs, the Luxembourgers, Angevins and the Jagiellons. Boundaries continuously shifted and changed over a short period of time, and the ingredients of aggressive expansionist nationalism were taking on even more meaning.

While the major growing countries such as France and England were engaged in territorial gains on flimsy excuses, in the East of Europe, the Hussites continued their struggles into Saxony and Silesia and Hungary, but they also had their own internal dissensions. Nowhere in Europe during this time was there any sense of security for the ordinary people. There were ramifications with the union of Lithuania and Poland, possibly instigated as a defence against the Teutonic knights. The Jagiellons rose in power and were assured of their ascendancy at the time after the defeat of the Teutonic knights at the Battle of Grunwald in 1410, and for a time ruled a major part of Christian Europe. It was the Habsburgs who eventually inherited Central Europe.

Religious belief and adherence played a leading role. As these dynasties rose and fell under the auspices of Catholic Christianity, it was claimed that all was done in the service of God as an act of justification. The division between Orthodox and Catholic was no longer of major significance, but there was a theocratic basis for these early European developments, which was not based on New Testament Christianity, but upon the interpretation of belief which could be manipulated for political purposes, and superstition for those in the lower social orders. The Church influence during this period was considerable playing a major part internationally, nationally, and at all levels of the social order. While medicine and science had started to emerge as serious studies, superstition remained a powerful component in everyday life. The Mass was spoken from a distance in the old Latin tongue, relics were believed to have miraculous qualities, hell and damnation were a serious hazard, and excommunication was seen as a threat more serious than a torturous death. Money could purchase the forgiveness of sins with larger amounts purchasing redemption. The Church played a major role in the development of law. There were varying systems ranging from Canon Laws, Ecclesiastical Codes, the King's Courts, and local laws also dominated many areas. Spanish law tried to codify its structures, and in England with King Henry II there had been the well-known development of Common Law. The punishments against breaking the law were normally capital punishment, frequently preceded by torture, amputations, brandings to act as a warning to others.

During this time of emerging nations progress was made on many fronts. Education made some limited progress and renowned universities were founded, even famous schools such as Winchester (1382) started. Literature made progress, not as much as devotional work, but there was some interest in the vernacular, such as the well-known *Anglo-Saxon Chronicle*. Military development saw the longbow and crossbow being developed during the fourteenth century, and the Turks used gunpowder for artillery, albeit primitive by future developments. Life for the late medieval person was changing, but it is easy to speculate that these advancements were only available for the leading houses and the rich. At the bottom end of the social ladder life remained one of impoverishment, survival, at times brutal. It has been suggested that these factors indicate that the fifteenth century was a time of transition between the medieval world and the modern, but it was limited to a few areas and to fewer people. However, the various monarchies were becoming aware of the need to create a sense of 'nationality' as descriptive of their domains, and to foster the sense of belonging, usually within the monarch's ownership.

There remained the issue of Islamic Christian boundaries, and especially in the Spanish area of Granada, where Muslims had retained a precarious grip in Western Europe. However, in the East, the Muslims were on the edge of taking Constantinople, and still controlled the North African coastal regions and dominated in the Middle East. A major event took place when the Turks took Constantinople in 1453 finally ending the old Roman Empire, but only to be followed in 1492 when they lost Granada to the Christian motivated Spaniards. In Rome, the fall of Constantinople had raised hopes of unifying Eastern and Western Christianity under the Papal banner, but there was the usual political friction with its traditional bigotry.

Moscow was standing on the brink of a new future. Various Kremlins (citadels) were appearing, and in Moscow, under Ivan III (by 1493) their Kremlin had become a vast red structure. Ivan III is regarded as the Tsar who cast off the Tartar yoke, and Ivan the Great, as he was known, is viewed as the restorer of Russian hegemony though some saw him as the Anti-Christ. Through the Habsburgs he sought the procurement of official recognition by the Pope, but the rift in the Christian corpus stopped this happening, and in the 1490s he took the Habsburg emblem of the double-headed eagle. In Russia, the state and their brand of Christianity were becoming inseparable, and from time to time the idea of Moscow becoming the Third Rome started to flourish as the Russian Orthodox Church took on its own particular shape. The Church and country became intertwined in their bid for their form of a recognisable nationalism. By the end of the fifteenth century Russia had a controlling oversight of territory from the Baltic shores to the Black Sea, with eyes turned towards Lithuania. By the 1490s Russia had surrounded Lithuania and soon there was a series of frontier wars. 'It is one of the wonderful coincidences of history that modern Russia and modern America both took flight in the same year of 1493. Europeans learned of the Americas, as they saw it, at the self-same moment that Muscovites learned that their Old World was not yet coming to an end'.[3]

Other major changes can be found in the emerging European life or habits in the early fifteenth century, when Prince Henry of Portugal (1394–1460; known as the Navigator) sent maritime expeditions down the West-African coast, occupied the Madeira and Canary Islands, and eliminated the inhabitants. This action would prove to be an enduring characteristic of invasions of new territories overseas, invoking the concept of expansionist nationalism as if by right of force of arms. This was part of the beginning of the European colonialism, which would soon become a dominant feature of European life, with future wider ramifications around the globe.

In Spain, Castile and Aragon were merging under marriage arrangements, but it was the time of the Grand Inquisitor Torquemada and Jews and remaining Muslims found they were obliged to convert to Christianity, which had the long-term ramification of making Spain a staunchly Catholic country. The fall of Granada in 1492 provided many converts and in the same year Christopher Columbus sailed to America though he had no idea where he had landed or what he had discovered. Significantly, Pope Alexander VI agreed to Spanish and Portuguese insistence that the borders between the two countries on the Iberian Peninsula be recognised, from which it may be assumed there was a growing sense of nationhood.

This period of European history saw parts of the map of Europe beginning to take shape, but it was still remote from the modern map. What was prominent and has remained is the constant bickering and conflict over borders, internal friction as to what the nation should be, the involvement or use of the Church, the perceived threat of Islam, and the constant suspicion of the next-door neighbouring country. Nations were not the modern nation-state, but they were clearly embryonic, and there is little doubt that the ruling classes invoked their sense of aggressive nationalism in times of military conflict. The working classes may have toiled at their labour in the fields to survive, but if called to die on the battlefield it was demanded because they were defending their nation. In Shakespeare's plays of Henry IV (Parts I and II) and in Henry V, though written later in about 1599 involving the battle of Agincourt of 1415, there is a distinct sense of nationalism. This is enhanced not only in the battle against the French, but there are the competing nationalistic figures of the Welsh soldiers Captains Fluellen and Gower, the Scottish officer Jamy and the Irish officer Macmorris. It is noticeable that each glory in his own nationhood but significantly they come to battle under Henry V against the French. The French must be opposed and the British Islands in this play appear as united under the King. Not too much should be read into this, but Nationalism's various configurations have similar ingredients in the mixing bowl of history.

The Renaissance

While the battles for territory and wealth by the various European dynasties continued there were growing signs of intellectual development. The precise dating of the well-known phenomena of the Renaissance and the Reformation remains difficult to define because they varied in different countries. The Renaissance reflected gifted individuals and had major ramifications during the Reformation. There was progress in science, overseas exploration was growing with vast changes in the expression of religion, but superstition and poverty remained a hallmark of the masses, especially those working in isolated country areas. The Renaissance was not simply the rebirth (*renatio* – Renaissance) of classical arts and ideals, but it produced some interesting individuals who questioned what was happening in their world. It could be argued that the Renaissance made room for the Reformation, and helped prepare for what would be described as modern Europe.

The Church started to lose much of its authority, because individual thinking was gaining a sense of freedom from habitual church control, the time had arrived when its claims of access to divine truth became contested. The Renaissance touched different but not all areas, much of it focused on some outstanding figures in Italy, such as Leonardo da Vinci (1452–1519) and Michelangelo (1475–1564). The Renaissance was not confined to Italy, and it started the road to freedom from the Church monopoly of always being right.

In the Renaissance there was a sense of growing intellectual freedom and liberation, but it is difficult to try and precisely delineate the depth or parameters. What was to become modern Italy produced some outstanding individuals who are now world famous, especially Leonardo da Vinci (1452–1519) and Michelangelo (1475–1564), but there were many more and not confined to Italy. Leonardo da Vinci had an inquisitive and inventive brain even stretching to the helicopter, submarine, and machine-guns, in theory. It was a new lease of life, which deepened the rift between West and Eastern Europe.

The Reformation involving Nationalism

This was a period when the traditional structure of the Church as long accepted as the Vatican came under scrutiny from those who no longer felt bound by Papal authority. One leading name during this development was Erasmus of Rotterdam. His real name was Gerhard Gerhards (which depends on various authorities) better known by his two very familiar pen-names Desiderius and Erasmus, (1466–1536). He was well-known for his intense study of theology, which was referred to as the 'Queen of Sciences'. In many ways Erasmus and others started to free Europe from the yoke of Christian hierarchical domination.

The Reformation had its roots in the freedom of the Renaissance, encouraging those who saw the need for the Church to reform, but not with the intention of dividing Christianity, which it eventually did, resulting in the two different and hostile forces of traditional Catholics and the Protestant Reformers. This was a critical stage in much of Europe's development and was often used as a means for nations attacking one another using religious belief as a motive for what is now called aggressive and expansionist nationalism. The traditional Roman Church had descended into the abyss of decadence. Chaucer's work offers today's readers some revealing insights, including the selling of indulgences for money. At the Papal level the various accounts of the Borgias (Rodrigo de Borgia, Pope Alexander VI 1492–1503) revealed the Pope, instead of praying for peace and love, was busy accruing wealth and enjoying sex, while ruthlessly pursuing the interests of his children. Pope Julius II (1503–13) followed on his heels, seeking political power and riding into battle with full armour.

There was the well-known backlash by Martin Luther (1483–1546) who nailed his '95 Theses' against indulgences to the door of Wittenberg's Castle Church. This action had wide ramifications, and divided the German princes, and Catholic and Protestant camps were soon in evidence. This was the start of many forms of protests. Huldrych Zwingli (1484–1531) in Switzerland challenged the Catholic Church on ecclesiastical and doctrinal matters. He also denounced indulgences with his theory of justification by faith, challenged the authority of the bishops and argued that the Mass was a purely symbolic rite. The rapidly emerging protests directed at Rome occurred in numerous ways across many countries. The Anabaptists were among the first fundamentalists who were crushed with outright barbarity. In England, Henry VIII became a Protestant Head of the English church not so much out of religious concern, but for political reasons, and needing a divorce as he had no male heir. It helped him economically because he found a new wealth in the sale of Church treasures in the dissolution of the many religious houses. The English Protestant Church looked doubtful for a time under Queen Mary, but soon became the national Protestant Church still known today as the Established Church of England. This development would later create nationalistic calls for Catholic Spain to invade Britain, using religious faith as the reason for aggressive nationalistic expansion.

John Calvin in Geneva (1509–64) came to prominence and was more radical than Luther, establishing an influential branch of Protestantism. It was the influence of Calvin which motivated John Knox (1513–72) and this form of Protestantism became the state Church of Scotland in 1560. Calvin also influenced the French Protestants known as the Huguenots, who were slaughtered on St Bartholomew's Day in appalling massacres on 23 August 1572. In Norway and Denmark, Hans Tansen became known as the Danish Luther, and by 1537 Protestantism became the state religion. It was the end of a united Catholic Europe now contested with various strands of Protestant versions, providing amongst the various motives for territorial expansion the Christian religion versions all based on love of one's neighbour.

Although the Catholic Church's decadence resulted in reform, the Reformation was cruel for many people. There were infamous massacres such as the Anabaptists and Huguenots, and as with the interfaith tensions many had to adapt new patterns of their beliefs for sheer survival. As the politics of the Christian faith became nationalised and changes were made, people sometimes found themselves having to change beliefs, then revert and change again. Political machinations used the Christian faith to its own ends, and England was targeted for reconversion and even conquest, aggressive nationalistic territorial gains and religious claims having been duly mixed as in a cement mixer. Some countries never settled comfortably. Ireland, for example, was first a strong Catholic country, but this was followed by a punitive and brutal expedition by Queen Elizabeth I (1598). Not long afterwards the Scottish Presbyterian Church was established in Ulster (1611), and the ramifications are still felt to this day because of the linking of religion to a specific territory, and thereby encouraging a sense of nationalism. As religious faith had long been in the melting pot for stirring up nationalistic feelings, now it became wider and with more venom.

In Germany they tried to resolve these problems in 1555 at the Peace of Augsburg where Princes tried to decide which interpretation of faith they should adopt. This was followed by the Catholic and Protestant leagues, which resulted in the Thirty Years War between the years 1618–1648 with its unbelievable cruelty, and an estimated eight million killed. The Thirty Years War had many causes and phases and was widespread and bitter. The causes were the traditional conflict between the German princes and the emperor, a war between Protestants and Catholics, and the ongoing conflict by states seeking more territory and power. The Treaty of Westphalia (a series of treaties signed between May and October 1648) in Osnabrück and Münster was an attempt to end this vicious conflict by trying to organise some international order. Germany was in poor condition, and hopes for a united Christendom appeared out of sight until the ecumenical movement in the twentieth century. The seeds of nationalism based on Christian denominations was a marked feature for centuries. It was a time of religious intolerance, but the safest place was Poland, ardently Roman Catholic and which was seen as the Christian barrier against the infidels, where necessity demanded tolerance, because this military defence border was deemed critical.

In Eastern Europe religious problems emerged with the Muscovite Patriarch extending his jurisdiction. At the Union of Brest in 1596 a new Uniate Communion was founded, namely the Greek Catholic Church of the Slavic Rite, which Moscow would not accept. There was a similar movement in Hungary with the Uniate communion when the Orthodox Ruthenes chose to look for union with Rome (1646).*

This religious war effected Europe into the seventeenth century, with still occasional rumbles to this day. The French suffered their religious wars from 1562 to 1598, Germany 1531–48, the infamous Thirty Years War already mentioned, and in England it surfaced continually and especially with the Pilgrimage of Grace (1516). There were no simple theological delineations as these religious wars were supported by dynastic aspirations. There was some form of resolution in what has been dubbed the Age of Reason, when some people queried burning heretics and the barbarous Inquisition, justified by the ridiculous claim that it saved souls.

---

* Ruthenes (Rusyns) were a diasporic ethnic group who spoke an East Slavic language known as Rusyn, and they descended from the Ruthenian peoples who never accepted the name Ukrainian.

Eighteenth Century and Beginning of Colonialism

During this era of development various names have been given to describe aspects of this period, the most popular being the Age of Reason; for others it represented growth of Absolutism. The Age of Reason is often associated with coming to rational terms with religious conflict which was essential, whereas Absolutism reflected a political system and its control, and the acquisition of territory now including overseas, and trade, power, and wealth. This was true of all countries, having greater ramifications in the more powerful nations. Each and every country was developing in its individual way. Switzerland with its mountain borders had republican confederations, the Holy Roman Emperor hereditary but elected, the British monarchy was slowly heading towards a constitutional base, but still holding considerable influence, especially in the new colonies. Absolute monarchs still played a major role, even in Sweden and Denmark. This was also the case in what could be described at the time as the strongest European nation of France, where Louis XIV, whose reign was one of the longest in European history, subdued his nobles with his absolute power and personal domination. His system seemed to work for him and a few successors, but it resulted in the total restructuring of France after the French Revolution of 1789.

During this era, the conquest of territories overseas expanded rapidly, and colonialism became the key word and frequently the centre of contention on land and at sea. Spain and Portugal made vast inroads into South America, and sea trade increased causing much friction. The Dutch founded colonies in Guyana and Curaçao and the Russians moved eastwards even claiming Alaska, which in 1912 they sold to the Americans for some seven million American dollars. The Russians even forced the Chinese to cede land between the Ussuri River and the Sea of Japan to build their principal Pacific port of Vladivostok. However, the French and British took full advantage of this development, claiming considerable territory in other continents. The French founded colonies in India, North America and Canada, and were constantly in commercial competition and military confrontation with the British, in their frantic efforts for territory, influence, and wealth. It largely went in Britain's favour because of the strength of their Royal Navy. This colonisation fell more to the control of the maritime states, and countries such as Austria and Germany, with few naval forces, remained somewhat in the background. When these European nations took distant territories, placing their national flag of ownership on the coastline, it was an extension of expansionist and therefore aggressive nationalism. The political forces of Europe were greedily expanding their power in places less developed in military resources and where they were unwelcome. The vastness of discovery around the globe, revealing the remotest of places to maritime navigators was almost seen as cherry-picking. It was safer than fighting in Europe, which was developing the well-known Balance of Power. However, the growth of colonies had its own ramifications on this so-called 'Balance', but religion was rarely involved, except the excuse to convert the primitive barbarians, but it was simply a blatant demand to increase territory, power, prestige, and wealth, at heart nationalistic as it set one nation against another as being superior. The Vikings and other tribes had used sea-routes, but now it was being exploited on a global level, and British naval superiority would gain the upper hand, giving West Europe's offshore Atlantic islands a world empire, for a brief time.

A Brief Overview of Europe

This colonisation also produced a new class of wealthy men and professional classes who carried more influence within the social structure than in previous times. It could be argued that during this era developed the wealthy patronage cities such as Paris, St Petersburg, Vienna and Dresden with their buildings and gardens becoming the exhibitions of Europe. Music, art, and literature flourished but the religious problems continued to rumble on in various places. There were occasional outbursts of bigotry as when Louis XIV suddenly attacked the Huguenots, but overall, the religious strife settled, and in England the established Church of England in time tolerated the emergence of Methodists, Baptists and other branches of the Christian faith. This spiritual and intellectual aspect had many benefits of tolerance and gave some sense to the term enlightenment. There were of course some fraught moments but not the brutal behaviour of the religious wars. It would no longer be a characteristic of national enhancement to call upon one denomination to attack another on these grounds, as Catholic Spain had once tried to attack Protestant England. Kant once wrote that 'mankind grew out of its self-inflicted immaturity' but whether humanity could move away from its brutal parental roots still remains questionable to this day with ongoing nationalistic types of wars in the Ukraine and Middle East at the time of writing (April 2024).[4] The sense of rationalism was not universal in Europe, but often limited to a few gifted people such as Immanuel Kant, John Locke who studied knowledge (epistemology), along with Berkeley an Irishman and Hume in Scotland. Some philosophers in pursuing rationalism tried challenging religion itself leading to a form of Deism popular in France. Voltaire (whose real name was Françoise-Marie Arout, 1694–1778) sought religious tolerance, peace between nations, liberty in politics and commerce. Rousseau (1712–78) was more challenging but never had Voltaire's appeal. These centuries, as inferred above, have many sub-titles to describe the historical developments, many of them motivated by a handful of highly gifted individuals.

England was busy building up its territorial gains in other countries, which were many times massively larger in land and population than Britain, and during this era in Europe France was regarded as the major dominant power, starting under the long reign of Louis XIV. It would remain powerful until the defeat of Napoleon in 1815. Under Louis XIV, France, a massive territorial expanse was economically well off and militarily strong, albeit surrounded by enemies. Spain was showing signs of decline, Germany had suffered from its Thirty Years War, Austria was more worried by the Ottomans, and Britain was tucked safely away some 20 miles across the stretch of the turbulent channel.

Louis XIV, who reigned for seventy-two years, was known as the Sun-King, and typified by his absolute rule. His palace of Versailles became an international symbol of his power from where he subdued those nobles who questioned his authority. He developed his power and publicity through the Versailles Palace producing his well-known quip that *L'État, c'est moi*, meaning that his word was law. It was undoubtedly the type of leadership which had ruled in the early tribes and re-emerged powerfully in the mid-twentieth century with figures like Hitler, Stalin, and Franco. This was a dangerous hangover from primitive times and persists to this day, indicating that it is part of humankind's makeup. Louis XIV was not a benevolent despot but carried all the characteristics of a dictator. In matters of religion, and for reasons of power like Henry VIII in England, he clashed with the Papacy with his Declaration of the Four Articles (1682). This was an effort to limit Catholic influence, claiming the Pope was not infallible. He claimed to have a passive acceptance of religious toleration, but suddenly attacked the Huguenots, with financial ramifications, because these Protestants had been a valuable part of the French economy. His army was powerful, and some neighbouring countries were concerned about him expanding, but there are no indications that he wanted to control Europe. However, he had four major wars, two against the Netherlands, the third resulted from his wish to acquire German territory, and the fourth was the result of Spain's failing dynasty which became the War of the Spanish Succession (1701–13). This was financially draining for France and their opponents resulting in the Treaties of Utrecht (1713) and Rastatt (1714).

Louis XIV died, and Louis XV (1723–74) who was only interested in personal pleasures, so the financial crisis deepened, with the gulf between most French people and the monarchy widening, indicating potential problems. These occurred during the reign of Louis XVI leading to the French Revolution of 1789 with monumental consequences for France and Europe, because the nationalistic traits which increase the possibility of conflict and war increased.

France had dominated Western Europe for a prolonged period of time during this period, but Britain, seeing itself as a United Kingdom, which it was by force and somewhat tenuous to this day, was also emerging as a noted power with its Royal Navy and merchant sailors, some of whom were pirates. The Cromwellian period was followed by the restoration of King Charles II, Britain survived two Dutch Wars and two Scottish rebellions by the Covenanters. Charles was succeeded by his brother James II who was a staunch Catholic, which led to two rebellions one by the Duke of Argyll in Scotland, and the better known one of the Duke of Monmouth. Religious issues still marked the British Isles. The Protestants were victorious and the Dutch Stadholder, William of Orange together with King James' daughter Mary came to the throne. It resulted in the victory of the Orangemen in the bloody battle of the Boyne (1690) in Ireland, and the British Islands had its famous so-called Glorious Revolution of 1688–9 which gave British history the legend of the absolutism of the British Parliament, but it was a hope more than a reality. It was not an easy relationship with Scotland and in 1715 and 1745 there were the Jacobite revolts which resulted in the Battle of Culloden (1746) and the decimation of the Scottish Highlands. Ireland also had its problems stimulated by the Protestant (typically British landowners) reaction towards Catholics, indicating that the Age of Enlightenment and Reason had not shone very brightly in this part of the European scene. There was brutal repression, bigotry, famines, and the abortive rebellion of Wolfe Tone (1798), but eventually Ireland was forced into the United Kingdom through the Second Act of Union in 1801. As from this time the United Kingdom was more widely known as Great Britain which was, 'however, a euphemism for great England. No eighteenth-century monarch visited Wales, Scotland, or Ireland', and the first two King Georges took their holidays at home in Hanover.[5]

When the United Kingdom chose the new monarchy, they selected the Hanoverians, the first four King Georges (1714–1830), and the country started to acquire the first fragrances of a constitutional monarchy. It also led to the inevitable loss of the American colonies but with colonial expansion elsewhere. The loss of the American colonies was significant from the point of view of this study because it was, from the American point of view, a secessionist form of nationalism, which was more acceptable as it could be defined as falling within the justification of self-defence.

As noted above Spain was in national debt and losing its assertions of power, as well as many of its colonies while the ordinary masses suffered under the wealthy nobles (known as the Grandees) and the Church's Inquisition. Its partner Portugal on the Iberian Peninsula was in a similar state, suffering from the Lisbon earthquake on 1 November 1755, which ironically happened to be the religious festival of All Saints' Day. Italy remained divided with boundaries frequently changing with constant tensions between the Habsburgs and the House of Savoy.

In the northern regions in Sweden Charles XII (1697–1717) tried once more to achieve greatness, but after this failure 'the Scandinavian countries settled down to an existence of inoffensive obscurity'.[6] Sweden developed a strong reaction to royal absolutism, and the emphasis was upon the Diet and the monarchy weakened.

Meanwhile in Eastern Europe there was continuous contention over borders characterised by the threat of the Ottomans, but also with the emerging powers of Prussia and Russia. The Ottoman power during the late seventeenth century was under the grand viziership of the Köprülüs of Albanian extraction. In 1683 they started another siege of Vienna, trying to free the Dardanelles from the Venetians along with disputes over Crete. They attacked Poland but were held back (1681–2) and declared Hungary as an Ottoman vassal. The siege of Vienna was a serious encroachment occurring because of the Western pre-occupation with Louis XIV. The threat of the Ottomans faded over the next two centuries, later being known as the 'sick man of Europe'.*

In 1699 by the Peace of Carlowitz Hungary became a domain of Austria. The frontier issues along with seeking territory and power through dominance vacillated and three Russian wars against the Turks between 1735 and 1792, left the north coast of the Black Sea in the hands of the now expanding Russian Empire. The Ottomans were no longer regarded as invincible, which was confirmed when the Serbians organised themselves mainly under the Habsburg flag, but Serbia showed at the time that it wanted its independence, and has done so ever since. Bulgaria suffered during this era as it was on the natural route for various armies. The area became well known for its growing number of bandits who established their little fiefdoms, giving the impression it was a few centuries behind compared to the West, with a similar pattern of local rule in Albania. Only Gora (Montenegro) escaped Ottoman rule because of its mountainous features. The grandiose titles of Western Europe such as the Renaissance, Reformation, Enlightenment, or the Age of Reason hardly entered Eastern Europe where kinship and bribery remained the convention. These ingredients could be found in Western Europe, but it was somewhat concealed by the pretence of civilisation, with the consequence of leaving a noticeable gulf between Western and Eastern Europe.

---

* In 1853 John Russell prior to the Crimean War quoted Nicholas I of Russia as describing the Ottoman Empire as the 'sick man'.

When the Ottoman threat decreased the Habsburg dynasty was on better ground for extending its influence. Joseph I (1705–1711) and Charles VI (1711–40) had mastery over an empire which included Hungary, the Netherlands and much of Italy. As elsewhere the lack of a male heir was a major issue, and Charles VI tried to ensure his daughter Maria Theresa succeeded him. However, the throne was taken by Charles Albert the Elector of Bavaria, who ruled as Charles VII with French support as the only non-Habsburg in four centuries. It then reverted to Maria Theresa's husband Francis I (1746–65) making Maria Theresa the well-known and major leader in Vienna for nearly forty years. She was not the typical royal leader because she was concerned about agrarian reform and the state of the working serfs, a feature often referred to as 'enlightened despotism'. As early as 1780 there were reforms announced ordering religious toleration which included the Jews, the serfs were emancipated, and Austria also established a professional class of office holders (known as *cameralism*) who were trained in the University of Vienna establishing a professional Civil Servant class. Despite these forms of progress, the Empire was constantly under threat by the dynastic policies and demands of its various princes. The various Electors such as the Wettins, (kings of Poland-Lithuania) and the Hohenzollerns (of Prussia) and the Electors of Hanover (who ruled Britain) wanted to increase their personal prestige and power. Hungary, free of the Turks, now fell subject to the Habsburgs who despite Hungarian Diets and proclamations, were largely ignored by Vienna, and there was a rebellion (1704–1711) by Francis Rákóczi II when the Habsburgs were preoccupied with Spain and the Turks. Austria and Hungary were treated as one entity, but the Hungarian desire for independence was constant, and the work of Maria Theresa helped form the modern state.

In European development during this period Prussia, albeit small in size, was emerging as a powerful force. It would soon be a critical state because of its later role in German unification. Prussian efficiency was well-known, as was its military capability with an army officered with minor to major aristocrats. The Hohenzollerns created their own dynasty which demanded loyalty and military ability, giving the sense they were growing their own nation and using the early cries of nationalism for their cause. This was more than evident with Frederick the Great (1740–86) when war was the national policy for aggrandisement, and it was little wonder that Hitler always had Frederick's portrait on his walls. In 1740 Austrian Silesia was taken, and later using diplomacy armed with threats, they occupied land in the first partition of Poland. There were two Silesian wars (1740–2 and 1744–45), and in 1745 Frederick occupied Prague, and during the Seven Years War he attacked Saxony. Under Frederick-William II times were less belligerent, and the Russians kept them at bay, but despite this, during the later partitions of Poland, Prussia acquired both Danzig and Warsaw. Prussia's activities had distinct similarities with earlier times turning that part of Europe into an area of instability of who dominated who. All this occurred because of the dynamism and impetus for national aggrandisement, carrying all the ingredients of aggressive and expansionist nationalism.

However, Russia was beginning to dominate the East of Europe, because it was the largest country, and as aggressive as Prussia. The Romanovs during the seventeenth century had placed Russia on the major stage. After many battles reflecting the expanding passions of two controversial Tsars, Peter I (The Great – 1682–1725) and Catherine (1726–96), both of whom had reputations varying between the great and the monstrous. During what is called the Second Northern War (1700–21) against Charles XII of Sweden, Tsar Peter managed to take the Swedish provinces of Livonia and Ingria where the foundations of St Petersburg were to be laid. Tsar Peter the Great had soon taken control of the north and faced the West. He started a long-standing feature of Russia as a powerful state of major proportions.

Catherine, like Peter had moral shortcomings, having murdered her own husband Peter III (1761–2) followed by a long retinue of lovers. She ruled a country which 'already possessed more land than it could usefully exploit and kept on indulging its gargantuan appetite'.[7] The Russians took possession of much of Sweden-Finland as well as Poland-Lithuania. Eventually they occupied the Ottoman areas of the Black Sea provinces including the Crimea (1783) and reaching as far as Alaska. It was the base tribal passion for territory which was the driving force. The Ukraine always desperate for its own independence as witnessed today (2024) with President Putin's attack on that country, was ruled under Russian supervision by the Dnieper Cossacks, Kiev became a Russian city, and the Russian Orthodox Church was forced on the Slavs. In 1794 Odessa was made the capital of what was called the 'New Russia'.

Amongst those to fall to Russian domination was the Republic of Poland-Lithuania, which had first been subject to indirect which soon became direct domination. Poland-Lithuania had always been subject to diplomatic and military threats and incursions. It was after Sobieski's death in 1696 that Russian pressure intensified assuming a protective patronage, but also providing a long-term buffer state between Russia and the West. The last King of Poland, Stanisław August Poniatowski (1764–95) had been one of Catherine's lovers, and he was tasked with reform yet accepting Russian supremacy. On three occasions the Russian army arrived to ensure their orders were kept, and devised partition as a punishment, which happened many times. It did not involve any significant wars but the three partitions (1773, 1793, and 1795) were always underwritten with the threat of violence. Lithuania like Poland always recalled its independent past, continuing to develop its own identity despite being subject to aggressive neighbours, but Poland and Lithuania were Russian captives.

Europe's sense of the balance of power, with each nation watching others with nervous anticipation was becoming a feature of international life. It was not a clash over ideologies, religious faith, or system of government, or even pride in nationhood, but the growing dynasties keeping their territories safe against potential intrusion, but always the possibility of expansionism fermenting in their aggressive nationalistic minds. At the end of the seventeenth century America, closely related to Europe, was forming a Republican Institution, the British were assuming a world empire, Russia was looking towards Turkish domains, the Prussians were even considering interfering in the Netherlands. In France Louis XVI was faced with national bankruptcy. It was often entitled the Age of Enlightenment, but Europe remained always on the edge of territorial friction, and the ordinary masses continued to suffer under dynastic ambitions, which would later support a major revolution in France with European consequences.

This era has also been dubbed the Age of Reason and the Age of Enlightenment, and there was some progress in intellectual circles, advances in science, and religious conflicts were showing some signs of receding. However, international conflict remained as tenuous as it had been in earlier times. Seeking power by territory was Europe's enduring characteristic. It was the time of royal despotic leaders and aristocratic nobles, always based on the concept of their nation, invoking a sense of nationalism to stir up their nations fervour of supremacy, especially in the masses expected to die for the cause. It was notably the aggressive form of nationalism which demanded expansionism as a right, and the subjugation of their own people to this purpose.

Europe and its Expansion in Colonies

Europe's countries were starting to take on a recognisable albeit vague shape, and during this era humankind made some intellectual and technological steps forward despite the religious upheavals. However, a major feature of national life was finding roots in aggressive expansionism overseas in the discovery of new lands and by occupying them, namely the start of extensive colonialism. It started with those nations who had seaports and vessels capable of crossing oceans. As mentioned above the Portuguese explorers had travelled down the African coastline, and Christopher Columbus had crossed the Atlantic. The motivations for further investigations rapidly heated up on grounds of seeking wealth and territory, even if from the seaman's viewpoint it was genuine curiosity.

By 1513 the Pacific was seen for the first time by a European who wandered across the Panama Isthmus, and the first inquisitive steps were taken towards

China. The Spanish were amongst the first to occupy other lands ignoring the natural inhabitants causing considerable bloodshed in these new occupations. This was characterised in 1519–20 when Cortez (1485–1547) seized the Aztec Empire in Mexico, and Francisco Pizarro (1476–1541) subdued the Incas in Peru. The Dutch, French, and English promptly followed in seeking new land and wealth. This resulted in international sea trade routes being established causing wars at sea and with the arrival of the well-known pirates in greater numbers, many becoming national heroes.

These maritime traders flew their national flags, and the usual European nationality rivalry soon stretched across the oceans, as they contested with one another in this new form of expansionist nationalism. As early signs of modern Europe emerged it has been suggested that this distant colonisation divided Europe on the old East-West lines, that 'Europe was almost cut in two. The West was preoccupied with the sea. The East preoccupied with itself'.[8] Apart from this political factor these overseas discoveries followed by occupation and claimed ownership, led not only to the now recognised immoral slave trade, but 'another, still more dramatic and far-reaching consequence of European global outreach was ecological. Plants and animals, as well as people were carried across the oceans, transforming the ecological balances, the economics, and the landscape of the entire world, though most rapidly and sweepingly those of the neo-Europes where large numbers of settlers clustered'.[9]

As the European map was shaping the privilege and power remained with the hereditary power-classes, but this new overseas growth witnessed the arrival of the new monied classes, and capitalism started to grow exponentially. It was evident in the growing cities and ports, and although it has often been suggested that the Protestant work ethic was a driving force, the fact remains that religion had meant less for many of the new rich, happy only to increase their wealth.

The military life was also developing with the long pike, muskets, and artillery, and especially at sea with ships becoming floating artillery fortresses, developing more manoeuvrability and navigational aids. The coastal fortifications were designed to resist artillery attack, which was rapidly becoming the key instrument in many forms of war. These developments indicated that Europe was changing and the nation state emerging. However, the problems and issues of tribal days was still prevalent with the human instinct to increase territory, assume power, seek personal wealth, and was epitomised by the monarchical leaders who would use race, religion, culture, and their sense of superiority. The excuse of Christianising the so-called pagan concealed the political drive for power, as tribes in distant lands were baptised at the point of the sword. This is often illustrated by the conduct of the Spanish conquistadors in what is now South America, but other European nations often followed the same patten.

Some writers have projected the view that 'nationhood' or nationalism in the modern sense was emerging, but this is debatable because this view is only based on the premise that the seeds are more obvious to identify. During this time, the royal dynasties were, as always, changing shape, growing, or diminishing, and in some cases dependent on the commercial success of trade and overseas acquisitions in the continuous search for power and wealth.

Nevertheless, there was no sense of a significant totalitarian control in most of Europe, and under the authoritative figure of King Francis I in France there was consultation with the nobles. In England, the Tudors had asserted their monarchical authority only to have it damaged when the lack of an heir resulted in the Stuarts and the rise of Parliamentary power. Even in the Holy Roman Empire, the Diet occasionally held some influence over the emperor. However, while control over the military had always been essential, the mercantile life was now a critical factor for many leaders.

At this stage in Europe's development there was a growing acceptance of internationalism signified by the increasing number of ambassadors in foreign lands. Venice was the first to start this trend, others followed, with the Papacy demanding that their ambassadors were given precedence. The diplomatic corps came into being with one country's representatives seeing themselves as superior to others. There had always been spies (in tribal times 'lookouts') but it was during this era that the Secret Services evolved, gathering information about other nations and cliques. This was the time when codes and secret agents began to have significance.

A Cross-Slice of European Aggressive Nationalism

At this stage of the study, it seems appropriate to take a recap of what was happening across the European scene, because aggressive nationalism appeared fully unleashed, with the various dynastic houses across the continent fighting to expand territory, gaining dominance one way or another. This section of the chapter explores the nineteenth century the precursor to the modern era, and it is important to picture how the map of Europe was taking shape.

The Habsburg House associated with Austria was one of the most significant of the dynasties, and for a time continued enlarging because of weakening neighbours and through matrimonial arrangements. Maximilian I's marriage gained him Burgundy and in 1490 he inherited Tyrol and a year later Bohemia. This continued in 1515 when Hungary and the Habsburg growth took on a vast stretch of Europe through the marriage-bed and subsequent treaties. His grandson Charles was elected the Holy Roman Emperor despite opposition by France and the Papacy. 'He was the last Emperor to cherish a dream of universal unity and has been invoked by some in contemporary times as patron of a united Europe'.[10] There were frictional and military moments of confrontation with France over territory ranging from the Netherlands to Lorraine, Savoy, and the Pyrenees.

At one time Spain, for a brief time, appeared to be the greatest power in Europe especially under Philip II (1556–98) with its wealth, overseas acquisitions, and military powers. It suffered from internal problems and was opposed by France and England, meeting much resistance in its occupation of the Netherlands. For Philip II religious friction remained a problem, especially when he used the offices of the Inquisition to crush the Dutch and other Protestants, even intervening against the French Huguenots. His famous Great Armada (1588) against England was confronted by Drake and destroyed by storms. To maintain an army in the distant Netherlands cost Philip II far too much in financial terms, making Spain once again bankrupt in 1596.

The Netherlands had started their revolt in 1566 until 1648 against the Spanish, a form of secessionist nationalism, which under the guidance of the Just War theories was an acceptable war as it was one of national self-defence. The Low Countries had all forms of Christian denominations, with the Catholic element being dominant amongst the Walloons of Hainault, Namur, and Liège, against the Calvinist influence of Holland, Utrecht, and Zeeland. There had been attempts at some form of ecclesiastical reform under the regency of Margaret of Parma (1599–67), which had been repressed with the characteristic brutality of Philip II, with only the well-known William of Orange fighting on. The Netherlands was a substantial distance from Spain, and the Dutch were encouraged and helped by the French and English, for political reasons of opposing Spanish power. Eventually, the Netherlands became a powerful maritime power and developed its own governance, with a degree of religious toleration making it a relative safe haven for dissidents.

France, always surrounded by potential enemies was entering a period of fresh dynamism. France had continuously fought wars of acquisition from Naples to Angevin claims, and it was from this period that the long-lasting Franco-German feud may be traced, once again indicating the main ingredients of aggressive and expansive nationalism. France descended into a conflict of internal religious wars. The power of the Catholic Church remained strong and even during the reigns of the monarchs Louis XIII (1610–51) and his son Louis XIV (1643–1715), churchmen such as Cardinal de Richelieu and Cardinal Mazarin carried major influence. France asserted itself on the German border, and in 1558 had taken Calais from the intrusive English, effectively locking England out of Europe. The passion for territory mixed with religious problems was a hallmark across much of Europe.

England, having lost its last foothold on the European mainland, turned inwards, but also had its own contentious conflicts. However, the Church of England, the Monarchy, Parliament, and the Royal Navy emerged as the basic foundations for English life. Despite its habitual resentment over English domination, Wales came under English control, but Scotland, had already formulated its own tradition of nationhood. This perpetuated border problems with well-known battles fought as the English sought supremacy. When Elizabeth I died without an heir, the problem seemed to be resolved by the house of Stuarts with Mary's son King James VI of Scotland and James I of England. The Scottish desire to retain its independence continued into the eighteenth century and has politically and almost successfully reasserted itself in this the twenty-first century. In 1534 Henry VIII had declared himself King of Ireland, which was to cause trouble in the centuries ahead. The Scottish and Irish problems have always dogged the British Isles, and in the late twentieth century riot and mayhem in Northern Ireland was met by military force. During the seventeenth century England was accruing territorial gains not in Europe but overseas. Familiar names such as Maryland, Virginia, New England, Jamaica, New York, New Jersey, and countless others enlarged England's start for what would be dubbed the British Empire in years to come. The English may have been kicked out of Calais but were more than busy taking French colonies helped by the growing strength of the Royal Navy.

Religious issues persisted, and during these complex years Scotland felt able to riot and cross the border and even to help the Irish. To raise taxes for these wars King Charles I was obliged to summon Parliament, but this all eventuated in the English Civil War, spreading to Scotland and Ireland. This Civil War had its own religious undertones, the Catholics and Anglo-Catholics supporting the Crown, while Cromwell and his men tended to be of the Calvinistic and Puritanical tradition. Cromwell's New Model Army won the day (with decisive battles at Marston Moor 1642 and Naseby 1645), and the republican zealots executed Charles I on 31 January 1649 from Whitehall Palace. Cromwell became the Lord Protector, a form of despot, and when he died it was decided a tamer despot was needed. King Charles II returned from exile in 1660, this was all very British, but there were similar religious-political struggles across Europe in the tussle for power.

While the British were seeking unification, in Scandinavia they were demanding independence. Sweden had been under Danish control but in 1520 there was a revolt over the coronation of yet another Danish King. Under Gustav Eriksson Vasa (1526–60) the Swedes managed to rid the country of the Danish army leaving Denmark and Norway under Frederick I (1523–33), while in Sweden 1527 Gustavus Vasa created the Erastian Church and abolished the

Catholic Rite. No one nation in these northern climes was able to establish control of the Baltic region, but Sweden during this time tended to be the most powerful force.

During these centuries Poland and Lithuania were controlled by the Jagiellons making it the largest state in Europe in this period. It had not suffered from religious wars and had resisted the Ottoman incursions. In 1569 in the Union of Lublin the Republic (*Rzeczpospolita*) resulted over the issue of dynastic heirs, so it was governed by a common elective monarchy and a Diet, and this unusual experiment lasted until 1648. The only wars were over control of borders and not by seeking new territories. However, in 1648 the Cossacks in the Dnieper brought them into conflict as far as the Vistula, with Catholics and Jews slaughtered across the Ukraine. Other invasions occurred with the Muscovites in 1654–67 and the Swedes in 1655–60. The Transylvanians and Brandenburgers followed bringing the country to the point of collapse, but Poland survived and with the Swedes defeated, the Muscovites pushed back, and the Brandenburgers were bribed. The result of the Truce of Andrusovo (1667) handed Kiev and part of the Ukraine to the Russians for technically twenty years, but this became an ongoing problem to this very day, with this era reflecting the growing power of Muscovy and Prussia.

At this stage Prussia had been in decline, the Teutonic knights fighting to convert found the pagans of Lithuania were now Christian inclined, and they had lost the major battle at Grunwald in 1410. Early in the next century diplomatic links were forged and the Hohenzollerns of Berlin permitted the twin titles of Elector of Brandenburg and Duke of Prussia. Frederick-William was known as the Great Elector, and it was his troops who in 1656 occupied Warsaw, and as one historian noted, 'the Prussian spirit was on the march'.[11]

In the emerging nation of Russia, following Tsar Ivan III who rid them of the Tartar yoke, Ivan IV (1533–84), known as Ivan the Terrible, unleashed his reign of terror. He virtually erased Novgorod, founded the independence of the Russian Orthodox Church, and through fear made his domination subservient to himself. It was during this era that Russia began to assert itself, in the time of his son Feodor (1598) it was known as the 'Time of Troubles' which was followed by the rise of the Romanovs some fifteen years later. There was internal friction and attacks by the Swedes, Tartars, and the Poles, reflecting the era of the Dark Ages. The Polish threat was stemmed in 1619 and Smolensk was recovered in 1654. The most significant development was the seizure of the Ukraine from the Poles, and the contest for power between Russia, Poland, and Sweden as to who would set the course of Eastern Europe.

The Ottoman Empire reached it pinnacle at the time the Habsburgs were expanding, when it was decided that the Sultan would be the leader of the Sunni branch of Islam. As with Christianity and most religious beliefs Islam had its own factions and consequent battles. Sultan Selim I (1512–20) made a series of aggressive moves against Persia which was followed with the occupation of Damascus, Cairo, and Baghdad along with the holy centre of Mecca. This action sent out warning signals that Islam was expanding again, and in 1529 the Turks were just contained at the Siege of Vienna. A truce in 1533 was arranged resulting in the partition of Hungary. The Islamic expansion under the Turks effected the Mediterranean area with successful attacks on Rhodes, (1522) Algiers (1529), Tripoli (1551), Cyprus (1571), and only Malta survived these incursions (1565). The Ottoman activity managed to turn Christian Europe's attention away from its own religious and political problems.

In this brief overview of European development, some intellectual progress by a few brilliant individuals had surfaced, a new world overseas was appearing. However, humankind's problems remained focused on the pursuit of territory, prestige, power, and wealth. Religion and politics were intertwined like a complex undergrowth, dynasties rose and fell depending on military and marital arrangements, while the masses had little choice but be influenced by their various leaders to support one cause or another. The map of Europe by 1700 was taking a shape, but somewhat distant from today's parameters. The modern nation was formulating, and always with the distinctive elements of aggressive nationalism. Some of this impulse for nationhood came from the masses, but it was utilised if not stimulated by the powerful rulers and their dynastic houses, stirring up emotional feelings in their populations. When Englishmen fought against the Armada, or the Netherlands against Spain, it was all a matter of convincing their people that it was done for their country or their adopted Christian denomination, but for the rulers it was their power which was central to their motivations. The need for national survival grew, thereby increasing the demand for larger national armies and military progress. This was always coupled with a dislike of neighbours because they were foreigners, or held to a different religious belief, and the helpless masses had no choice but to obey. This growing aggressive nationalism, which for this writer was part of the human genetic makeup, was often enhanced and imposed by the political leaders of the day.

The Time of Revolution

The final phases of the eighteenth and the start of the next century were highly significant, mainly because of Revolution, not just the political upheaval in 1789 France, but revolution as producing major new trends at a social level. This was the period when the first signs of the Industrial Revolution, started to blossom and grow dramatically in the nineteenth century. It was a blanket title to describe the technological, scientific, and engineering advances which also led to demographic, social, and organisational changes. It was generally characterised by new machines, steam power, the science of metallurgy, and growth of coalmines. These advances led to factories, communications, and agrarian changes. This developing era is also regarded as the time of the Agricultural Revolution, mainly because the new inventions changed the nature of farming. Machines needed durable steel, coalmining became an industry, and in Lancashire and Yorkshire the growth of huge textile factories, with rural places like Manchester becoming industrial cities. Communication links were essential, and roads, rivers, canals, and later rail-networks proliferated.

The distinctive changes in demography were significant because industrial sites needed people living outside their gates, and not widespread across the traditional rural landscape. Rural and city poverty had not been much different, but the new industrial poverty, of living side-by-side was known to be more dangerous. It was not just the spreading of illness brought about by insanitary conditions, but criminality increased with the desperate poverty. The individuality of the rural scene gave way to the larger conurbations, and for those in authority they perceived dangers as a collective force which could be used for mass dissent. Landowners and the new mercantile wealthy accrued the wealth of the industrial era, some artists, writers, poets, and musicians flourished under their patronage, but nothing changed for the masses. However, there was a growing awareness of the potential strength in numbers, and since the French Revolution the fear of revolution was a concern for any government be it monarchical, republican and all the alternatives.

The word 'Revolution' has wide meanings, but for most people prompts thoughts on the French Revolution, for some the English Civil War, or the 1689 Glorious Revolution, and more pertinently the Russian Revolution when the Bolsheviks chased from power the last Romanov Tsar Nicholas II. It was the French Revolution which had far-reaching consequences in and beyond the French borders. At the time for many people outside France, the Revolution portrayed mob-rule and the reign of terror, for others it was the dawn of the modern political world. It certainly projected Europe into a state of turmoil for twenty to thirty years. The causes of the Revolution in France are still debated to this day but there were similar stirrings elsewhere in Europe.

In France it was the bankruptcy of France and its *Ancien Régime* which had the undivided attention of its finance ministers such as Turgot, Necker, Calonne and others, who failed to stop the financial cataclysm. King Louis XVI had planned reform but many French people at all levels of society had tired of total absolutism. Ironically, it was the King and some nobles who called for the changes to the French system, not realising it would provoke a revolution where violence bred violence. The nobles of the French court were as divided as many of the intellectuals. The storming of the Bastille has stood as the historical image of these times in France, leading to armed camps, which gained momentum and came as a shock to the whole of Europe. In the early years of 1789–94 it was radical as it destroyed every aspect of the monarchical regime, and in 1791 introduced a new constitution which called for elections, but too many laws were passed to process as the Jacobin grip took a two-year control. Rumours abounded that the Prussian army was near to Paris, the king's Swiss guards were killed, and Louis XVI guillotined with the Republic being proclaimed.

Governmental control fell to committees led by Danton and Robespierre. The second phase started with the new French Republican calendar known as Thermidor II 27 July 1794, when the Revolution appeared to pause. Robespierre fell from power, and in 1795 another constitution appeared. By 1798 a three-man Consulate was declared under a referendum and in May 1802, France's world-famous general became First Consul, and in May 1804 Napoleon was proclaimed Emperor. The fear of foreign interference and Napoleon's success had replaced one absolute monarch with another.

It had not been a Revolution without internal rancour, the Girondins with their attempts at cooperation and moderation fell, while the Jacobins (mainly lawyers) had led the mob with Danton at the head, sometimes known as the 'Archangel of Terror'. By 1792 atheism appeared to be the order of the day and clergy lost their many assets and the Church was widely attacked. Bonaparte organised a Concordat with the Papacy in 1801, but the French Catholic Church lost their power, and the repressed French masses found freedom, making them the victors of the revolution for a brief time.

Discontent at various levels and on different issues continued and in places such as Vendée there was a three-year civil war. Bonaparte raised a conscripted army, introduced new ranks, and gave aristocratic titles to those who served the new developing community. When he was crowned at Notre Dame in 1804 Pope Pius VII was present, but Napoleon placed the crown on his own head. It was a time of war, commerce was limited by opposition to free trade with a maritime struggle with the British, and in 1806 Napoleon announced (Berlin Decree in 1806) that the British Isles were to be blockaded. However, the British were more capable of enforcing their actions with their maritime powers.

This phase in French history had deep ramifications. The belief in human rights may not be identifiable in Revolutionary France, but the 'Declaration of the Rights of Man and the Citizen' reflected part of the English Bill of Rights in 1689, offering a sense of direction for much of humanity. The laws of the state applied to all citizens giving a sense of impetus through this ideology of a 'nation apart' with a keen sense of nationality. However, militarism was seen as essential, providing the means of enforcing policy, and the conscripted armies of France gave an almost nationalistic sense of achievement, and nationalism in its various forms remained as a characteristic of European politics leading to conflicts on a major scale.

Europe were shaken by the French Revolution regarding it as a dangerous threat, with Russia, Sweden, Spain, Prussia, and Austria suggesting intervention. This international fear was undoubtedly based not on love for the Bourbon monarchy but the danger of a people rising up in protest. This revolution, much more than the Peasant's Revolt, had changed the structure of society and the ruling families across Europe felt the potential dangers. There was already a revolutionary war in Eastern Europe with the Russian-Polish conflict of 1792–3, but Catherine of Russia was equally interested in what was happening in the West. Europe was now on the brink of a major continental wide conflict. As the French threat increased three international coalitions (1793–6, 1799–1801, 1805–14) were formulated, which rose and fell in significance. The major powers were Russia, Prussia and Austria, with Britain supplying the maritime threat and an army in Spain, and the expanding colonies soon became involved in the conflict.

It appeared that the little Corsican corporal understood military strategy and tactics better than most of his opponents, and he was unquestionably a natural leader. Within a year Northern Italy fell to the French forces when Napoleon demonstrated his military skills at the Bridge of Lodi (May 1796), and the Austrian resistance was crushed at Rivoli. It was no surprise that Napoleon played excellent chess. He claimed he was bringing democratic republicanism to the conquered, but he was ruthless against any opposition. The French (now run by a Directory) looked to Egypt conscious of Britain's commercial trade with India and the Far East. Malta was occupied, and French troops appeared in Alexandria. The French armies were maturing in experience and power, but the British Royal Navy remained superior, with Nelson crushing French hopes in Egypt by the sinking of their fleet at Aboukir Bay in 1799. Napoleon's rise to power would take volumes, but for this study it is only necessary to note that it was a combination of his enemy's weaknesses and his military skills which made him the fear of Europe.

This exploration of nationalism can only outline some major events. During the attempted domination of Europe by Napoleon there were many battles having more significance for some countries than others. In 1805 the maritime battle of Trafalgar meant that Napoleon's threat to invade the British Isles was impossible, but the French army seemed invincible and in 1805 the battle of Austerlitz saw Austria defeated, and at Jeda and Auerstadt, Prussia was crushed.

It was believed that the French invasions of the smaller Italian and the German states might accelerate unification in those countries, by giving a sense of national identity to these territories. The exiled Baron von Stein in St Petersburg denounced Napoleon as the enemy of mankind, and he was already proposing a federal union of German speaking peoples claiming, 'Germany must assert itself in its strategic position between France and Russia. Here was the kernel of the concepts both of *Gross Deutschland* and of *Mitteleuropa*'.[12]

National identity during this Napoleonic era became apparent to many of the ruling dynasties and smaller countries, giving hope to the working masses called to arms for the nation. During 1797–8 there had been naval mutinies at Spithead and the Nore along with Wolfe Tone's rebellion in Ireland. However, the British naval victories gave the British a distinct sense of national identity but made them more insular in European terms. Interestingly Denmark had a period of their own enlightenment for civil rights, a free press, emancipation of serfs and religious toleration which included Jewish citizens. There were uprisings against the Ottomans in Serbia, a form of secessionist nationalism, and it was clear that the French phenomenon of revolution and military success was having a marked effect across the European scene, especially in terms of national identity for the future.

The critical moment in the Napoleonic era was Napoleon's decision to invade Russia when his army crossed the borders on 22 June 1812 making the same mistake as Charles XII (and later Hitler) by neglecting Russian winters. Of some 600,000 French soldiers who entered Russia barely one in twenty returned. As is well-known Napoleon was placed in exile in Elba but escaped raising the flag again at Waterloo. The British fought under Wellington, but the day was lost for the French when Blucher's Prussian army arrived. Napoleon was sent to St Helena deep in the South Atlantic. The Congress of Vienna was intended to resolve issues arising from the Napoleonic wars by an effort to establish peace in Europe. Land was parcelled out (as it would be at the Treaty of Versailles in 1918) with Prussia benefitting against Austria, the United Provinces was granted the Austrian Netherlands, Sweden took Norway and lost Finland, and Britain was content with Ceylon (Sri Lanka). The victors restored Europe as they thought fit, hoping there would be no repeat of the attempted French dominance by another state, and thereby reorganising the Balance of Power. The Congress in Vienna was reactionary in spirit, and the famous Quadruple Alliance of Russia, Austria, Prussia, and Britain was reached, deciding there should be further conferences if necessary. Unlike the Treaty of Versailles in 1918–19 the losers were not humiliated, and in 1818 the Congress of Aix-la-Chapelle readmitted France to the powerhouse of major nations. There were other Congress Meetings (Troppau 1820, Laibach 1821, and Verona 1822) which tended to set the pattern for nineteenth century Europe in terms of the balance of power. It virtually arranged a map of Europe which would not change until after the Great War of 1914–18.

During the hundred days following Napoleon's escape from Elba Louis XVIII had to flee, while Europe remained concerned, wanting the status quo of pre-Revolutionary days. The monarchy was regarded as the norm and no attention was given to the democratic claims of the masses. Most critical in terms of this study, was the continuous presence of aggressive nationalism, which was growing rapidly as war, whether defensive or aggressive, and demanding greater manpower. The sense of nationhood and belonging was the same as with the tribe but becoming focused on the masses as they, despite their lower caste, were the strength of any army or nation. The 1789 French Revolution followed by the spectacular rise of Napoleon indicated a significant feature in European history. The Revolution had marked 'the people' as the nation and the nation as sovereign. It had given rise to a political nationalism which executed its absolute monarch, spreading these impulses of change across Europe, growing the military forces to a major level, tending to justify Max Weber's belief that the modern state is defined by its monopoly on violence. It became a time which focused on national self-awareness in many countries. In European history it was a major fault-line, indicating that nationalism traversed small communities and regions and demanded public involvement. The sense of nationalism had for centuries been inspired on the masses from above, but for a time in France it was reversed. The old French Order, the *Ancien Régime*, had failed to adapt and had collapsed to a new order, not instigated by the masses but rapidly taken up by them. France was just one country in the European jigsaw, but this revolution had widespread significance. The Habsburg Empire fragmented into smaller components, and by this very feature survived because they could be controlled region by region. The superior French monarchy, isolated in Versailles with a weak unpopular king, had become easy prey to the revolution. Other countries had no choice but to learn from the French and not only watch what was happening in neighbouring countries, but ensure the masses remained onside. Britain surrounded by sea and wealth, had a constitution whose politicians stood between the masses and the monarchy and survived, although there was a high degree of anxiety.

This development was the legacy of the French crisis, with the image of France, a large territorial state dependent on aggressive nationalism, which led to European borders becoming much more controlled and enforced. The French decision that the nation existed before anything else, including monarchies, the privileged or monied classes, and the Church, was a substantial claim and worrying for many traditionalists, as all were subservient to the Nation.

The people, the masses, were called to arms to either defend or expand their territory, making this a nationalistic rallying call to the nation. Compared to the rallying call of tribal chiefs the numbers involved were greater, but it was the same motivation of 'our country first'. In revolutionary France it was not always idealism, there were desertions, but by 1794–5 it has been estimated that 95 per cent of recruited soldiers had enrolled since the revolution.[13] The ideal for these new republicans was that all citizens should be involved in the sacrifice for the nation. However, in military life it is generally agreed that many soldiers were more attached to their units and senior officers than higher concepts. It was the tribal chieftain still in place, as it was Napoleon's charismatic leadership style which stimulated the military support of his role as leader. As such, when Napoleon rose to power it was evident that the focus on nationalism was in reality a cult based on his heroic image. He was now France, and the focus was again on the leader, to be repeated over a hundred years later with Hitler's influence in Germany. The Napoleonic Constitution of 13 December 1799 made no mention of national sovereignty or the rights of the people, and in 1804 he took the grandiose title of 'Emperor through the Grace of God and the Constitution of France' – a monarchical form. His behaviour emulated previous French kings, having the power to grant pardons amongst his despotic rights. He made substantial territorial gains, while his marriage to Marie Louise of Austria evidenced his dynastic policy. The republican claim of the equality of citizens soon appeared as mere packaging.

The effects following the French wars were widespread, and in Prussia Karl von Stein and Karl August von Hardenberg suddenly became reformers looking for more self-government. When Hardenberg introduced a new fiscal system, he said it was initiated 'because we want not to perpetuate provincialism, but rather establish nationalism'.[14] When King Frederick William III became aware of unrest within his domain, he appealed 'to my people' while busily forming an alliance with Russia. The reference to 'my people' was intended to have a unifying sense alluding to the family. It was repeated in the next century by Stalin who suddenly addressed the Russian people (to their surprise) during Operation *Barbarossa* as 'my brothers and sisters' as it was an emergency which needed the country bound together. However, 'the extent to which this effort represented a broader popular nationalism…is a question which historians have sought to answer' and will probably always remain elusive.[15] The Prussian king's appeal tried to emphasise nationalism's significance needing to gain the people's support. How far nationalism grew in Prussia during these times is uncertain, but the reaction to the French dominance paved the way.

Another consequence of the French wars and its appeal to nationalism were the country's borders, which were no longer mere frontiers but policed. Nationalism was now embedded in political rhetoric, and as in previous centuries, used as a device by governments and leaders to aid mobilisation of forces and public opinion. European rulers and governments were recognising the incipient power of nationalism in the masses, which since tribal days had always lurked beneath the surface.

Nationalism had been intrinsic in Europe scene for countless years, mainly emanating from leaders and nobles in projecting their territory as significant in national and cultural terms. However, the 1789 French Revolution had witnessed the internal upsurge from a discontented population that caused concern for traditional rulers and governments beyond French borders. The simmering ingredients of nationalism were within the human condition and development, stimulated by leaders and nobles to protect their territory, but the French Revolution initially exposed a nationalism with a new element when the masses demanded the right of governance of France and destroyed their traditional leadership. It was a significant break from the past which had international consequences, it would simmer again during the nineteenth century, especially in 1848, and at time reappear in extreme forms.

Chapter Four

The Nineteenth Century

Introduction

In nineteenth century Europe, the French Revolution and wars had increased the need to stay stable and retain the structures of previous years, and it also brought to the surface the perceived necessity of the Balance of Power. Napoleon had used the nationalistic cry of France and Empire to attempt the takeover of Europe, but even after Waterloo for the French it became their victory as 'a celebration of courage in the face of overwhelming odds, of patriotism and self-sacrifice for the "Great Nation."'[1] The British were the same with their rallying cry after Dunkirk in 1940. This type of nationalism often held countries together in danger and defeat.

Revolution did not finish in France and erupted again in 1848 when across Europe there were political upheavals. This was sometimes dubbed the 'Spring of Nations' because it indicated democratic and liberal motives and intentions. Efforts at political and social reforms were made in various countries, if only to maintain stability amongst the growling discontented, and the unfairness in most European societies.

Amongst the questionable tools of rampant nationalism language, race, and religious belief were always evident. Serbs and Romanians shared the same territorial areas, but the linguistic differences were often a problem. The Germans, and Magyars considered themselves superior to lesser nations such as the Czechs and Croats, while the Habsburgs exploited these inbuilt divisions. Language always appealed to nationalistic fervour. In Bulgaria, the West Bulgarian dialect was used for the upmarket language of the country, and in Italy the Tuscan dialect. Not just languages but their dialects were often divisive. The same applied in Britain where, as previously noted, acceptable English had to have the Oxford sound, later re-defined as BBC English. Language and its dialects were frequently utilised by nationalists. The Finns often spoke Swedish, but Finnish became the national language in its struggle for self-autonomy from Russia, in an effort to establish national identity. These were constantly the ingredients used by aggressive nationalism, the more sinister or dangerous variety. There were also signs of the more acceptable secessionist nationalism to rid oneself of a foreign domination, such as the Finns wrestling with the Russians as well as the Poles.

Secessionist Nationalism arose periodically during this century with the demand for independence, and on 27 January 1822 a self-styled Greek National Assembly at Epidaurus issued a declaration of independence from Ottoman rule. They appealed for outside help, but most smaller nations were in the grip of the larger states and empires, often with the consequence of anarchy. The year 1848 is always associated with the various revolutionary outbreaks which occurred and for many seemed infectious. In Moldavia and Wallachia, the two Romanian speaking areas mainly under Ottoman and Russian oversight, prepared for revolution. The Slovaks were demanding that Slovak be used as the national language, this element is often the identifying factor for many groups. These eruptions encouraged other national minorities such as the national Serbs living in the southern part of Hungary to raise their claims. In Italy Giuseppe Mazzini (who argued for a United States of Europe) inspired a sense of Italian nationalism, but the Habsburgs were resilient against such attempts. Metternich an Austrian diplomat who was at the centre of affairs for nearly forty years, declared membership of such organisations as punishable by death. Rival forms of nationalism were constantly vying with one another in East-Central Europe, where unrest in Vienna and Berlin was presenting impetus for national unity and autonomy. The major states during this century were building their economies and lines of communications through railway networks, bridges, roads, and canals, not just for economic reasons but unifying their power. Major figures during this century rose to leadership of historical relevance, such as Bismarck, Cavour, Napoleon III and Disraeli all of whom had recognised the need for stability both within their nation and internationally. These prominent figures realised nationalism could be potentially dangerous, but they preferred to harness its power. Napoleon III of France had recognised the need for popular support, so he used a voting system to be declared Emperor. In reality he was a dictator and as in many cases to this day, the elections were controlled and manipulated. The historian Richard Evans noted that national self-determination became the characteristic of this period, and 'from 1848 onwards, nationalism was a major driving force in European politics' and organised political parties, with mass communication possibilities emerging, used this for their propaganda, which became a characteristic of this period.[2] What was happening during these years was, at last, the recognition of the powers, values, and dangers of the various shades of nationalism. As noted in the previous chapters the seeds and ingredients of nationalism had been part of the community base and was virtually part of man's genetic makeup. However, from the time of the French Revolution onwards into the nineteenth century, this driving force of nationalism was being politically recognised.

The need for territory and power, first felt by the primitive tribes continued, and following the Franco-German War (1870–1) history shows that Europe's various countries had continued with grasping power from one another, along with the passion for colonial expansion. The continuous diplomatic wrangling, military preparations with novel resources brought nationalism clearly to the surface following a period of peace. The ongoing international rivalry led to the industrial type of conflict of the modern war, resulting in a greater loss of life and barbarity than in the medieval period.

New military weapons were developed on an industrial scale, the days of arrows and clubs, ships powered by sails would soon belong to a distant past. Europe was militarily superior when colonising most other parts of the planet. The nineteenth century was a period of sudden growth, and not all the results were for the advancement of humanity. Wars continued, and events were building up during this and the next century when new conflicts made the Napoleonic Wars appear almost mild. The masses generally were less suppressed but suffered just as much under economic duress.

To understand this century, it is critical to grasp the backdrop of peoples' lives before looking at the political situation. It is believed that the vast industrial growth occurred at first in Britain, but this was followed in mainland Europe in Belgium, in the Ruhr and Silesia and rapidly became widespread. During this century developing countries were based on economic success. This industrial growth, helped by advancing technology and science, was rapid and by the third phase of the century Britain fell behind the dynamism of German industry. It appeared to create within Europe industrial zones with their centres in the north and west of the continent, whereas the south and east were considered undeveloped by the lack of industrial effort. The British expanded their colonies, but the growing power of Germany was not invested in the seas, tending to look for expansion towards the east. Many of the past religious divides were mainly superseded by economic factors, but not forgotten.

In some countries the peasant/serf population had been released from their agrarian bondage into new inner-city poverty. They were poorly paid, high rents, unfairly taxed, all of which sowed dissent and revolt. It was this way of life which gave Marx his impetus to attack 'class-war, seeking the seeds of political change and by revolution'. Industry had brought about massive changes and sociological movement. In the farming world horse-drawn reapers of the era were replaced by steam-driven thrashing machines, and by the end of the century petrol-driven tractors were being thought about and produced by 1905. The sources of power changed, and oilfields were opened in Galicia and Romania and at Baku on the Caspian Sea. Nevertheless, by the end of the century '92 per cent of the world's energy still came from coal'.[3] Steelmakers such as Krupp became the critical key to industrial progress, and John McAdam's roads, the new industrial canals, and railway lines typified the recent changes. A train journey cut across the landscape and was able to reduce a week's journey to hours. At the end of the eighteenth-century Montgolfier's hot-air balloon was airborne to public bemusement and military interest. By the end of the nineteenth century Zeppelins were in flight, gliders followed, and just at the turn of the twentieth century (1903) the Wright brothers started the development for planes. In many different ways modern history was characterised by this almost frenzied development. It was not surprising, with the benefit of hindsight, that social changes occurred. It has been noted that women's status started to change, first from the rural wife to the new industrial world where the man was the source of income, and the wife was left as mother and housekeeper. This gender relationship stayed this way until the twentieth century, when the demands of two World Wars changed the social structures again as women helped in industry, developed a sense of having their own freedom to join the professional classes by right of ability, eventually the vote, and much later becoming political leaders.

However, discontent in the masses grew as a new type of poverty increased, with unhealthy slums remaining characteristic of industrial development until today in some areas. Cholera and typhus were common, and the poverty so appalling that crime grew and police forces were introduced. There was, as always and still today the well-known gap between the poor and the wealthy. There were the first calls for school education, especially in the middle to upper classes as the government needed civil servants, scientists, secretarial help. Some churches started to play an active role in the lower regions of this changing social structure. Most of the traditional Church of England parish churches lived comfortably in countryside areas, but there was an effort to build churches within the developing industrial areas, especially from the Anglo-Catholics (often associated with John Keble and the Oxford Movement) but also the more Protestant elements of the established Church.

These social changes instigated by industrialisation gave a sense of greater national consciousness even though workers were not tied to the land, but had become wage-earners, living in large communities, where they developed more of a political consciousness of what was happening. It was during this century that male suffrage was demanded, and even female suffrage was raised. It was not always easy as some changes were resented. Some powerful landowners were against railway lines near their grand houses, angry workers who watched machines doing their traditional work. The Luddites have never gone away and are now re-appearing with AI (artificial intelligence). Newborn babies died at an alarming rate, and wages rose and fell always with new tax demands. Famine remained a problem, especially in rural areas. Galicia on the Volga was a rural area and suffered as did the Irish in the Potato Famines of the 1840s. Being an island Britain with its population growth needed to import, and even in the middle of the twentieth century rural poverty existed, notably in Spain and parts of Eastern Europe.

The major growth of population in Europe raised some concerns, and the first population census was started by Sweden and copied across Europe. Britain and France started their first attempt in 1801 noting the expanding numbers of people. Today there are still concerns about the unsustainable growth of the human breed, but some countries such as Hungary in 2019 (February) made a plea for more babies to avoid the need for immigration.

The religious conflicts were less critical, and although the Catholic Protestant divide remained for some, it was no longer death-threatening, and for many it was irrelevant. Some churches were by now part of the national structure, notably in England and Prussia, but more pertinently toleration was widely accepted, except in Russia where the Orthodox church still imposed major restrictions. Theological debate was now more open, and Papal infallibility was debated, with some sectors of the Church of England moving closer to the Catholic doctrines with the emergence of the Tractarian or Oxford Movement. Pope Leo XIII (1878–1903) was known as the Pope of Peace, however, Catholic leadership with its insistence on Papal Infallibility was no longer well-received in the developing Europe of the nineteenth century.

The world of art produced many well-known names still appreciated to this day, the well-known Pre-Raphaelite Brotherhood of poets and painters, the appearance of widely read novelists, such as Dickens, Honoré de Balzac, Charlotte Bronte, Thackery, Victor Hugo, Tolstoy. In the world of Philosophy Hegel appeared (1770–1831), Sociology produced its founding father in Auguste Comte (1798–1857), and in the sciences famous names such as Faraday, Pasteur Mendel, Darwin were emerging with their innovative ideas and experiments. Darwin's famous *Origin of the Species* (1859) provoked a clash with some churchmen, as the Christian fundamentalist took time to accommodate to this shocking discovery that *homo sapiens* appeared to be some form of advanced ape. During this period of the nineteenth century there were significant changes in human society which at one level offered hope for a better future, but aggressive nationalism with it inherent dangers was becoming more apparent.

Colonialism Continues

During this century, those European countries which had maritime facilities continued to occupy other peoples' lands, which was nothing more than a greedy scramble for territory, and indigenous populations were regarded as irrelevant being viewed as sub-human. From 1870 to 1900 a few European nations took control of nearly a quarter of the planet, driven by the need for power and more wealth, using the spread of Christianity as an excuse. The military took an interest, and colonial regiments became part of the military arsenal. The other excuse was civilising the barbaric natives, hypocritically dressed up in altruistic terms. In 1908 a French writer and artist Georges Deherme wrote that 'the most important result of colonisation is to increase world productivity. It is at the same time a great social force for progress. The earth belongs to humanity. It belongs to those who know best how to develop it, increase its wealth, and in the process augment it, beautify it, and elevate humanity. Colonisation is the propagation of the highest form of civilisation yet conceived and realised, and the perpetuation of the most talented race, the progressive organisation of humanity'.[4] Many have agreed with these views, others may argue that colonisation was simply a form of aggressive nationalism, which forced the European way of life on indigenous peoples which was morally wrong. The history of colonisation could be regarded as an invasion, and in the earlier days there were attempts at eliminating the indigenous races or they were treated as sub-human, leading to slavery and apartheid.

The British grasped the lion's share, the new territories were settled by British immigrants, and self-governing states were given dominion status. The major areas granted this new form of government were Canada (1867), Australia (1901), New Zealand and Newfoundland (1907), and South Africa in 1910. It was a repetition of early tribal migration, as settlers travelled to new areas where they intended to settle and dominate. France pursued a similar policy demanding its new populations should have tight integration with the French nation which led to its own problems. Famous missionary explorers such as David Livingstone spent years in the endless jungles during the 1870s. The usual European arrogance assumed that Africa was just a land of tribal savages, knew of their inability to withstand modern weapons, and looked with distaste at their lack of modern sanitation. These scorned indigenous people were leading the tribal life once lived by Europeans, who had lost such days in their memory banks because of their assumed sense of superiority. This epitomised expansive and aggressive nationalism as each country with colonial ambitions was seeking to gain prestige, power, and wealth.

Unlike complex Africa and remote small islands in the major oceans, China was a vast territory and civilisation under its own emperor, and European interests were focused on trading rights and leasing territory. This part of the globe had not developed like Europeans who arrogantly tended to see China as somewhat tardy in making progress. Some have looked to this backwardness as a result of imperial exploitation, but as one historian noted 'this is in large measure an illusion; rather it was the decadence of Eastern empires that made European dominance possible'.[5] Later modernisation began in Japan and it is becoming clear that this current twenty-first century might well be the age of China and Asia, with China already recognised as a formidable super-power. In the nineteenth century the Europeans with their usual arrogance felt able to see the area as a protectorate, resulting in the Boxer rebellion. By the late nineteenth century, the closed country of Japan was showing its potential power, occupying Korea and Manchuria, and in 1904–5 inflicted a defeat on land and sea against the Russians. Nationalism was not limited to Europe but an obvious feature of much of humankind. America, a one-time colony emerged as an intruder on the colonial stage taking Hawaii (1900) and using maritime power, the key to colonial success, defeated Spain overseas in 1898 by taking Cuba, and other Spanish possessions in the Philippines. The Americans often denounced empire building, but they were still expanding on their own northern continent and would spread their influence world-wide.

State of Europe

Germany, the major power of central Europe having accrued little territory overseas, was later a source of frustration for Wilhelm II who associated national pride with military power and possessions. The German philosopher Friedrich Nietzsche (1844–1900) caused controversy then and to this day with his philosophic ideas impacting on political thinking. He challenged religion and democracy, producing his superman theory, and in preaching the thesis of the power of the strong. He appeared to deride the 'masses, as a burden', wanting the best men to rule a humanity which needed control. It was no surprise that later Nazi theorists tried to utilise his works.

In terms of international relationships European nations had, on the whole, attempted to maintain peace since the Congress of Vienna, which was often referred to as the Concert of Europe. Some fissures appeared which became important as the international community feared any form of revolutionary outbursts, such as regional problems in Italy, the Balkans, and Germany. The main tensions in Western Europe tended to centre on the old issues between France and Germany, which had started in the time of Charlemagne and continued in the Napoleonic Wars. It reached a further crisis level in 1870 when the French tried to impose their military superiority but were crushed by one of Bismarck's lightning wars and invaded instead. The French Emperor was obliged to flee to England, Alsace-Lorraine was conceded, and this French fiasco enabled Prussia to confirm the United German Empire under the first Emperor William I (1871–88).

In Eastern Europe nationalism resulted in Russian expansionism and the decline of Ottoman power, notably in the Balkans. The Russians had long awaited the opportunity to move south with their eyes on the Bosporus Straits and access to the Mediterranean. This resulted in the well-known Crimean War with the French and British combining to stop Russian aggrandisement by defending the Danube principalities. This halted the Russians but only for two decades. It has been observed that 'Russia's compulsive expansion continued at a rate which for the period 1683–1914 has been calculated on average, perhaps conservatively, at 55 square miles per day'.[6] The Russian Empire was not looking west, but south, to the Caucasus and Central Asia. As the West was accumulating territory overseas the Russians took Amur from China, occupied Turkestan in 1864, and in 1875 Sakhalin and Kuriles were taken from Japan. In 1900 they occupied Manchuria which led to their humiliating defeat by the Japanese in 1905 mentioned above.

Typically, of European nationalistic impulses, problems followed one after another. Revolts broke out in Bosnia, Herzegovina, and Bulgaria, there was military interference by Austria in Serbia and in Montenegro. Efforts were made to control the new Sultan, and at the Congress of Berlin (June-July 1878) there were changes to the San Stefano Treaty to curtail Russian ambitions. The emerging power of Germany should be noted at this stage. It was towering in the lofty heights with Britain and France, and the smaller states were often in peril. Bosnia and Herzegovina were occupied by Austria, Bulgaria was divided, Britain took Cyprus, and Russia, frustrated by not having the Straits, took Bessarabia from Romania. None of the smaller states had their views considered, and it was no surprise that the Balkans were always discontented, with violence regarded as the norm. One colleague historian told this writer that tribalism had never left the Balkans, but it was simply the larger tribes, now called nations or empires seeking expansion, who were behaving the same way. It could be argued that his theory could be applied on a much wider scale. Sometimes in the distant past the early tribes found it useful either for defence or attack to unite with other tribes, and this policy continued with nations seeking support in power groups. In the late nineteenth century various nations grouped together for the same reasons. In 1879 there was a dual alliance between Germany and Austria, which in 1882 became the Triple Alliance with the addition of Italy. In 1893 the Franco-Russian Alliance was signed, and despite past colonial problems and a long enmity, Britain and France signed the *Entente Cordiale* in 1904. These major treaties were founded on mutual defence and dominated European international politics into the twentieth century. It could be argued that Europe was dividing into large military power pacts, and the concept of *geopolitics* became a significant word with wider ramifications than Europe.

As is characteristic of humankind to this day, peace was always a delicate matter and not helped by the arms race, diplomatic friction, and mutual suspicion. There were concerns over minor crisis points such as Bosnia in 1908 and the Agadir crisis in 1911. The Bosnian incident happened when Austria-Hungary annexed Bosnia. In 1912–13 there were three Balkan wars, and Italy seized Rhodes, Tripoli, and Cyrenaica from the Ottomans while the Balkan League (Montenegro, Serbia, Bulgaria, and Greece) attacked the Ottomans in Macedonia, and in June 1913 Bulgaria attacked Serbia. What could happen next was almost like watching a roulette wheel. By the end of the nineteenth century for those who knew what was happening the European structure of nations must have felt like a melting pot. The Russian Tsar arranged two peace conferences in The Hague in 1899 and 1907, but the growing nationalism across Europe was evident and was readily accepted by many without political criticism or evaluation, but the twentieth century would lead to a series of global disasters to be explored later.

The colonial wars were calming down which eased some pressure points in Europe, but 'from the point of view of indigenous peoples it meant little more than a change from one variety of European colonialism to another, and usually a more aggressive version'.[7] Colonisation, a term for expansionism was still seen as a civilising influence with missionary work, and this view was helped by the growth of popular newspapers encouraging the attitude that colonisation was indicative of a country's vitality and growth, a form of banal nationalism mentioned earlier. It was presented as the benevolence of the occupying power.

There were exceptions to this banal nationalism when a nineteenth century newspaper correspondent William Russell, working for *The Times* explained his insights on the matter in his observations in Egypt. He wrote 'it would stir our blood, exhaust our Reserves, enrol our militia, volunteer our Volunteers, increase our income-tax, create wholesale land and sea peerages, GCBs, KCBs, brevets, and honours; revive patriotic quotations from Shakespeare and Dibdin, "Nought shall make us rue, if England to herself do prove but true"'.[8] Russell also offered a perceptive view after meeting young British officers in Egypt in 1882, who had been influenced by the popular thinking, that 'the only way to deal with a native is by force', with Russell adding that 'I see that all the newspapers in England have made up their minds that there is no such thing as the country Egypt, and there can be no such sentiment as that of Egyptian nationality. This is purely a military revolt…all the men who are Arabi-ites are thieves, rogues, forgers, murderers, robbers, lunatics, and the like'.[9] Russell was educated and aware that Egypt had been a recognised civilisation and nation for millennia, and he challenged this jingoistic nationalism, making him a reporter well ahead of his times. These colonial expansions created a sense of what

The ancient Israelis pleaded with the prophet Samuel to have a King-leader to crush their neighbours with nationalistic fervour. 'Nothing changes under the sun.' (*Qualiesin via Wikimedia Commons/CC BY-SA 4.0*)

Genghis Khan (an artist's impression). (*Adobe Stock*)

A monotheistic Islamic warrior battles with a monotheistic Christian, not for the One God but their nations, c.1250. (*Wikimedia Commons/CC BY-SA 4.0*)

Henry V of England, known for his nationalistic attempts to occupy France. (*Public domain*)

Henry VIII of England. (*Public domain*)

Louis XIV of France.
(*Public domain*)

Philip V of Spain.
(*Public domain*)

Frederick the Great. (*Painted by Arthur Kampf, sourced from Wikimedia Commons/CC BY-SA 4.0*)

Napoleon Bonaparte, a French Nationalist who wanted to govern Europe. (*Public domain*)

Adolf Hitler. (*Bundesarchiv, Picture 183-S33882/ CC BY-SA 3.0 DE*)

Benito Mussolini. (*Public domain*)

Joseph Stalin. (*Public domain*)

Francisco Franco. (*Public domain*)

Oswald Mosley, leader of the British Union of Fascists, always based his appeal on being British and the British Empire, using this nationalism to try and make himself popular. (*Public domain*)

Nationalism is worldwide, Juan Perón of Argentina based his propaganda on this concept. (*Public domain*)

Tribal Vikings re-enacting the past. (*Photograph by Silar/CC BY-SA 4.0*)

Alt-rightists in August 2017 in Charlottesville, Virginia, with Nazi and Confederate flags. (*Anthony Crider via Wikimedia Commons/CC BY 2.0*)

Map – 1899 cynical map of Europe. (*Drawn by Fred W. Rose/public domain*)

some called patriotism, but which in reality is a form of aggressive nationalism. Nationalism has some distinctive traits, such as the claim that the British were superior even against a country which once had the engineering ability to build the pyramids so precisely, when Europe was tribal. It was a form of aggressive nationalism at the expense of other peoples, by claiming ownership of their entire inheritance, even by removing valuable artefacts from their past to place in European museums. Another aspect important to the larger European nations was the strategic control in vital areas, such as the maritime and land routes for trade and military movements. These areas of interest included the Cape, the Persian Gulf, the Suez, (the canal was completed in 1869) the Red Sea and the Mediterranean, the latter being regarded as critical by the British and French. A major component in this nationalistic drive for land and control was the projected viewpoint that it was essential for national survival. It was a time 'to strengthen the grip of the nation on the mind of the masses', and in British schools, classrooms were decorated with maps of the empire coloured in pink.[10]

One of the extremely sensitive areas was the Middle East, as it still is, but in the nineteenth century it was with Egypt under Ottoman rule. It was argued that it was necessary to liberate the Christians of that country from Muslim oppression, but in reality, it was Egypt's position in terms of the Suez Canal. Britain militarily intervened in Egypt in 1882 (as noted in Russell's report above) for no other motive than securing the Suez Canal, a repeat of such an exercise would happen seventy-four years later in 1956 which would prove disastrous. There were political concerns that Russia's expansion was heading too far south, reaching as far as the Caucasus; all this threatened, or was perceived to threaten the routes to India. The European areas of nationalistic unrest were global. Africa had become a treasure trove, China became a centre for Europeans accumulating power, commerce, concessions, and influence. French, German, and British diplomatic tensions were at times intense with Britain forming an alliance with Japan against Russian and French activities. It was a form of competitive coexistence; while hoping to avoid direct conflict, it was like standing on a precipice.

Political Changes

Political changes were emerging which in this historical survey need noting, because it was during this era that politics and the masses were of greater interest to the ruling elite. In democratic forming countries the public appeal to the masses was growing in importance, and for non-democratic areas there was the reminder of the French Revolution with the Russian one just around the corner.

There were two mainline developments summarised by the words conservative and liberal, (in England the Tories and Whigs) though this could be regarded as a gross simplification. Those who tended to move in the general right-wing direction belonged to 'conservatism' implying the need to preserve (Latin *conservare*, meaning to preserve) what was already custom. It was not opposed to the developing democracy, but wanted the traditional bases of monarchy, church, property, and the social order maintained. The conservative element has throughout the last two centuries tussled with the liberal elements, but its most feared opponents have been the extreme left-wing and anarchists.

Anarchists challenged the political structure and the conservative way of thinking, but it was considered less serious than Socialist Internationalism, because its appeal was wider. It challenged conservative nationalism on the grounds that it was a mere class struggle making national borders irrelevant, and it promised to bring peace by avoiding war. For many people it was just intellectual aspiration, but it offered hope that would bring not only better conditions for the masses, but peace. The various strands of conservatism vary in every country and have different names, but this traditional political divide remains extensive.

Liberalism demanded political consent in all national actions and reactions, as seen in American development with its base lines in France and Britain and their parliamentary systems. The critical features were Rule of Law, personal liberty for the individual, a constitution, religious toleration, and the universal rights of man.[11] In the area of economics Liberalism concentrated on free trade and the policy of *laissez-faire*, often directed against governmental control through tariffs and protectionism. This was projected by Adam Smith, and John Stuart Mill (1806–73) who had initially outlined a balanced prototype of political Liberalism. Liberalism drew its name from the *liberales* of Spain, but its drama was fought out in France.

The emergence of socialism occurred early, sometimes claimed that its roots can be seen in the protests and riots during the medieval period, with the common ideal of fairness and justice for every individual however poor (derived from *socius* the Latin for companion). It looked to a time when the poor should benefit from the wealth which was always in the hands of the elite minority. Its main platform was for even distribution of wealth, and often argued that the impetus arose from the teachings of the Christian faith. It has always been associated with the emergence of trade unions, cooperative movements, and utopian theorists. It was natural that it appealed to the masses repressed by poverty and also caught the attention of many intellectuals. The trade unions looked to binding the interests of the workers, and the Dorset Tolpuddle Martyrs in Britain helped found the movement. The roots of this political attitude may be traced to the French Revolution in terms of general concepts, and several French theorists during the nineteenth century proved influential, as was the rise of early German socialists. Karl Marx (1818–83) and Friedrich Engels (1820–95) had first met in Paris and based their thinking on what happened in the French Revolution, and in 1848 the *Communist Manifesto* made its appearance. These men were expelled from Prussia, fled to Paris, and Marx had worked on his world-famous *Das Kapital* in London, where he was eventually buried. The intellectual content of Marx's work has come under intense scrutiny, but the power of his ideas became more effective than his theories: for some people Marx's work provided an alternative form of religion. The Socialist movement at times became the work of middle-class theorists such as the Fabian Society. In Germany, the SPD (German Social Democratic Party) was established in 1890 having been banished for a time by Bismarck. 'Given their situation in the multinational monarchy, they were particularly concerned with nationalism, a subject hitherto rather neglected in the Marxist tradition'.[12]

Following this very brief survey of the nineteenth century and the developing political viewpoints it is essential to pause and take a brief overview of how nationalism not only became focused on by the leading figures of European leaders but also in the reaction by their various citizens.

Nationalism into the Modern Era

It was during the nineteenth century that various aggressive forms of nationalism found a major focus in the lives of nations. For many historians this is seen as the time nationalism originated based on the fact that nations were now firmly in place. It is the contention of this writer that its hidden roots had always been just below the surface, simmering in different ways, but it could be argued that the nineteenth century certainly exposed the dangers of the worst type of nationalism in its aggressive and expansionist forms.

The historian Norman Davies identified two types of nationalism, the first was a state or civic form supported by the ruling classes, and the second was the more popular or ethnic form of nationalism.[13] As noted in the introduction there are more shades to nationalism than a twofold classification, but his description offers an analysis of potential aggressive nationalism best described as internal nationalism, with State nationalism as a feature of the top echelons of leadership preserving their own values, whereas the popular variation came from the lower parts of the social orders with the opposite intentions of overthrowing the current order. It could be seen in modern developing politics with the conservative traditionalists wanting to preserve and increase their current values, and the socialist left wanting changes within the social structure. For centuries tribal chieftains, despots, monarchies, and military leaders have appealed to the masses for nationalistic support, and as the tribe became the nation and the masses grew in numbers, congregating in large numbers with the industrial revolution, many developed their own form of nationalism. State Nationalism was driven by the leaders as when the British in 1707 brought the United Kingdom into existence. The English, Welsh, and Scots were informed they were British, which given the predominance of the English and their institutions meant they often associated British with being English. This was reflected, for example, when the Welsh language was banned from Welsh schools and the so-called unity was introduced by legislation in 1801 together with the Union Jack. Under state nationalism citizenship and nationality became the binding theme which is still upheld by British law. To this day there are strong elements in Ireland, Scotland, and Wales, who when the British State ruled that the Isles were one country, objected and still reject this form of nationalism responding with their own version. There is still a strong Welsh political party, in Scotland constant calls for freedom from London government, and the twentieth century witnessed appalling violence in Ireland. This scenario of clashing nationalism can be identified in many European countries. A century after their unification Italians still tended to associate themselves with their old regions first. Nationalism created a sense of some nations regarding themselves as being historically superior to others, and some states claimed the position of being an established power, especially France, Britain, Russia, Austria, and Prussia.

Popular nationalism tended to thrive on deprivation and repression to stir up protest and revolution. Language was used as a tool by nationalism, and as it grew efforts were made to show that vernacular language had the same authority as Latin. Folklore was researched (one of Heinrich Himmler's obsessions) in a desperate effort to connect the present with its so-called deep significant cultural roots. 'When Himmler joined the Nazi Party in 1925, he was already a member of the Thule Society, which preached that the greatness of Germany reached back to the Teutonic tribes' defeat of the Romans'.[14] Himmler was a political fanatic and fantasist, but reaching back to the distant past in the cause of nationalism was widespread. The more level-headed Ulrich von Hassell recorded in his 1940 diary that he had heard of one German historian stating that 'there is now such hatred between the two contending branches of the Germanic peoples', referring to the British as a natural branch of Germanic origins, as if tribal origins implied it should be one large happy family, which for some it did.[15] It amounted to an almost frenzied effort in the search for identity.

Survey of European Nations

As this century ended its final phase, nationalism entered an even more aggressive stage, not just as a means for unifying a nation, but it rapidly degenerated to a sense of the exclusive rights that Germany was only for Germans, and Britain is British and only for the British. This insular British attitude is a problem which persists to this day with the Brexit referendum making this all too clear, and a built-in resentment against immigrants fleeing danger and seeking a safer lifestyle. In Germany, the phrase *Blut und Boden* (blood and soil) was propagated, while in France, Charles Maurras co-founded the movement of *Action Française*. This form of integral nationalism was widespread ranging from Poland to Zionism. The violent activities of the IRA and their opponents, and the Basques on the Iberian Peninsula demonstrated many of the problems. While in Britain and France there was progress towards a form of modern democracy both countries were still under the influence of the elite and wealthy. The French Revolution and the English Civil War had ongoing ramifications, with the leading elements in France forever watching a population who may object on the streets causing mayhem as they can still do to this day. In Britain, the power of Parliament was now embedded, but the monarchy often had to be reminded of this factor, and it would take a long time before the people in the various workplaces had the right to vote. The politics in France and Britain were slowly moving towards a democracy but not without revolts and protests in both countries, and it would take until the next century before the modern democratic system would be recognisable.

During this century national movements were being powerfully activated. There were moves for nationalistic unification across Europe, especially in Italy and Germany. In Italy it was known as *il Risorgimento* (the Resurgence) and after seventy years succeeded in 1871. It originated in Sardinia and was organised by a group of secret societies, the main one being the Carbonari who started revolts in Naples (1820), Turin (1821), and Rome (1830) under the claim that Italy was one country with one language. Unlike Poland and other countries, Italy had no background of a recognisable state, as it consisted of a mixed pot of provinces, regions, and city states, with no national assembly as in the German Confederation. Every region in Italy had its own formulae of nationalistic reactions. It was the unrest in 1848 which caused Pope Pius IX (the longest elected Pope in history) to react against nationalistic fervour when obliged to flee Rome in November 1848. In Piedmont, the King of Piedmont-Sardinia (Charles Albert) was inclined towards dynastic expansion, and gained support from nationalists, but he was defeated by the Austrians in 1848 and again in 1849. In 1859 Louis Napoleon had apparently turned to the French tradition of supporting nationalist movements and waged war against Austria in Northern Italy. Piedmont was the junior partner, but the Prime Minister Cavour ensured his control started to stretch over that northern region of Italy.

Giuseppe Garibaldi epitomised the radical movement whereas Piedmont was playing a political game in the north. In May 1860 there was upheaval in Sicily, and Garibaldi's well-known march of the 'thousand redshirts' to Italy managed to take over most of that region followed by the mainland. The Piedmontese moved south to halt the radical nationalist Garibaldi moving north which involved the capture of the Papal States. Garibaldi crossed the mainland and took Naples in September 1860. It was a mixture of radical nationalism and political vacuums, but it 'was contingent rather than what one might call an organic relationship which became manifest in subsequent events. Garibaldi surrendered leadership and handed over to Piedmont in November 1860. This was not simply an individual decision but an act of political realism'.[16]

The same mixed development took place in Germany tracing its call for unification to the Napoleonic times of 1813–14. The various princes managed to stifle any liberal legislation, wanting to retain their own domains. The significant year 1848 had witnessed reactions with revolts in Vienna, Berlin, Prague, Dresden, Baden, and minor ones elsewhere. Frederick-William IV had turned down the offer of a united crown, but there was a change of attitude during the 1860s because Prussia was entangled with Austria, and significantly Herbert von Bismarck (1815–88) was appointed Premier to resolve the problems. 'His aim was to put Prussia "in the saddle" in Germany, and Germany in the saddle in Europe' which he intended to do by creating a North German Confederation without Austria.[17] Bismarck was an authoritarian leader who once said, 'you can do everything with bayonets except sit on them'. His policy was a series of minor and tightly controlled wars such as in 1864 Denmark, which was attacked for annexing Schleswig, and this was later followed by the defeat of the French in 1870–71, which led to a united Germany and Wilhelm I declared Emperor. It was not a case of emancipation from foreign domination but a desire for unity. The German impetus was more political and ran itself along the line of democratic elections, as in 1848 Frankfurt am Main where the local leaders argued for a national unity. Many tended to look to Austria or Prussia for leadership, raising the issue as to who should hold the power of the state between Prussia and Austria. The Habsburgs established their form of domination in 1848, the year of agitation. The German National Assembly vacillated but soon there was a leaning towards a smaller Germany under Prussia. The Prussian king was not impressed, and the Habsburgs were battling on all fronts. In 1866 the Austro-Prussian war excluded Habsburg influence from both Germany and Italy. As noted, it was the Franco-German War of 1870–1 which resulted in the German Second Empire and saw the final unification of Germany about the same time as Italy.

'The Polish national movement had the longest pedigree, the best credentials, the greatest determination, the worse press, and the least success'.[18] Between 1733 and as far as 1944 there were continuous revolts with various resultant partitions, but powerful nations such as Russia in the East and the pressure from the West meant that a settled and peaceful Poland was a distant hope. Poland was divided by four differing partitions, the fourth was known as Congress Poland after the Congress of Vienna (1814–15), along with the historical kingdom bound to Russia, the Duchy of Posen under Hohenzollern influence, and the Habsburgs controlling Galicia. It must have felt like carving up and sharing the hunted prey.

Poland's geographical position between East and West gave the country major problems because of interests in their land from greedy neighbours. Its landscape had no natural geographical borders to make invasion difficult. Many Poles took to exile in Paris and London agitating for independence in various centres. In 1830 they took control of the kingdom's army, only to be crushed by the Russians in the following year. Poland with its domination by three major powers was never going to succeed despite its history of nationhood. Germanisation and Russification attempts sustained a sense of Polish nationality, and Poland became a sovereign state but dominated by communist Russia until 1989–90. Poland had its own form of nationalism but was dominated by the aggressive and expansive nationalism of its more powerful neighbours.

The national problems in Austria-Hungary were complex. It involved a dual monarchy and imposing the German language was a divisive task. There were three distinctive races struggling in this territory, the Germans, Magyars, and Galician Poles, each with its own brand of nationalism. Francis-Joseph I (1848–1916) later declared himself the last Emperor of the old style ruling a polyglot empire.

Language continued to play its role in nationalism. The nationalistic spirit stirred, and touched many areas of Europe, not just at the state-political level but there were provincial impulses. In Provence in France there was a cultural effort to revive their old language and culture, and in Wales in 1819 the old bardic meetings of the *Eisteddfod* were revived. Hungary had included Croatia and the Grand Duchy of Transylvania, but the latter eventually came under Ottoman rule. However, Hungary managed to retain a form of autonomy within the Habsburg Empire. It was a multi-ethnic country with the Magyar language spoken by their elite, who with their own inbuilt sense of nationalism, insisted on this language's supremacy. The Magyar Hungarian nobility was deeply conservative rejecting many of the rational reforms by Joseph II in the 1780s.

They wanted Magyar spoken and not German nor written Latin, which was proposed in their reform Diet of 1827, and they pursued this policy for the next 20 years. It became sidelined during the turbulent times of 1848, and while the Magyar 'political leadership envisaged a centralised nation state with Magyar as the official language', this provoked considerable opposition.[19] The Austrians used other ethnic groups to control the Magyars, notably the Croatians. Hungary possibly had the most robust national-type movement of 1848–49, and unlike Poland, was not concerned at being overwhelmed and partitioned. It was able to confront the Habsburg power, preparing for reform. The Russians crossed the border in aid of the Habsburgs to crush the rebellion in 1849. Under the leadership of Ferenc Deak, who used negotiation, the Hungarians reached a compromise (*Ausgleich*) in 1867, and the dual monarchy of Austria-Hungary came into being. However, by the 1860s Hungary possessed a degree of autonomy with influence in Vienna over matters of foreign and military policies. Most of the Magyar elite felt a loyalty to the monarchy which lasted until the end of the First World War in 1918.

It was not until the defeat of Austria in 1914 that the new nation of Czechoslovakia found a place on the European map. This convoluted process started with nationalistic urges in the medieval kingdom of Bohemia, which had come under Habsburg rule during the fourteenth century. However, Czech literature flourished, but a rebellion in 1620 was crushed. It was during the latter part of the eighteenth century that Czech intellectuals concentrated their efforts on researching their history and language. German was the dominant language amongst the elite, but Czech was spoken by the masses. Joseph II, known for his reforms, encouraged a number of Czech intellectuals to identify Czech identity. They used their common language which demonstrated the power of language, as well as their traditional culture. It also encouraged the growth of a Czech speaking elite and in March 1848 a programme of political aims was prepared. There was a fissure between those wanting German identification, and others who sought Czech autonomy as a distinct identity. Centralisation by the greater powers was their theme of the day, but in the 1860s nationalists started to win municipal elections, especially in Prague. Cultural nationalism became critical, and the German speaking University of Prague was divided into two, with German language in one, and Czech in the other. They were demanding autonomy within the monarchy, but it was not until the First World War that Czech politicians started to understand that the ties to the Empire were a matter of the past.

The nature of language as noted was critical to the cries of nationalism, with speakers of their language trying to gain the upper hand. In Eastern Europe Slavic speakers tended to be rural, but with various dialects, and intellectuals studied Slavic to identify their common language. People who spoke this language were given the name of Slovenes, and a Slovenian dictionary was published. These intellectuals looked to the creation of a Slovene nation, raising this during the turbulent year of 1848. There was a small degree of some success in 1860 when Slovene parties gained election votes, but the Germanisation was also accelerating. There was never enough power to pursue political independence, and following the First World War the Serbians held the movement at bay. It was not until June 1991 with the introduction of a multi-party democracy that Slovenia was able to extricate itself and become an independent country. It entered the portals of NATO and the EU, later the Eurozone and the OECD. This country had evolved from its persistent adherence to its cultural nationalism and its language. As a curious note, the Slovenes had made more progress in the last forty years, and Major General Alenka Ermenc was announced as Head of the Slovenian Army, promoted to Chief of General Staff, and was the first woman in a NATO member state to hold this position.

In the early twelfth century Croatia (which had included Slavonia and Dalmatia) had been unified but in a union with Hungary. Dalmatia had been lost to Venice, and most of the other regions in this area became borderlands in defence against Ottoman incursions. The Croatians tried to hold their own land but lacked the manpower against the Habsburgs. Once again language was an issue with two dialects in operation, the *Kai* and *Sto* dialects, the latter more widely used by the Serbs and Bosnians. There was an effort made to reach a common language using *Sto* as the basis, but this failed. During the 1840s a Croatian national movement was formed becoming an identifiable political force in 1848, seeking its own independence, but Germanisation was powerful. There was another effort in the 1860s, but divisions remained on how independence could be fulfilled. There were those who were more interested in the pro-Hungary lobby, another grouping which demanded South-Slavic cooperation, and a right-wing party wanting the unification of the medieval territories. After the Empire's collapse in 1918, and despite the Croatian demands they became part of Serbia. To go ahead chronologically, when there was a degree of unrest in the 1920s it was followed by the abolition of democracy under King Alexander. This King had failed to unify the rival nationalistic groups, and politics became bloody with some Croat deputies killed in a parliamentary session by a Montenegrin deputy, causing Croat members to withdraw. Alexander felt he had little choice but dissolve the parliament (the Skupština) and replaced it with a royal dictatorship, changing the name to Yugoslavia. There were protests, and King Alexander was thinking about a return to a democratic system when he was murdered on a State visit to France (1934).* The right-wing nationalistic demands for independence grew stronger receiving support from Germany. Hitler cunningly created Croatia as a state run by his appointed puppets, who treated non-Croatians in a savage fashion. This had ramifications following the collapse of Germany, and under Josip Tito, Croatia retained its historical borders as an autonomous republic, but within the federal state of Yugoslavia. In Croatia political nationalism played a much more active role than the cultural nationalism of the Slovenes.

Most of medieval Serbia had been destroyed by the Ottomans, and the only factor which helped maintain a sense of the past was the presence of the Orthodox Patriarchate. This gave a sense of cultural identity and nation, but the Serbians were constantly resisting the Ottomans who in turn persecuted them. In 1804 with Russian support there was a revolt which lasted eight years, and in 1830 the Serbs achieved autonomous status as a principality. They were not yet a nation since 'three important obstacles remained. First, only about 20 per cent of Serbians lived in the territory of the principality. Secondly, its traditional patriarchal society lacked a nobility and middle class and was subject to the power of the Orthodox Church. Thirdly, the new state elite lacked modern political education and only slowly and unwillingly accepted elements of civil rights and constitutionalism'.[20] These three statements defined a nation in a critical sense, nevertheless, Serbia had its own distinctive identity, and amongst its inhabitants and neighbours it was generally accepted as such, although deemed to be under the oversight of the Habsburgs. The more educated and elite lived outside the principality where they indulged in a cultural nationalism. Although it was in the 1840s and 1850s that the concept of a Serbian State in the modern sense started to formulate, the Habsburgs kept a sharp eye on the region, which responded with a rallying cry to the Orthodox religion and the Serb language, not normally natural partners. Nevertheless, it functioned as an ideological basis for an independent country. The Bosnian enclave, as it was often called, was regarded as Serbian Muslim because they spoke with the *Sto* dialect mentioned above. From the point of view of the outside world Serbia's nationalism was seen in the kinder light of unification nationalism, which looked askew at the Croatian variation. Already built into this Balkan region were problems for the future.

Montenegro is a small mountainous area and today has a population of just over half a million. For most of its history it was a patriarchal society based on clans and ruled by princes. In 1910 it became a kingdom as a result of

---

* He was assassinated in Marseille by a Bulgarian revolutionary named Vlado Chernozemski during a state visit, which was embarrassing for the French.

the Balkan War in 1912–13, when the Ottomans lost their Balkan holdings, and it sided with the Allied powers during the Great War, but was occupied by Austria-Hungary, and King Nicolas went into exile in Bordeaux, France. Following the breakup of the Empire in 1918 Montenegro was incorporated into the Kingdom of the Serbs, Croatians, and Slovenes. During the Second World War it was occupied by the Italians, and it was there the first uprising against the fascists took place in July 1941. When Italians changed sides, the Germans occupied the area which was later liberated by partisans in December 1944. This all meant that in 1945 it gained the status of an autonomous republic. Nationalism in such a tiny region was easier to ignite but demanded courage. There were many problems ahead for this small state during the Balkans conflict in the early 1990s, not least being bombed by the Western forces. Nevertheless, in June 2006 the Montenegrin Parliament declared independence and Serbia raised no objections. This was more a history of secessionist nationalism, as the people of Montenegro only wanted freedom from outside domination.

Unlike most of the Balkan countries Greece had an ancient national identity which had suffered destruction by the Ottomans, but who had left intact the Greek Orthodox Church, and Greece retained its cultural identity. Many of the Greeks of the elite class had risen to positions of administrative power within the Ottoman rule and were known as the Phanariotes. The Greeks like the Jews had their smaller diaspora living out in enclaves in Russia, and in surrounding areas around the Balkans. After the French Revolution, as elsewhere in Europe there was a new hope of their nation becoming autonomous again. As elsewhere, there were differing views on the nature of the projected national identity. Language again played a role in this upsurge of nationalistic feeling as the Phanariotes preferred the developing modern Greek which was lost on the masses. The Phanariotes tried to organise themselves under the leadership of Alexander Ypsilanti, a leading Greek personality in Russia. Meanwhile there was some resistance amongst the peasant groups on the Greek mainland. The Ypsilanti rebellion was defeated in 1821, but the revolts in the Peloponnese were more successful. From there efforts were made to occupy the mainland and volunteers from other nations came to help (including Lord Byron), and a new assembly tried to organise an appropriate constitution. The surprised Ottomans prepared themselves, but Greece had the support of the British and French who defeated the Ottoman navy in 1827. Because of Greece's classical past which influenced much of Europe, the Greek nationalistic movement had the support of major European countries, but the Habsburgs kept a discreet distance. The Greeks were helped by other European countries who were constantly suspicious of the Ottomans. A new Greek nation entered the scene, with only part of their original territory and soon came under the autocratic rule of King Otto of the

Bavarian dynasty. The struggle for constitutional reform and uniting all Greek areas continued until the First World War. In terms of nationalism there were the usual divisions between the moderates and the radicals, with a few looking to expansionist nationalism. Generally, in Greek history, it was more secessionist nationalism associated with releasing the country from foreign rule, made easier by having once been a well-known identifiable nation, and assisted by the apprehension of other major nations towards the Ottomans.

Romania's background consisted of three distinct areas in Wallachia and Moldavia where the people spoke Romanian, but in Transylvania they were subservient to the Magyar. Romania had three shades of Christian belief, the Greek Orthodox, Roman Catholics and the Uniates, who followed Orthodox liturgy, but regarded Rome as their head. Typically, language was a nationalistic driving force, and in Transylvania under the Uniates it became a matter of major importance. This form of cultural nationalism was prevalent in Transylvania, but the political motives came from the other two regions. Wallachia and Moldavia were partly independent but ruled on behalf of the Ottomans through the Phanariotes mentioned in the Greek survey. A nationalistic impulse came from the elite, the Boyars who reflected a feudal leadership. In 1848 they had concentrated on various reforms, but the Russian authority was overpowering, and Russian occupation soon followed. There remained the desire to unite the two principalities, but the end of Ottoman domination led to the two states differing over their international views, with Wallachia leaning towards supportive France and Moldavia influenced by Russia. During the Crimean War both states were occupied by Austria giving them more impetus for unification. It was initiated by Alexandru Ioan Cuza in 1859 who had been a prominent figure in 1848, and who offered the idea of a liberal state but without too many reforms. As such the new nation took on the form of a monarchy under kings drawn from the Hohenzollern royalty. It was not until the 1880s that a degree of political emancipation and liberalisation started. Transylvania continued its pursuit of language identification, but unification with the Romanian State was not successful until the end of the Habsburg Empire in 1918. In smaller countries the nationalistic motives and intentions always existed but were governed by the same nationalistic drive by larger more powerful neighbours.

Bulgaria had virtually lost its sense of identity under the Ottomans, but some intellectuals renewed a study of the Bulgarian language and its ethnography, by outlining its older history. Some clergy in the 1830s had requested the Ottoman rulers to be permitted to use the Church Slavonic language in their liturgy. This was granted, and the Bulgarian language was taught in some schools, which meant merging the dialects together into a recognisable shape. The Church had driven this request, but during the 1850s there was a revival of Bulgarian ambitions, and some of the elite living outside Bulgaria argued it should be based on more secular needs. The more moderate Bulgarian nationalists wanted to arrive at an agreement with the Ottomans, but there were others who wanted their own government. As elsewhere, the Bulgarian nationalists watched with focused interest Garibaldi's movements in Italy. This encouraged local uprisings which failed, and during 1875 there was a general insurrection brutally suppressed by the Ottomans, but which led to a further uprising in 1877. This time the Russians sent an army, and the Ottomans had no choice but to withdraw. The new state of Bulgaria was established in 1879 with a constitutional monarchy promising civil rights. Bulgaria had made it to the state of nationhood but was backward economically and educationally. Language and cultural nationalism, along with the Church, had started the process of a political nationalism demanding the right of autonomy, a form of secessionist nationalism.

Amongst the smaller countries, many of their histories are little known, the name Macedonia was virtually forgotten during the Ottoman rule and used more as a mere geographical expression for an area. Greek and Turkish were the languages, and it was under the control of the Ottomans, emerging as a state in its own right only in 1870, when the Bulgarians wanted to unite the territory under their nationalistic impulses. Macedonians had mixed reactions, but by 1900 some of the intellectual elites were arriving at the wish for a Macedonian identity, which was, as usual, founded on linguistic differences. In 1918 Serbia occupied the region on the dubious grounds that the Macedonians were just Serbs with a different dialect. The Macedonians resisted the Nazis in the Second World War which helped create an autonomous republic within Yugoslavia.

In Albania, the inhabitants called themselves *shquiptare*, a distinctive ethnic group who had resisted the Ottomans for a brief time, but most became Muslims. They reached out to their form of nationalism in 1878 during the Balkan Wars. They associated themselves with political and cultural intentions under the Prizren League (an Albanian political organisation) which the Ottomans in 1881 and 1897 had repressed. In the Balkan Wars of 1912–13 the Albanians recognised the growing weakness of the Ottomans, declaring themselves an independent state in November 1912. During the Great War they were occupied but their independence was restored in 1920. Albania remained an unknown quantity as it continued to be governed by a feudalistic system suppressing any liberal proposals, and from 1928 King Zog (1895–1961) ruled, though under Mussolini it was seen more as a client state of Italy. After 1945 Albania reidentified itself with the ideology of communism.

There had been a Slavic kingdom of Bosnia during the medieval period under Catholic and Orthodox influence. The Ottoman invasion in the late fourteenth century changed the religious situation, and Muslims became the leading elite. The religious differences led to an uprising in 1875 which was crushed, and Austria-Hungary occupied Bosnia with Herzegovina in 1878 and governed the area until the outbreak of the First World War. After this war Bosnia was merged into Yugoslavia and the Muslim issue lessened. However, during the next World War the Bosnians fought the Germans through a partisan movement with the Muslims in an active role. After 1945 Bosnia remained part of Yugoslavia, but it was not until 1968 that Muslims were given official recognition.

The Ukrainians constantly found themselves under powerful autocracies, once controlled by Poland, then Austria, and later Russia. Part of their nationalism was to rid themselves of their given nomenclature of *Rusini* or Ruthenians widely known as 'little Russians', and as this part of the survey is written, there is a serious war between Putin's Russia and the Ukraine, again dividing East and West.

Finally in this overview the Russian Empire which was famously described by V. I. Lenin as a 'prison of nations,' with a similar description applied in the 1990s referring to the Soviet Union in its final days'.[21] More space must be allotted to Russia because of its long influence in Europe as friend and foe. All objective histories of Russia rule in the years before Bolshevism clearly indicate the Romanovs created serious impoverishment for the masses, while a tiny minority controlled the wealth leading comfortable lives, which is an ongoing issue in human life and its history. The economic deprivation and consequential social injustice existed in most countries but in Russia, it became a crisis because of the extreme injustice under their regime. As one historian noted, 'It is clear that revolutions do not usually break out unless there is a situation so bad as to invite revolution'.[22] When the British diplomat Bruce Lockhart arrived in Russia before the First World War, his opening autobiographical pages indicated he was struck by the wealth of the few, and given that it was the same in Britain and other European countries, it must have been a starker picture for this dichotomy to be noticed.[23] The Romanovs had ruled Russia since 1613, and Tsar Nicholas II was the last of the royal line. He was not a sound leader and disliked more than Kaiser Wilhelm II and Emperor Franz Joseph of Austria-Hungary. He was noted for his repression of political parties, especially the developing Trade Unions. His secret police known as the Okhrana and his military were an uncompromising defence against any challenge to his authority. Nicholas II had a massive Empire to govern, Britain's empire was larger, but it was overseas, and unlike the British Nicholas II was concerned about his land borders. Even patriotism was limited because in this vast empire traditions were local, and personal survival was more important. The main identity for most in the Russian Empire tended to be religion, more important than language in a multilingual empire. By the nineteenth century Russia, calling itself Holy Russia, was identified by the powerful national Church of the Russian Orthodox. During the nineteenth century national consciousness and political organisations were limited, but the Russian rulers were aware from watching Europe that nationalism was of many shades, be it aggressive expansionism or secessionist potentially dangerous.

However, Russification was the constant policy ensuring the regions in their area regarded themselves as Russian whether they were or not. The realists recognised that this was an impossible task, but there was for some reason always suspicion of the Polish and Jewish elements. Poles were restricted in the use of their language and the University of Warsaw was shut down, and in 1863 the Minister Petr Valuev stated that there never had been nor would be a Ukrainian language. Following the failed Polish revolt in 1863 the Russians decided to block all separatist movements in Poland, the Ukraine, and the Baltic regions.

By the latter half of the nineteenth century the Russian Imperial leaders were all too aware of the nationalistic upsurge raging across Europe, especially in the Caucasus which had a vast variety of ethnic groups still with old tribal affiliations. Jumping ahead to the time of the Georgian Stalin, even he was acutely aware of ethnic sources in that region, and his infamous henchman Lavrenty Beria was Mingrelian by birth, the man whom Stalin used to run his secret police. In the huge tract of territory called the Ukraine the Russians had called them 'little Russians' and suppressed their language. The Russians held the nationalist spirit at bay in every square mile of their territories.

Some mild reform in Russia started with the arrival of the Duma but it was too late. Under Tsar Nicholas II it was a devitalised institution and the electoral process, so named, was divided along ethnic-national lines. During the First World War, the Tsar was declared the main protector of Russia, resulting in the Duma being further curtailed. The Tsar during his lifetime was often criticised for not offering any sense of patriotism, which prior to the Great War was deliberately stirred with patriotic exhibitions and a general rallying cry, a form of banal nationalism soon to turn aggressive. As the war developed and Russia was struggling, sudden nationalistic calls for independence emerged in Finland and Armenia, but the Bolshevik revolt was underway, a major political revolution, which would later shake the world even more than the French Revolution.

To jump ahead again in time to Stalin's days, any sense of nationalism never died out as Lenin had anticipated. The question of various leaders and the developing circumstances had been clearly foreseen by Marx, who had written that 'people make their own history, but they do not make it just as they please; they do not make it under circumstances chosen by themselves, but under circumstances directly encountered, given, and transmitted from the past'.[24]

Lenin had preferred the policy of self-determination, having to acknowledge there were problems as to how national self-determination could fit in with a unitary Soviet state. The arguments were bitter leading to internal disagreement. Nationalism was regarded by many as 'a uniquely dangerous mobilising ideology because it had the potential to forge an all-class alliance for national goals'.[25] The idea of motherland and nationalistic expansion was referred to as chauvinism, and Russian past history was virtually discontinued.

Nevertheless, under Stalin during 1934, a new policy called 'the great retreat' began. It was an effort to change 'Russia into a country with much more fervent nationalism than she had before the attempt of international transfiguration'.[26] Russia's past and present was exhibited as the greatest nation. Their history was re-written with nearly every invention and scientific discovery being allotted to some famous Russian in the past. The whole cultural aspect was transformed, often known as Zhdanovism named after Andrei Zhdanov, and he chose any target which he suspected 'of fawning on the West'.[27] It was an extreme form of Russian nationalism leading to many minor purges. Stalin was a Georgian and used this language often with his sadistic henchman Beria so others in the room could not understand, but later stopping this habit insisting he was Russian through and through. Lenin had wanted the other countries within the old Russian Empire to have soviet ideology but looked to a federal relationship. Stalin at first doubted this concept but agreed, probably from ambition, and once in total power entrenched the empire as one entity, and following the great retreat as described above he became an ardent nationalist, as with President Putin to this day.

Not to be forgotten in this myriad view of Europe was the Jewish element spread widely across Europe. The Jews found some countries more accommodating than others and their diaspora was widespread. They had found a haven in the old Poland-Lithuania, but they were obliged to keep their migratory habits by the necessity of having to flee sudden bouts of persecution and purges. During the nineteenth century this migration increased for many reasons, ranging from Russian pogroms and the need to find work in a rapidly changing world. It was mainly because of the Russian persecution and the infamous pogroms that they tended to move west. This was encouraged by the French who offered full civic rights to Jews, though they suffered to an unexpected degree in later Vichy France.

The prejudice against Jews is difficult if not impossible to explain, but it was sadly prevalent throughout Europe, and especially in Russia. The Jewish tended to be intellectual and had business acumen, which made them a gift to some communities and resented by others. In 1841 Baron Lionel de Rothschild became a member of Parliament, and Disraeli, also Jewish, served as a British

Prime Minister, though he had converted to Christianity. In Europe generally, especially in the East, Jewish people tended to speak Yiddish (mainly in Eastern and Central Europe, originally a German dialect with Hebrew words and still used today in the USA, Russia, and Israel) which for some would have set them apart, and Zionism was also growing. Nationalism during this period tended to be increasing in its aggressive nature, and in places it even developed signs of anti-Semitism. It has been noted that 'the spread of political ideologies such as anti-Semitism reflected in part the rise of nationalism in a more exclusive and aggressive form than it had taken in the early decades of the century'.[28]

As early as the 1860s efforts were made by Jews to access their original homeland in Palestine. The World Zionist Organisation was founded in Switzerland in 1897, but it was not that successful because of anti-Semitic bigotry. The Ottomans were not sympathetic while the British offered an unattractive settlement in Kenya. Nationalism as a movement in Europe was not conducive to this migratory people, tending to be aggressive towards the Jewish racial and cultural differences. This nationalistic anti-Semitism, always prevalent in Russia even surfaced in liberal France over the infamous Dreyfus affair. The hope for a Jewish homeland was only resolved when the British took Jerusalem in 1916, later to be followed by the Balfour Declaration in 1917. Following the Second World War with the Nazi extermination efforts Jewish nationalism re-emerged powerfully in Palestine/Israel where it remains a dominant force. In the Jewish scenario the sense of nationalism was very much attached to ethnicity, language, and religion, but it needed its homeland for identity. Today (2024) the world is watching a nationalistic Israeli government ignoring the wider-world pleas for peace as they hammer Gaza with modern weapons in retaliation for terror attacks.

Chapter Five

The Twentieth Century

Introduction

The two World Wars of the twentieth century killed more people than any other previous conflicts in humankind's history, mainly because of technological and scientific advances. These wars spread, encompassing much of the planet leaving Europe in a state of degeneration. It also indicated that Europe was no longer the continent which could dominate the world as hitherto. It has been proposed with much justification that the war which started in 1914 lasted to virtually the end of the twentieth century. When the French military leader Marshal Foch claimed that the Treaty of Versailles which ended the First World War was merely a truce, he was being more perceptive than most people thought. This treaty was so badly prepared it has been argued that it contributed to the causes of the Second World War. In the old Roman style, the spoils of victory went to the victors, but this time expressed through financial and political dominance. It is now possible to see that the First and Second World Wars were contiguous.

After the First War World came a period of ideologies with the growth of Communism and Fascism opposing the developing Liberal Democracies. As the Second World War was being fought there were signs of hostility between the Western Allies and as Germany was divided between the victors, the Cold War was developing another possible conflict with the fear of weapons of mass destruction. Many of the nations in Eastern Europe who had established themselves as independent states were suddenly under Soviet Russia's domination. It was not until 1989–1990 with the new Russian reforms that conflict for a brief time appeared to have been settled. It has been pertinently argued that the whole of the twentieth century was a period of European conflict which engulfed the entire world. The disaster started 'in the German capital, Berlin on 1 August 1914 with the Kaiser's declaration of war on Russia. It ended on 8 May 1945, in the Soviet Field HQ at Berlin-Karlshorst', but as proposed above it was far from the end of conflict.[1]

This was a time when patriotism and more especially nationalism in its shades and forms were utilised by the various states. Nationalism also influenced many individuals without state encouragement, and much of this was based on the maxim that war brings out the best and the worst in humanity. As the twentieth century gathered momentum nationalism remained as a driving force in humankind's history. Lenin's hope for a federation of states linked by political ideology was shattered once Stalin assumed power, as he became a totalitarian leader encouraging nationalistic views of Russia. During this century, the various shades of nationalism were driving forces, sometimes secessionist but more often aggressive expansionism, with a degree of irredentist nationalism. Territory, power, influence, domination based on language, race, religious belief, culture, all to be found in the tribal era rose to the surface and was used by leaders and many others, often deliberately confusing it with patriotism.

The First World War and Consequences

Archduke Francis-Ferdinand (heir to the Austrian-Hungarian throne) with his wife visited Sarajevo the Bosnian capital (against all advice) and was assassinated by a member of the terrorist Black Hand gang called Gavrilo Princip. Within a few weeks the outcome was explosive. The origins and causes of the First World War will always have several reasons suggested. In its simplest form Austria wanted action against Serbia and was supported by Germany. Tsarist Russia decided to support Serbia without consulting its treaty allies France or Britain. Kaiser Wilhelm II on military advice declared war on Russia on 1 August 1914, because of their mobilisation and then two days later declared war against France. The Kaiser could have a whole book written about him. Grandson of Queen Victoria, he is often seen as an aggressive nationalist who wanted Germany to be recognised as the leading nation.

The well-known Schlieffen plan meant Germany virtually marched through Belgium which promptly involved the British. Austria wanted Serbia punished and Germany supported them, although Serbia had not declared war, it was a terrorist attack. France and Russia had an alliance, and Britain had a treaty with Belgium dating back to 1839. There had been room for diplomatic manoeuvre as an assassination by a terrorist could not be deemed to have been the fault of Serbia. The so-called obligations of international support on both sides may have appeared sound in theory, but in reality, they created a major war instead of a local conflict.

Experienced historians have different views. From some studies Austria was the prime mover, others pinpointed Germany's Kaiser, others Russia for mobilising so rapidly. Individuals are selected for criticism, with names such as Sir Edward Grey (British Foreign Secretary) who had his supporters and detractors; Theobold von Bethmann Hollweg the German Chancellor for his lack of decisiveness; Berchtold the Austrian Foreign Minister made serious errors of judgement, but it could be argued that these men were already in a rapidly developing scenario over which there was little control, because the demands of nationalism were all too powerful. The build-up of armaments, the threats of mobilisation were the indicators of Europe's long history of contention based on wealth, power, and territory.

Historians have long had mixed theories, but it has been noted the 'reality is that the First World War was a shock, not a long-anticipated crisis'.[2] Most historians tended to blame the Germans, some the Austrians, 'yet that is surely to understate the shared responsibility of all the European empires'.[3] None of the acknowledged facts of the day form a coherent picture. It presented a 'fatal triangle of territory between the Baltic, the Balkans and the Black Sea which was a zone of conflict not just because it was ethnically mixed, but also because it was where the realms of the Hohenzollerns, Habsburgs, Romanovs and Ottomans met.'[4] It gave the appearance of a deep fault line with a long history of developing beneath the surface.

That the First World War was a surprising shock which can be seen by the economic experts who knew there were tensions across the continent, but never anticipated war. The volatility of economics had not helped, and 'it was precisely the unpredictability of twentieth century economic life that produced such strong shifts in what John Maynard Keynes called the 'animal spirits' of employers, lenders, investors, consumers and indeed government officials'.[5] The claimed *Pax Britannica* assumed peace, and felt reliable to investors, but neglecting 'it was just possible for one civilisation to make war on another, for the same base motives that actuated man in prehistoric times: to expropriate nutritional and reproductive resources'.[6] The human propensity of seeking wealth, territory and resources at the expense of others is a major overlooked feature in humankind history, especially its main strand of aggressive nationalism.

The war was expected to last a few months but continued until 1918, noted for the number of deaths and attritional trench warfare. It was in the trenches where thousands of lives were expended by machine guns and high-explosive shells for a matter of gaining a few yards of useless muddy territory. The French and British also had the aid of Russia until the Romanovs collapsed and the new communist state emerged. The central powers of Austria-Hungary and Germany were supported by the weakening Ottoman Empire. The Allies saw themselves to be the morally superior side, but both camps had plans of reshaping Europe after the victory. Spain, Switzerland, the Netherlands, and the Scandinavian block managed to remain neutral, and benefitted economically, but Bulgaria, Romania and Greece were not so geographically well-placed and were dragged in by the centrifugal forces of conflict.

Of considerable significance America entered the war in April 1916 under President Woodrow Wilson (1856–1924) who had work for peace in Europe, and he entered with a series of postwar plans. Although in the following interbellum years America went through a phase of isolationistic nationalism (repeated for a brief and recent time in the Trump years). America, whose roots in its immigrants was linked to its European heritage became entwined with twentieth century Europe to this day. Also significant in terms of future history, Russia experienced its Bolshevik Revolution in 1917. The famous February Revolution overthrew the Romanovs, and the October Revolution brought the Bolsheviks to power, who soon turned the new country into a totalitarian state despite Bolshevik pretences to be otherwise. As from 6 December 1917, there was a German Russian armistice at Brest-Litovsk, with Russia withdrawing from the war, forcing a change in the deployment of forces, causing a sense of unease in the West.

The Bolsheviks held a tenuous power-grip with their uneasy relations with the Socialist and Menshevik revolutionaries. Lenin, aided by the intellectual Trotsky, soon turned the opposition into enemies of 'The Party', which title was almost given divine status for many years. The many countries which had been part of the Tsarist expansionism all sought their own independence, which was sympathetically accepted by Lenin, but later, as noted above, Stalin ensured these countries would be part of the USSR.

The Versailles Treaty was organised by and for the victors. The major players were a Council of Ten, but its successors centred on the major three of Clemenceau, Lloyd George, Woodrow Wilson and occasionally Orlando from Italy. It was an imposed settlement by the victors, as Soviet Russia and Germany were now regarded as pariah states. Wilson had long preached the idea of a nation's right to self-determination based on the experience of the secessionist nationalistic war against the British. This sound ideal was nearly always ignored when it came to national self-interest. The Americans suspected the British of imperialistic designs as they had for decades. The British were concerned France wanted Napoleonic glory, and both France and Britain shared a concern over America's growing power. Various smaller nations in a series of conferences made bids for their own national identity, notably the Czechs. To ease these trouble-spots the League of Nations was created, but it lacked, in popular terms, credibility and the Americans entered their period of isolationism. Nevertheless, the League was not as entirely useless as is claimed, and there were sixty-six international disputes during its time, of which it resolved thirty-five, but as with its successor the UN, the larger powerful nations continued to dominate.

There were five treaties, and new states were recognised, but the errors of revenge in the war-clauses were immense. Germany was found guilty (the Guilt

Clause) of creating war, their military with imposed restrictions was another humiliation (their army was reduced to 100,000) along with the loss of military machinery. Not least amongst these demands was that the Germans were obliged to give their fleet to the British, and scuppered itself in Scapa Flow. It is not difficult to believe that had the other side won it would have been little different. The statesmen failed to comprehend that these humiliating terms and the financial recriminations left a once proud German nation in a state of serious disarray, which would be used by dangerous German politicians making the future somewhat uncertain, and only a gifted few foresaw this at the time. One of those commentators was a *Daily Herald* cartoonist who drew a picture of a baby crying out at the Versailles Treaty, and around its toe was a tag with the words '1940 conscript' – one of the most prophetic political cartoons ever drawn.[7] The British economist J. M. Keynes in 1919 had argued that the retributive repayments were excessive, and their punitive nature would bring future upheaval. The Congress of Vienna, following the Napoleonic wars, had been signed just over a hundred years before making a better effort for European peace than the Treaty of Versailles managed.

The Russian Civil War (1918–21) which should be dubbed 'Russian Civil Wars' was a series of armed confrontations in varying areas. It involved the Bolsheviks fighting for their new power, involving clashes between the Reds and Whites often with the support of other nations, and some republics fighting for independence. This was especially true in the Ukraine which Russia regarded as personal property, as today in the Putin conflict. It seemed to some that the new Bolshevik power was in danger, Trotsky was an intellectual, but also a sound military leader. The West became involved but at a very minor level, and the Ukraine was often seen as a Russian domestic matter as the Irish were with the British. Large territories came under Soviet control such as Georgia and the Caucasian area. Historical attention has been given to these civil wars, but the loss of life was horrendous, with people starving to death in their millions in the Volga area, leading to a loss of life greater than all sides in the First World War.

Communism, which Lenin wanted to be international, infiltrated Germany, Hungary, and many other places, as it seemed to offer more hope for the working masses. Postwar the Habsburg Empire collapsed with its loss of Hungary, which for five months in 1919 became a Soviet Republic. There was a rebellion by a Hungarian military officer and consequently Horthy, a one-time admiral, rose to be the regent and became a dictator for 24 years. Poland found itself at war with the Soviets (1919–20) with the climax reached when the Soviet General Tukhachevsky reached the Vistula in mid-August, only to be defeated by Piłsudski who had carefully planned a counterattack. Lenin realised that his version of Communism could not win through war, suing for peace at the Treaty of Rigain, March 1921.

The Ottoman Empire also collapsed, and the Allies dictated what would happen. However, Kemal Pasha (Atatürk) who had shown determined leadership at Gallipoli led a Turkish national movement. Kemal Pasha had objected to the Sultan and Mosque domination and a new Turkish Republic was established with an exchange, often forced, of Greek and Turkish populations in key areas, and the important Bosp(h)orus Straits were held by an international commission, (Treaty of Lausanne 1923).

The Great War, as it was popularly known, was a disaster on an unbelievable scale damaging the traditional Europe. It had demanded patriotism and the full enormity of nationalism had demonstrated its various shades of meaning and impact. More to the point the worst aspects of nationalism were fuelled by the conflict, and in the following years would escalate to dangerous levels. Technically the war had finished in 1918, but as noted, in Foch's insight it was a mere truce. It had called upon aggressive nationalism in the call to arms, and the Versailles Treaty had behaved like traditional victors, leading to a doubtful future.

Interbellum Years

The appalling casualty rates of the Great War, the loss of traditional monarchies, the emergence of new nations, not least Soviet Russia, left Europe changed and the various forms of government wondering about the future. Unless it were a single governmental unity, Europe could be policed, and a few perceptive people realised another conflagration was possible, if not inevitable. Russia and Germany remained large and potentially powerful nations being treated as unwanted pariahs. It should have been no surprise when Russia and Germany, who were historically bitter antagonists, signed the Rapallo Treaty (1922) on trade, with concealed military agreements (the so-called protocols). Europe was losing its sense of global supremacy, which was emphasised by the Washington Conference of 1921–2, leading to the Washington Naval Agreement agreeing to naval tonnage for each nation, with America and Britain claiming the greatest numbers permitted.

For some of the more astute it was becoming clear that the Versailles Treaty would not lead to a settlement for lasting peace. Germany had been wounded and made angry. The new Weimar Republic offered hope socially and politically, much more than is usually credited. It had attempted impossible simultaneous efforts 'to create a welfare state and to pay the reparations imposed under the Treaty of Versailles'.[8] However, this new Republic was financially weak with right-wing and Communist riots starting as early as 1919, if not earlier which were widespread and bloody. Walter Rathenau the Minister for Reconstruction was assassinated in 1922 mainly because he was Jewish, arising from the 'stab in the back' that Jews had caused the defeat. This ridiculous belief was used by Hitler and the NSDAP (National Socialist German Workers Party) and was already headlines by 1923. Anti-Semitism as noted above, was inexplicably rife in Europe, and one of the best novels ever written on Jewish persecution was the winner of the Booker Prize: *Brothers* by Bernice Rubens, only a novel but it explored European anti-Semitism from the early nineteenth century to the late 1940s from the Jewish perspective.[9] The racist strand for many was deeply rooted in humankind, helping to make nationalism more bitter and aggressive, as it had done for centuries.

Despite the Versailles Treaty Europe was never entirely at peace, and 'Between 1918 and 1921, the Poles fought small wars against the Ukraine, Germany, Lithuania, Czechoslovakia and Russia; the upshot was that Poland extended much further east than the peacemakers had planned'.[10] German communities came under attack by Polish mobs in Bydgoszcz (formerly Bromberg) and Ostrowo (formerly Ostrow). 'In Czechoslovakia the Germans were effectively excluded from the 1919 elections; in clashes with Czech gendarmes and troops, the so-called massacre of Kaaden of 14 March 1919' occurred when fifty-two Germans were killed, and eighty-four were wounded.[11] Across Europe ethnic minorities felt under pressure, especially the Armenians who were vulnerable as a religious minority, and like the Jews often seen as too wealthy. Their persecution had started with Kurdish troops in the previous century, but a murderous campaign against them started between 1915 to 1918. Most pinpoint this as the first true genocide, which may be true in the modern age, but the Turkish government deny it to this day. It was not only a mass slaughter of anyone aged over ten or twelve, but involved massive deportations, leaving women and their families naked at desert borders with no chance of survival. This was a classic example of the danger for ethnic minorities as a state tried to organise itself along nationalistic lines. The Armenian massacres as well as those of the Pontic Greeks exposed the reality of minority persecution, which is the curse of humankind history.

In postwar Germany, the Weimar Republic struggled to seek moderation and a degree of peace to Germany's political mayhem but lacked experience. Their Foreign Secretary Gustav Stresemann (1878–1929) permitted the German military to cooperate with the Soviets which contravened the Versailles Treaty, which eventuated in the clandestine build-up of German military power under General von Seeckt. Stresemann argued that the financial reparations were damaging all of Europe's finances, winning some Western sympathy because he made efforts to suppress the communist revolts in Saxony. He negotiated a loan from America (the Dawes Plan) to help national finances, and at Locarno (1925) Germany at last rejoined the international circuit by promising to respect the French borders. Noticeably, the Locarno Treaty guaranteed the Western borders but there was no commitment to Germany's eastern borders. In 1926 Germany joined the League of Nations and the following year the Inter-Allied Commissions which had stayed in Germany keeping an eye open, returned home.

The financial burdens were never resolved as the Western Allies had attempted to recover their own losses and repay American charges. If there had been no intervening second war the payments would have lasted to the 1960s and beyond. The French appeared somewhat remorseless in their demands, and in 1923 occupied the Ruhr as compensation, but this only fuelled a deeper resentment. Following the global Market Crash in the New York Stock Exchange the world's financial system was virtually stymied, with serious repercussions in Germany. Even in Britain the National Debt increased by a factor of twelve, and by 1927 'it was equivalent to a crushing 172 per cent of gross domestic product'.[12]

Beyond German concerns Europe was also changing, there had been nineteen monarchies and three republics, but five of the royal houses had disappeared and there were sixteen republics. Two small states came into existence. The Irish Free State was established in 1922 as a sovereign dominion, but real independence was hard fought for, with conflict with the British army and also their own civil struggles. The emerging leader was de Valera (1882–1975), and Southern Ireland became Éire in 1937 and severed formal ties with Britain in 1949. This led to an uncomfortable relationship in the British Isles which in some ways is still an ongoing issue, especially after Brexit. The other state was the Vatican, limited to about a hundred acres in central Rome which had been suppressed since 1870, and this brought some security to the Papacy.

It appeared at first as if the democratic system would at last find a footing in Europe, especially as the Weimar Republic appeared to be hitting the right notes, but these hopes evaporated with the upsurge of the dictators. This was the century dominated by the ideologies of Communism, Fascism and Liberal Democracies. The Soviet Union (as from 1923–4) was the sole Communist State but under Stalin (died 1953) it emerged as a totalitarian state. Fascist regimes of various shades emerged in Italy (1922), Germany (1933) and Spain (1936) and minor ones across Europe. Communism and Fascism were spawned from different ideals, but they held much in common. The historian Norman Davies in his outstanding History of Europe, which this survey has plundered for background purposes, drew up a comprehensive list of the points these ideologies shared, which the reader may wish to check.[13]

Communism and fascism were both a mixture of nationalist and socialist elements, although both sides made every effort to appear unique. Both adopted pseudo-sciences, the Nazi regime studying eugenics and racial theories, the communists the theories of Marxism. They portrayed their own versions of the future, the communists to a classless society, the Nazis to an Aryan paradise, and Mussolini looked back to the grandness of the Roman Empire. They all established bureaucracies, governed on strict hierarchical lines with the power emanating from such titles as the Führer, the Duce, and Caudillo, all intimating 'the leader'. They had much in common, behaving like the proverbial boss or tribal chieftain, eliminating enemies, using fear to suppress opposition, and portraying their efforts as a means of defending their community. They nearly always claimed their country was surrounded by enemies, making their leadership essential for the nation's well-being. Franco in Spain was the expert in this game, but Hitler and Stalin used this fear of the external threat, claiming they were surrounded by potential enemies which naturally led to the rise of militarism.

Propaganda is used to this day by every form of leadership, but the rising German Nazi Party took it to extremes, and Joseph Goebbels was probably the most infamous for his clever style of telling lies and yet convincing the public. His style of propaganda controlled the press as the so-called communist Party did in the USSR. Censorship was blatant and controlled every area of life, even in art, literature, cartoons, and posters were examined before being allowed to go public. The political leaders used propaganda for appealing to the masses for nationalistic support. The confusion between Nazi fascism, Russian communism and nationalism is difficult to describe, but nationalism was there and presented using different ploys. In August 1937 the German diplomat Ulrich von Hassell wrote in his diary regarding the Molotov-Ribbentrop Pact, that 'it remains an open question to what extent the pact is merely a dishonest expedient for both authoritarian regimes or how far it goes towards drawing the two states closer together – the Soviets more nationalist and the Nazis more Bolshevist'.[14] For any political observer at that time it was confusing.

The sense of hatred was seen as necessary in totalitarian states to stir up nationalism of the worst type, and in Germany the Jews and communists became the focused targets, for Stalin it was aimed at the Kulaks, the fascists, and capitalists as representing the West. It was their way of arousing primitive tribal passions. It was also a useful tool for control of their own populations, the NKVD/KGB in the USSR with a similar arrangement typified by the Gestapo in Germany, both organisations provoking a sense of fear if not sheer terror. The barbaric behaviour in the Nazi extermination camps is well-known, and Solzhenitsyn's literary works later exposed a similar brutality in the camps of the Gulag. Whereas the Nazis exterminated people, the Gulag camps worked them to death. The state even tried to control family units with youth organisations, the Komsomol groups in the USSR, and Hitler Youth in Germany. This effectively ensured youngsters put the nation's leader before their parents. The Church was banned in Russia (until the war crisis), suppressed in Germany, and used in Spain. In Germany and Russia, the only social gatherings were those permitted by the state. Lenin and Stalin had looked to international communism, Hitler wanted to conquer Europe, while Mussolini was content with the Mediterranean land and seascape following the Roman theory of domination. Both these ideologies of fascism and Stalin's communism regarded themselves as world saviours, communism fighting off the fascist threat and challenging capitalism, and the fascist stopping the spread of communism. Morally they shared the threatening policy that the end justifies the means.

The Nazi leaders were carried to power by the tribalism of the well-known street brawling, and it is now known that personal power was more important to them than their ideologies. The upsurge of communism in the streets gave Hitler his means to power, and Mussolini, a one-time street fighter, had little political principle. For him fascism had its own formula, of 'socialism plus nationalism plus war'.[15] Stalin's form of communism would have been unrecognizable to Marx but these dictators, including Stalin, rose to total power with global ramifications, which scarred Europe and the world to this day. They all used nationalism by claiming their countries were superior to others which meant they should occupy them. As one historian noted, 'Considering the emphasis the new dictatorships laid on their supposedly distinctive nationalistic traditions, they all looked remarkably alike: the coloured shirts, the shiny boots, the martial music, the strutting leaders, the gangsters of violence'.[16] The Nazis used tribal instincts of nationalism, even referring to their mythical ancestors the Aryans, while Himmler studied tribal gods. The fascist states and their leaders made the most of nationalism with territorial claims, irredentist to start with, but swiftly followed by unashamed aggressive expansionist nationalism. There was the appearance of racialism, as noted above, which is one of the most sinister ingredients of nationalism, religious belief was crushed or utilised, language was used as a distinguishing marker, all underlining the perilous nationalistic impulse that 'they are not one of us', an early ingredient in humankind's early history.

All these developments across Europe, from Russia to Germany, from Italy to Spain were like political earthquakes announcing the possible arrival of a catastrophic volcano disaster. In the West there was a genuine fear of repeating the First World War, in the postwar era appeasers were often sneered at, but it was an understandable hope for peace amongst nations. The Americans had retreated into isolationism, the British failed to sign the important Geneva Protocol of 1924. The French tended to be the most active, and in 1928 led the Briand-Kellogg Pact renouncing war and encouraging over sixty states to sign this pledge. It had high ideals but little chance of upholding them. Briand was an outstanding statesman, even proposing the need for a European Union in 1929, a 'moral union', but he was years ahead of his time.

In the West communism had invoked more fear than fascism, with Stalin and his cohorts offering their propaganda picture of socialist idealism. Many Russians were not taken in by this propaganda, but some foreigners were, not least Sidney and Beatrice Webb who following a visit to Russia, tried to explain that Russia was not a dictatorship.* Visitors were easily persuaded, and when the Webbs spent time with a British diplomat he noted in his diary, 'it is evident that on the whole they have seen what everyone sees, the show pieces, and I think they have been too prone to accept at their face value such statements'.[17] The current writer of this exploration visited Russia as a Komsomol guest during the Brezhnev period and experienced the same style of influential posturing. 'The Soviet propaganda machine was so efficient that it managed to hide monstrous atrocities at home while projecting a utopian vision abroad', managing this for decades.[18]

The Roman Catholic Church had a greater fear of communism than it did for fascism; the Catholics were aware that Mussolini was no threat, and Franco in Spain was an ardent Catholic. However, in 1937 Pope Pius XI published two encyclicals, *Mit Brennender Sorge* and *Divini Redemptoris*, which basically stated that both communism and Nazism (not just fascism) were incompatible with Christianity. The Eastern European countries also found themselves with the complex problem of finding their geographical position had left them trapped between the communist USSR and a different and potentially dangerous Germany.

Tsarist Russia had always attempted to expand its territory, and it was soon apparent that Soviet Russia under Stalin was the same. Stalin was as feared as much as Hitler and along with Mao Zedong these three national leaders were all responsible for millions of deaths. Stalin was later joined by the Western democracies to eradicate Nazism, and Stalin was known almost affectionately as Uncle Joe. However, he was as criminal as Hitler, interested in personal power. The political purges of the 1930s and the show trials demonstrated what happened to anyone who dared oppose or were critical of him. He dictated what the Party required, even if it meant the death of his cohorts such as Bukharin (1938) and Zinoviev (1936).

Stalin rose to power through the Revolution, Mussolini bullied his way to power, and Hitler used and abused the democratic process. Hitler's rise to power was assisted by the financial depression, the fear of communism, but he never won an outright majority. The Nazi plebiscites were common and used with

---

* The Webbs wrote an apologia called *Soviet Communism: A New Civilization?*

manipulative propaganda and the ominous presence of Nazi Party members at the polls. The burning down of the Reichstag confirmed the Nazi control over communists, an enabling Act granted the Chancellor dictatorial powers. It was a plebiscite which led to the withdrawal from the League of Nations, and from the Disarmament Conference, winning with a simply unbelievable 96.3 per cent vote. In another plebiscite Hitler won approval for a party-state and the title of Führer with 90 per cent. It was viewed as a democratic triumph despite the massive evidence that the plebiscites were rigged, leading the historian Norman Davies to note that 'democracy has few values of its own: it is as good, or as bad, as the principles of the people who operate it. In the hands of a liberal and tolerant people, it will produce a liberal and tolerant government; in the hands of cannibals, a government of cannibals'.[19] Hitler rose to power from a humiliated and economically depressed country, and a once superior military only too willing to offer support even if it disturbed some of them. Hitler's *Mein Kampf* was a boring monologue of his political thinking. In 1939 the Queen of England sent a copy to Lord Halifax advising him to skip through it because it would give him a good idea of Hitler's mentality. The trouble was that too few read it because it indicated many of his political aims, such as *lebensraum* (living space) implying the German right to move east, and the word *herrenvolk* (master race) indicating his racial bigotry. His use of expressions such as Aryan and Jew carried his threatening actions for the years ahead. Nazism like Stalin's communism used coercive powers to control by suppression the free will of their citizens and eradicating any opposition. Both Hitler's Nazi regime, and Stalin's Communism were simply evil, and their rise to power is easier to explain than their amoral behaviour.

By the mid-1930s the suspicions of Hitler's intentions were growing, and France and Britain looked to Stalin, a known predator, to save them from the other. In Poland, Marshal Piłsudski signed a non-aggression pact with the USSR (1932) and two years later another with Germany, only to be invaded by both in 1939. The Serbs, Croats, and Slovenes since 1929 had become Yugoslavia but remained unsettled with their main crisis being Mussolini's Italy. During the decade of the 1930s Mussolini sent troops to Abyssinia, and to the Spanish Civil War, which financially cost Italy too much. The Abyssinian invasion was condoned by the Hoare-Laval Pact in 1935, which caused such public outrage that both the British and French political organisers lost their posts.

Spain was torn apart by their Civil War because it had never resolved its feudalistic background, and Spaniards were sharply divided. Franco had a bitter hatred of communists and any form of opposition. He had military support as well as that of the extreme right-wing Falangists led by José Primo de Rivera (whose father had been a dictator in 1923–30) and the support of the Germans and Italians. The Republican government had Soviet support in return for gold bullion, many international volunteers turned up to fight mainly for the Republicans. Francisco Franco was a fascist dictator who lasted until 1975, and he was still executing his Civil War opponents in the mid-1940s. The bombing of Guernica (1937) is often regarded as the embodiment of the Civil War, but there were many more appalling deeds, but it was Guernica which registered warnings to other countries concerning the changing nature of airpower and bombing. The Italian military theorist Giulio Douhet (1869–1930) had already written on the strategic possibilities of aerial bombing to avoid wars of attrition of the trenches, and all the major countries were busy looking at airpower from the point of view of attack and defence.

Germany was rapidly becoming recognised as a potential threat by attempting a coup in Austria in 1934, a year later the Saarland's accession to the Reich, the re-introduction of conscription, and the announcement that the Luftwaffe had denounced the disarmament clauses. In 1936 they entered the Rhineland and signed the Anti-Comintern Pact with Italy. In 1938 Hitler engineered the Anschluss taking Austria into the Reich, and he was making objections to the way German speaking people in the Sudetenland region of Czechoslovakia were being treated. In these incidents and events were the signs of irredentist nationalism in which one country claims by historical right the return of land which was once part of its territory. It was a claim based on a sense of justice or natural rights, and even the anti-Nazi Ulrich von Hassell noted in his diary that because the Polish negotiator had failed to appear 'there was nothing left for Germany but to take action to secure its rights'.[20] This anti-Nazi diplomat assumed that Germany had right of occupation because of the invalidity of the Versailles Treaty, a view shared by many Germans, even gaining a degree of understanding from other countries.

Britain and France, recovering financially from the Great War, were desperate to keep the peace. Chamberlain visited Hitler three times, eventually returning with the famous 'Peace in our Time' proclamation, and most people were jubilant. It was peace because Hitler had the Sudetenland handed to him on a plate, increasing his support amongst the German public. Britain was the slowest to react. The monarchy faced the abdication of Edward VIII but more pertinently the military, especially the army, was well under strength. They were short of cash and the British had kept to their 'Ten Year' rule (introduced in 1919), that if another war was not predicted the budgets would reflect this hope. It was reaffirmed annually until 1932, but there was an assumed reliance on France which reputedly had the largest army in Europe. However, by 1939 all nations were busy rearming, and Churchill persistently argued for the expansion of the RAF which would later help Britain survive the war. Germany and the

Soviets had built up their military, while America's army was small and almost insignificant. It soon became clear that the Poles were not going to give up any of their territory, as the Czechs had been obliged. There was a last-minute French-British effort to work an alliance with Stalin, but the Western Democracies lacked the necessary commitment, and when the pro-English Litvinov (married to an English woman and strongly anti-fascist) was replaced by Molotov, it was a clear signal that Stalin was looking towards Germany. In March, the Slovak government was deposed by the Czechs and their leader, the priest Father Tišo appealed to Hitler and the Germans marched into Prague without resistance. The Hungarians seized Ruthenia and Europe's map was once again showing signs of change. The British made a treaty with Poland, a mere bluff, and the French General Gamelin immorally assured the Poles that if invaded then French troops would cross the Franco-German border within fifteen days. The infamous Molotov-Ribbentrop Pact was signed, based on trade agreements, but with the secret protocols regarding the division of Poland. The outbreak of war was launched by the deception that the Poles had attacked, and German ground and air-forces, later dubbed the Blitzkrieg War, were successful.

Nationalism during Interbellum Years

As noted at the start of this exploration of nationalism the word has so many shades of meaning, ranging from the acceptable, to the immoral, with some elements fluctuating dependent on different viewpoints. The nature of nationalism during this period of the twentieth century tends to indicate the severe forms of nationalism (aggressive and expansionist which scarred European history, with long-lasting ramifications). Nationalism is often associated with fascism and military conflict, but it raises 'questions that need analysing...they should not be taken as foregone conclusions'.[21] The types of nationalism during this era can be seen in the post-First World War successor states, where displacement of ethnic or minority groups caused by the upheavals meant to counter the revisionist nationalism of the defeated states, and the entangled relationship between nationalism and fascism.[22]

Cultural nationalism, closely related to revisionist nationalism focused on by intellectuals trying to define a nation's culture, led to romantic nationalism, which was safe enough, but during this period the tendency developed from defining a nation and its membership, to denouncing those who did not belong. It amounted to the tribal thinking of 'them and us' but taken to the immoral extremity that they had no right to exist. The surrounding political and military events of the period 1918–1945 tended to shape the thinking of nations emerging into a disrupted world, caused by wars which changed the map of Europe. In the interbellum years this map-changing found many ethnic clusters trapped as minority groups in a new nation. The well-known Rabbi Hugo Gryn once said in one of his popular radio talks, that over a period of twenty years he lived in three different countries but never moved from his home-village, which was a feature for many people during this turbulent time, especially in Eastern and Central Europe.* Some people were stateless and especially in areas such as Romania, Poland, and the brand-new state of Czechoslovakia. The Jewish people had to face the rise of extreme anti-Semitism. The destruction of the Ottoman and Habsburg Empires caused a seismic shift, and the collapse of the Romanov dynasty led to its problems as the Bolsheviks re-established what they had refused to call an empire. Across these domains of Eastern Europe many regions were historically mixed ethnically and in language.

In the period following the First World War, little or no attention was given to these ethnic groups within the evolving states, who were now foreigners in their own homes. 'These nationalistic projects were fuelled in part, by the irredentist nationalism of the defeated states'.[23] This form of irredentist nationalism was and remains a global problem and has been the cause of many major conflicts. The revised states of Romania, Poland and Czechoslovakia were all aware that Germany, Hungary, and Russia believed they had claims on the revised territories, leading to violent clashes, and what could be described as a European civil war.

Too often the ethnic minorities were the excuse for revisionist nationalism, which demanded the restoration of what was perceived to be territorial rights based on ethnic demand. Many ethnic minorities were under suspicion by their governments and popular opinion. This effort of national re-building became a vicious circle with some disastrous consequences.

During the 1920s Polish people constituted some 70 per cent of the Polish population, and the rest were Germans, Jews, Ukrainians, and Lithuanians with a smattering of other ethnic groups. Much of Poland was multi-cultural, causing, as it often and sadly does, feelings of resentment amongst much of the population. In Poland, the Ukrainians and Belarussians tended to be rural labourers, and the Jewish element was associated with commerce and artisans. The minorities were excluded from the constitution-making process, while the German minority were treated as a fifth column, with suspicions of their loyalty. Many Germans left Poland, but it was not so easy for those whose traditional homes were in the ex-Prussian regions.

The same issues existed in Romania whose population and territorial size had nearly doubled. As in Poland ethnic Romanians were about 70 per cent

---

* Hugo Gryn (1930–96) was born Berehovo in Carpathian, which was then in Czechoslovakia, and now in the Ukraine.

of the population, and the remainder were Hungarians, Jews, and Germans, who were generally treated as foreigners, not least the Magyars who were often regarded as a threat. Romanian cultural nationalism expanded in its language and traditions within the educational system, it was intensified in Transylvania, where the Hungarian and other ethnic minorities were more prominent.

As with Yugoslavia, Czechoslovakia was a new country within the re-organised map of Europe. In Czechoslovakia, its western regions were industrialised and had a form of democracy, but its new additional regions of Slovakia (once Hungarian) and Ruthenia tended to be more rural. Czechoslovakia had some three million Germans in the Sudetenland and nearly a million Hungarians in Slovakia. The postwar armistice appeared to have been ignorant or unaware of the possible consequences of its decisions. The Czechs were not as repressive as the Poles and Romanians, but they dominated their state, and from the immediate post-Great War years the irredentist claims by Germany were loud and clear. The Germans in Sudetenland were often reminded they were just immigrants, which was unsettling with some wanting to be regarded as an independent province of Austria, causing the Czech government to occupy the region at one time.

This raised the difficult question over nationalism and the rise of fascism. The many studies on the rise of fascism indicate that certain shades of various nationalisms were part of this issue, but there are no straightforward answers. It has been argued that fascism succeeded because it enlisted the support of the conservative or right-wing elements, and it is most likely that aggressive nationalism played a significant role. Many historians and other disciplines have often noted the fascist reliance on nationalism, but it must not be forgotten that the First World War had created a sense of instability across Europe, mainly because its aftershocks prepared the way for political extremism. The groundwork of fascism can be found not only in this factor, but also with the mislaid ethnic minorities and boundary demands mentioned above. This led to the demand by many suffering the repercussions to shout that 'something had to happen', and in others that 'they needed decisive leadership', a cry heard in many nations to this day with a divided or weak government.

Nationalism in its various shades was not a novelty confined to Europe, but it became an aggressive force during this era. The fascists in promoting their view of the future linked this with their version of aggressive nationalism to encourage the masses to their way of thinking. Fascism became a challenge in Europe during the inter-bellum years because of this call to nationalism. However, it has been noted from the various case studies that 'the lines between nationalism and racism are complex and fluid', but mainly dependent on adopted variations, but it was to play a major role.[24] It could be argued that Hitler was a racist and a nationalist, or that he took nationalism to an aggressive level by using the racial ingredient. His variation of nationalism included anti-Semitism, accusing Jews and others of being sub-human, making fascism and racism part of the same weed growing around the trunk of nationalism. It can be cogently argued that it was always built into the themes of aggressive nationalism which had always tended to adopt the 'them and us' policy from the earliest of times, soon to reach the level of crimes against humanity with the onslaught of genocide. A brief look at the developing fascist countries during this period will indicate that fascism, like nationalism, had different forms in each country.

The Civil War in Spain saw the rise of a fascist dictatorship under Franco, which had not been a consequence of the First World War from which Spain had financially profited with neutrality. It was the result of a divided country which had retained elements of feudalism, and the eventual victor, Franco had ruled as the dictator. He had found support from Mussolini and Hitler during the Civil War and appeared to support them during The Second World War, but adroitly switching allegiance when their defeat became obvious. Spain was for years regarded as a pariah state, and this form of nationalism was Franco's projection of Christian Spain surrounded by enemies. Franco had wanted to retrieve Gibraltar from the British and take over the French colonies in North Africa, but although fascist nationalism was distasteful to the Western Allies, Spain was isolated in its impoverished war-weary peninsula and never carried the same international relevance as Germany.

For a moment Switzerland appeared to have developed a fascist movement with its main elements of anti-liberalism, anti-Semitic, anti-democratic with its National Front and Neue Front Parties, but it was thoroughly beaten at the polls and evaporated. In Britain, some unpopular fascists appeared under Oswald Mosely, an MP with inherited titles who led the BUF (British Union of Fascists) in 1932. This appeared in London with mixed responses, it was frequently opposed and a popular subject for cartoon humour. and Mosely was thrown into prison in 1940 to be released in 1943, as he was not thought to be a national threat.

In the liberal democracy of France, the right-wing was impregnated with nationalism, mainly as a result of the 1870 Franco-German war with the loss of Alsace-Lorraine, leading to the League of Patriots (1882), and more importantly *Action Française* (1899). France's first fascist party was the *Le Faisceau* which was founded by Georges Valois in 1925. This party was basically a far-right political party, and when it came to racial matters there was a time when some members wanted the Jews expelled, because of their hold in economic matters. They were strongly opposed by a republican nationalist movement, the *Parti Populaire Français*, which was founded by a one-time communist Jacques Doriot in 1936, and it was given a popular boost by linking Jews and Bolsheviks into the same sculpt. This movement was helped by popular reactions against the left-wing Jewish Prime Minister Léon Blum, who had little public appeal, but was a man who retained any sense of personal integrity. The *Parti Populaire Français* was never a strong party, but it attracted some intellectuals such as Pierre Drieu La Rochelle, whose novels associated Jews with decadence, and who preached a form of ethno-regionalism. Another similar collaborator was Robert Brasillach who wanted to exclude Jews from the French nation. Later, it was claimed that under the Vichy regime, Pétain was regarded as a fascist leader but although under the circumstances he may have appeared dictatorial, he was merely conservative. Interestingly the fascists survived more in the occupied zone. However, there is no question that Pétain with such leaders as Laval and Darlan were anti-Semitic, agreeing to transport refugee Jews to German transports via the Paris camp of Drancy to Eastern Europe for extermination.

In Romania nationalism with anti-Semitism had an existence from before the First World War, and was not helped by Romania's poverty, misleading many Romanians to believe it was because of the Jews, Germans, and Hungarians running the country's economy. 'A major difference compared to general fascism and especially Nazism was that the [Romanian] Iron Guard was overtly Orthodox Christian. Initially known as the Legion of the Archangel Michael, the guard was organised like a religious order'.[25] Their slogan was *Totul pentru Țară*, (everything for the country). It was Romania's sense of nationalism which stirred the irredentist nationalistic variation against Hungary. The rise of fascists with radical nationalism led to a power struggle between King Carol II and the infamous Iron Guard, and in 1938 the king suspended the democratic constitution. Eventually when General Antonescu assumed power he became a form of fascist dictatorship similar to Franco in style.

Hungary was reduced in territory, as after the Treaty of Trianon (June 1920) Hungary lost 60 per cent of its population, some Hungarians were placed in other states, and it lost half of its railway lines and roads, and 80 per cent of its timber and iron-ore resources. The Versailles Treaty was seen as a humiliation by the Germans, and the Hungarians felt the same way. In 1928 there was a call for a 'Greater Hungary' and Count Kunó Klebelsberg called on Hungarian nationalism to free itself from the humiliating treaty, hoping to transform Hungary into a racially pure kingdom. It followed the general trend of making Jews the targets as this aggressive and expansionist nationalism grew. It produced the infamous Arrow Cross (whose insignia suddenly re-appeared in the right-wing Hungary in recent years) which was racist, anti-Semitic, anti-democratic, benefitting from Nazi funding. Later in 1944 Hitler, not trusting the regent Horthy in 1944, re-instated the Arrow Cross which led to the elimination of the Jews. The expansive nationalism of Hungary seemed to work as Hitler returned them Slovakia and Ruthenia in 1938, but these gains were soon lost.

In Italy the fascists had joined the government in 1922, and within a few years had established the first new dictatorship in twentieth century Europe. Italy had only become a democracy in the full sense of the word in 1918 with what is best described as a form of liberal parliamentarism. After the First World War there had been massive demobilisation, a class struggle and serious discontent over the way Italy had been badly rewarded for its efforts in terms of territorial gains. There soon appeared a form of revisionist nationalism based on this perceived poor treatment which the Italians referred to as the 'muted victory'. The British and French had claimed after the war that Italy's contribution needed no reward of territorial gains, and Prime Minister Vittorio Orlando had to announce that Italy's hopes were dashed. This helped to account for Mussolini's major support coming from Trieste and South Tyrol where there had been hopes of nationalistic expansion.

Mussolini's encroachments in North Africa and the Balkans were all part of this Italian hope of aggressive expansive nationalism to give a sense of the country's greatness, which the fascists offered. 'Arguably the main constant in Mussolini's thinking was his conviction that violence was necessary to shape troops', and he knew he had many discontented military men from the Great War to assist his plans.[26] The brutal ramifications of nationalism were certainly felt in North Africa, but there were few signs of the racialism which featured in Nazi Germany and elsewhere. As Nazi influence grew in 1938 the signs of a racist approach appeared, and Jews were banned from prominent positions and forbidden to marry so-called natural born Italians. Various biographers have struggled over this issue, pointing out that Mussolini was not personally anti-Semitic but following all powerful Germany. The nationalistic school in Italy tended to be more cultural than biological, and although various Nazi leaders often requested that Mussolini rid himself of Jews many escaped compared to the fate of those who lived in Nazi Europe.

In Germany the year 1933 witnessed the collapse of the Weimar Republic and the appearance of Adolf Hitler. He used aggressive nationalism to the full extent, and he had inherited much of his perverse thinking. As early as the 1880s, just after Germany's unification, citizenship depended on ethnic background, which stopped Eastern Jews from becoming acceptable Germans. This was a Prussian led directive and 'recent research on popular associations [i.e. Choral societies and so forth] in the late nineteenth century suggests such organic understanding of nationhood was neither confined to the political class nor the conservative fringes of society'.[27] This underlined the powerful nationalistic drive for a Greater Germany. Prussian leaders wanted a unified race of people

The Twentieth Century 119

ready to fight external enemies in and outside their lands. Before Hitler had published his dangerous thinking on *lebensraum*, the nature of this subject had already started. The feeling for irredentist nationalism was used by the Nazis and supported at all social levels, while overseas there was some sympathy, but less so when it broadened to the total domination of Europe through the passion of aggressive nationalism.

From his early days Hitler was obsessed with the widely held belief that Germany was threatened by inferior races. Hitler's influence was overbearing on men like Gregor Strasser who had argued that the Party was more important than race, and even on Goebbels who as a young man was not extremely anti-Semitic. It was no surprise that the Nuremberg Race Laws were inaugurated as Hitler in *Mein Kampf* had argued for the preservation of the race, a feature his henchman Himmler took seriously.* There were discussions about exporting Jews to Madagascar, but after Poland fell, ghettoes and concentration camps were placed there for the so-called sub-humans.

Racism, culture, language, were the traditional features of aggressive nationalism which became major factors in the German fascist plans, providing the impetus for the Second World War. The major driving force in the interbellum years was the growth of the Nazi fanaticism projecting nationhood and a superior race. Hitler's warped thinking was reflected in Italy, Japan, communist Russia all seeking territorial expansion with anachronistic ideas of imperial glory. It has also been noted that economics played a part with Hitler's four-year plans and his theory of *lebensraum* driven by money. Hitler knew Germany needed oil, rubber, copper, and iron ore, which was a powerful driving force. The very word *lebensraum* was the primitive maxim that the other man's field is greener. In 1936 Italy had occupied Abyssinia, Japan was making incursions into China, with Hitler looking to the east of Europe, all driven by aggressive nationalism.

The Second World War

The Second World War was primarily a conflict fought on the grounds of aggressive nationalism with some countries trying to stay isolated or neutral. It also started and later ended with the irredentist form and after occupation

---

* In 1940 Himmler took a tour of Poland to establish German areas of settlement (although few Germans were happy with the idea of moving to Poland) and he noticed that many Poles looked Aryan which for him meant they were blue-eyed and fair-haired. There began a sifting of children looking for those who could be taken from their families and raised as Germans. German Aryan women known as *Brown Sisters* would patrol the streets looking for likely candidates. A Dr Erhard Wetzel wrote that racially the Poles contained the same racial strains as Germans. This was all pseudo-science but men like Himmler believed this nonsense.

by alien troops secessionist nationalism was prominent. It should be noted that had aggressive nationalism not played such a major part the other forms of nationalism may not have taken root and there may possibly have been peace or a more limited conflict.

The French, knowing they faced a war with Germany had the largest army, the Maginot Line, and having won in the Great War were probably overconfident, a feeling shared by the British who saw the French as militarily strong, and having the English Channel as a border. In 1939 the British only had two divisions prepared for the continent, and the Latin advice of *si vis pacem, para bellum* (if you wish peace, prepare for war) had been neglected. Roosevelt in America was clinging to isolationism (another shade of nationalism) having promised voters their sons were safe, and he suggested the Polish corridor should be returned to the Germans, hoping that a peaceful form of irredentist nationalism would resolve the problem. The British during the 1930s thought the Nazis threat would evaporate and appeasement was the keynote, with only the lone voice of Churchill objecting, and by 1939 the Munich agreement had lost its credibility. It appeared that the British politicians had failed to see the situation, even ignoring the Secretary of the German Foreign Office, Ernst von Weizsäcker's warnings. The benefit of hindsight is useful, prompting many historians to wonder why the West had failed to listen to advice about what was happening in mainland Europe. Appeasement had been completely understandable in the light of the First World War, but it could never work with Hitler. Of all the wars fought in Europe, this was to be a major confrontation which had to be fought, but with no adequate preparation.

Most books identify September 1939 as the starting date for the Second World War, Americans pinpoint 1941, but it was a global war with the Japanese invading Manchuria in 1931, and who had been fighting China since 1937. Even in Europe it had started earlier than September because the Germans had interfered in Lithuania in March 1939, and the Italians in North Africa. These different dates for a major global war indicate the egocentric attitudes of the various national powers.

Stalin, due to French and British incompetence and their inbuilt distrust of the communists, had decided to join Nazi Germany, a diplomatic failure on the part of the West. Poland was overrun by the Germans and Russians who halted at an agreed line on the river Bug. Aggressive nationalism was current in both Hitler's and Stalin's policies, and Stalin was hoping to outwit Hitler in the hopes of territorial expansion. The Poles fought bravely, confused as the Soviets invaded from the east and by the failure of the French to cross the German border, which they had assured the Poles they would. They also endured an aerial bombardment by the Luftwaffe which was to become a characteristic of this war.

The Polish defeat sent out signals to the rest of Europe, but three issues in this Polish war predicted a dubious future. First was the Nazi *Einsatzgruppen* killing helpless Jews and Polish civilians, secondly, the Katyń massacres indicating that Stalin and Hitler were equally amoral, and thirdly the Stuka attacks working with tanks demonstrated that this war would be different from the Great War, with the word Blitzkrieg involving speed and correlation between land and air power devised in the 1920s by General von Seeckt.

Many perceptive people realised that such were the potential dangers of this war that it had to be fought to the end, because of the immoral and criminal behaviour of the Nazi regime. It also stirred feelings of opposition to the Nazi regime within Germany especially amongst the senior military. In the West many recognised the same dangers in Stalin when the Soviets and Nazis held their victory parade together in Brest-Litovsk where the rivers Bug and Mukhavets meet, but Germany being a central European state appeared to pose the major threat to the West.

The more sinister aspects of aggressive nationalism were clearly outlined in Poland. Russia held what it considered to be its traditional share from the various partitions of the past, while the Germans took their portion for Germanisation, re-naming it the General Government. It was here where racial matters such as Jews and dissidents held in concentration camps were so brutally treated or liquidated. Hitler's racialism saw the Poles, Jews, and all Slavs as sub-human, and it was later revelations in Poland that made the world aware of Hitler's extreme racialism. The two totalitarian states were now not only allies but next-door neighbours. These two military giants were similar, with an apparent secured future, with *Pravda* announcing that the Soviet-German friendship would endure forever, when it only lasted a matter of months.

As the nervous phoney war was underway in the West, Stalin's expansionist nationalism restarted with his war against Finland in November 1939. He was opposed by Gustav Mannerheim and the Germans noted with interest that the Red Army had not performed as well as anticipated. The interest in Scandinavia raised more concerns, because it was well known that the Germans needed the Swedish high-quality iron-ore usually transported through Norway. Scandinavia would have preferred its neutrality, but the Swedish government had little choice given the perceived force of the Nazi military.

Following the creed of expansionist nationalism in April 1940, Denmark was overrun and later Norway, once the Germans had fought a few battles with the British. In the Norwegian campaign the Germans gained immediate dominance with its army, but British naval power was noted. It was during the Norway campaign when information was gained from the German enigma machine and when the code was broken this source of information was essential for the whole war, with only Admirals Raeder and Dönitz having doubts that the British had broken the complex code machine. It was also clear that German occupation was to a degree more civilised in the West than in the East.

In May 1940 Hitler's forces invaded Belgium and the Low Countries in less than three weeks, and Paris fell on 16 June. France had the largest standing army and even the Germans had been surprised at the speed of their success. The French historian and soldier Marc Bloch blamed it on the mediocre performance of the French generals. The British had sent only a small force (BEF) but had to retreat from Dunkirk, which was painted as a victory, despite being a major debacle in British military history. The so-called impregnable Maginot Line was by-passed by the Germans because the French had not extended it along the Belgium border. It had to be acknowledged that the German military was prepared with well trained professional officers.

It was not just a French military problem, but there had been so many French governments during the inter-bellum years cynics called it musical chairs. The French were obliged to seek an armistice, and Alsace-Lorraine was returned to Germany, the coastal areas came under German military zones, the northern industrial part of France was occupied but the south, known as Vichy was granted independence with strict frontier controls. While Pétain governed in Vichy France and avoided taking his government to North Africa, Hitler was in Paris saluting his soldiers in the Champs-Élysées. France and Germany had a long history of conflict, but this time Hitler's aggressive nationalism won the day and he appeared to many as a military genius as expressed by his Field Marshal Keitel.

According to Field Marshal Kesselring had the Germans launched an immediate attack across the Channel England would have fallen as well, but this will always remain questionable. He made this claim postwar over the radio which did not make him very popular. In worried Britain, they faced Göring's Luftwaffe trying to halt any British resistance by what has been called the Blitz. There had been much concern in Britain that Germany would attack cities with what is now described as carpet-bombing, not helped by Göring's claim that London would be reduced to rubble. In fact, the Germans tended to use their airpower as a tactical force as evidenced by their attacks on airfields and ports, including the London docks, during the Battle of Britain. Later the RAF and the USAAF would reply with more devastating effect with strategic bombing which came close to annihilating populated areas such as Hamburg and Dresden. As the Second World War progressed the hatred and barbarity reached new depths. The nature of mass bombing and its policy is discussed to this day, but young bomber crews had courage and moral judgements from this distance are inappropriate.

The Battle of Britain was eventually won by the British with incredibly young pilots (including Czechs, Poles, French, American volunteers, and others) flying their famous Spitfires and Hurricanes. By 15 September, the German plan of Operation *Sea Lion* (Invasion of Britain) was abandoned in the light of Hitler's plans for Russia. However, the Battle of Britain gave hope to the wider world, not least because it meant that Britain provided a reasonably safe platform to launch further aerial attacks, and later would become an American carrier for amassing troops and bomber aircraft. It was not until Japan attacked at Pearl Harbor (7 December 1941) that America entered the war with Hitler's help, who declared war on America, knowing the Americans had already helped the British.

Britain was on the defence not just in the air making the channel less of a border but struggling to feed its population and rebuild its armaments, a problem for the Royal Navy in the 'Battle of the Atlantic'. There were naval battles for control of the oceans, with the Germans sinking the *Royal Oak* in Scapa Flow, the *Graf Spee* tricked into scuttling itself, then the *Hood* sunk by the *Bismarck* which was pursued and destroyed. The serious menace was the submarine, in German terms the well-known U-boat (*Unterseeboot*). The Royal Navy would fight the U-boat for years but gained the upper hand through clever technology, but not before merchant seaman died in massive numbers. The control of the sea lanes was critical for essential supplies, for transporting troops, and later preparing invasions. The Axis powers had reached out to North Africa, Europe's conflict happening well beyond Europe's borders. The Mediterranean became a major theatre of war and witnessed the destruction of the French fleet at Mers-el-Kébir by the British, indicating it was already a war with no holds barred. In a ruthless nationalistic war, the British by destroying their one-time ally's fleet demonstrated that when the chips were down national survival came first. In Africa, the Italians were beaten by British troops, and then rescued by Rommel's Afrika Korps, who were later defeated at El Alamein (October 1942), which was seen as the first British victory, though many would point to the Battle of Britain. However, in the collapse of the Germans and Italians in North Africa, the Allies took the same number, if not more enemy PoWs than the Russians did at Stalingrad. As the natural inhabitants of North Africa knew, and had known for centuries, European expansionist nationalism often included their area as part of the Mediterranean.

Hitler, who had a magnetic hold over many of his own military, once dubbed 'the command bug', and he had many others admiring him and willing to do his bidding, but he had less success with his beneficiary Franco who was more cautious. Franco admired Hitler for his military conquests, but he was more concerned about his essential imports not being blockaded by the Royal Navy. He also had his own hopes of nationalistic expansion in North Africa but knew that Spain was impoverished after its Civil War. He met with Hitler on the border at Hendaye, and he refused to co-operate immediately, even with the prospect of German help to retake Gibraltar. This meeting left Hitler demonstrating his habitual hatred of anyone who did not jump at his command. Nevertheless, Franco, despite his later mendacious claims, always believed the Nazis would win and he later sent some Falangist troops to the Eastern Front, making Spain a pariah state postwar. This lasted until the Americans, during the Cold War, needed a military foothold on the Peninsula.

Mussolini continued to make military blunders in his effort for expansionism, advancing through Albania (April 1941) to Greece, but was stopped and humiliated by tough Greek resistance, and the Germans, as in North Africa, came to his rescue. Where the Italians failed the Germans were successful, and within a fortnight the Yugoslavian government fled to London leaving the Axis a large stretch of other nations' territories which later erupted into violent resistance. The resistance was brutal, first led by the Četniks, and followed by the communist partisans led by Josip Tito (1892–1980). The Germans followed through and crushed Greece and then after a fierce battle took Crete from the British, and it must have seemed that Germany's aggressive nationalistic approach knew no bounds, making the grand imperialist plans of previous centuries appear almost moderate.

The Balkan incursion by German troops had been as successful as their invasion of France, but many Wehrmacht divisions were gathering at the Russian border, indicating to the more astute that Operation *Barbarossa* (invasion of the Soviet Union) was about to happen. Stalin was not among the astute and he ignored warnings from their own well-known spy Richard Sorge as well as Churchill in London. As recorded, 'One recent Russian analysis provided a table of fifty-six intelligence reports from January to June 1941, each growing more specific'.[28] Stalin still insisted on transporting Russian goods to Germany: in 1940 alone some 52 per cent of all Soviet exports went to Germany. Stalin's stupidity in not listening to advice can only be matched by Hitler's blunder believing he could overwhelm the Soviet Union.

The German-Soviet conflict from the moment it started was a total war, bitter in the heat of battle, and fought in freezing temperatures. This would eventually be the main reason for the defeat of Nazism. To Western ears this may sound 'unpatriotic', but 75 per cent of German war casualties occurred on the Eastern Front. The initial German thrust took them to the outskirts of Moscow, but the same day the German officers saw 'the Moscow Kremlin in their binoculars, before (on the same day as Pearl Harbor) Stalin's secret reserve of fresh Siberian divisions arrived to drive them back', with the same devastating Russian wintry weather of Napoleon's retreat.[29] Stalin had turned nationalistic, speaking on the radio to his astonished listeners by addressing them as 'brothers and sisters', and demanding their heroic sacrifice. It was probably from this time that Stalin appeared to forget he was Georgian and insisted he was Russian. It is a curious if not ironical thought that two of the most seriously cold Russian winters occurred in Napoleon's war in Russia and during the German invasion. Under Hitler's orders the Germans moved south to the Baku oil fields and the wheat basket (as they hoped) of the Ukraine, but they met the results of a scorched earth policy and discovered that much of the hoped-for industrial resources had been moved beyond the Urals as they met stiff resistance. The Ukrainians may have preferred German rule under Hitler and not Stalin (and many Ukrainians joined the Waffen-SS) but the Nazi racialism and sheer barbarity made even Stalin look at the time the safer alternative. When Hitler's army rolled into Russia it was given a new form of propaganda for its justification and was frequently referred to as the 'crusade for Europe'. When in retreat the Germans continued this theme as if they were rescuing Europe from Bolshevism, as if they were suffering for the sake of all Europe. The Wehrmacht had some support of soldiers from other countries, from places such as Finland, Romania, Italy, Spain, and many others.

When Germany attacked the Soviet Union the world's diplomatic alliances with Communist Russia and the capitalist West becoming allies in an effort to defeat the Nazi forces. Churchill, who was always anti-communist, had once told the British Parliament that if the devil himself opposed Hitler he would be welcomed. The Western Allies then combined with Russia, thereby resurrecting the old triangular alliance of the First World War. Stalin needed this arrangement for American material supplies were often conveyed by the Royal Navy. The West as a matter of policy through its propaganda and populist journalism claimed that Stalin was a good man, addressing him as Uncle Joe (which he resented) despite the growing knowledge he was a totalitarian dictator. The new international structure was an issue of survival against the Nazi onslaught, a matter of cynical necessity.

Churchill and his top military commander Field Marshal Alan Brooke convinced the Americans that Germany, and not Japan was the main enemy. Hitler and his cohorts had failed to understand the economic strength of the USA. Göring had once claimed they could only produce razorblades and refrigerators, but this industrial expertise in mass-production was rapidly used for manufacturing the tools of war. The Americans equipped themselves and their allies at phenomenal speed, their small army grew rapidly, Liberty ships, tanks and bombers arrived from the American production line like kitchen utensils. The German political ignorance about American resources and industry revealed an ignorance of life outside Europe. Britain alone could not win the war, but Churchill had recognised that with America onside with the Russians, not only would Britain survive but could be alongside the victors.

The Anglo-Americans now fought the Atlantic War together, shared some military secrets, and with their massive bomber forces (the first 1,000 bomber raid against Cologne was on 31 May 1942) destroyed German cities. The Soviet Union wanted a second front to alleviate their situation, with Stalin constantly nagging for this to happen, as at that time Russia was carrying the brunt of the land fighting, and it was known that 'feet on the ground' was the only way to defeat the Nazi regime. When the second front eventually started the Germans deployed four divisions to resist the Anglo-American invasion, keeping 150 to fight the Soviet Union. The Italian campaign was not seen as the second front, and it was bitter in places, but it provided major airstrips for bombing Nazi-held territory. Mussolini had been deposed, rescued by German paratroopers, reinstated as a German puppet, and later lynched in public by Italian partisans. His downfall had started with the invasion of Sicily on 10 July 1943, but it was not the second front that Stalin demanded, and the Americans tended to agree with him. They wanted to head directly to Berlin, but the British with more experience of fighting the Germans managed to convince them to bide their time.

This nationalistic war was fought by the masses with millions of deaths, but as in the past directed by the leaders and governments fighting through changing alliances. Stalin, now an ardent Russian nationalist invoked the hitherto suppressed Russian Orthodox Church to the rallying cry of 'Holy Russia' and produced the T-34 tank. Hitler had stupidly blundered in demanding a no-retreat order, and Stalingrad with much justification, was often seen as the turning point of the war. Stalin was just as vicious as Hitler issuing no-retreat orders, probably based on Trotsky's claim that if a soldier advances, he 'may' be shot, but if he retreats, he 'will' be shot. Stalin was using the nationalistic cry of encouraging Russians to fight for their homeland, and communist ideology had taken a backseat compared to fighting for one's home territory. In America, the word 'patriot' became dominant but in the nationalistic sense of the word, in Britain there were similar feelings and in mainland Europe the growing resistance and partisan movements were united by the same exaltations. It was this global war which had nearly every shade of nationalistic drive, first irredentist nationalism when Hitler took back German territory lost in the Treaty of Versailles, followed by aggressive and expansionist nationalism as used by Hitler, Stalin, and Mussolini, consequently by secessionist ridding oneself of another country's domination. America had at first adopted isolationist nationalism until Pearl Harbor left no choice, but many countries in Europe such as Spain, Sweden, and Switzerland used isolationism for the hope of self-protection. Banal nationalism was utilised by all sides in the call for love of one's country right or wrong, revisionist nationalism came to the fore as communist partisans looked to a different political future with others desperate for a democracy or a return to their old world. It was during these turbulent years that the wide range of nationalism could be detected, acting as motivation and intention, offering the impulse for conflict for frequently immoral reasons alongside justified war for defensive purposes.

In Western occupied Europe resistance turned from passive to active, and in France after the Vichy zone had been occupied (November 1942) it increased rapidly to the delight of the British, with Churchill's efforts 'to set Europe on fire' helping to assist the resistance with arms, even as far as Tito in Yugoslavia. The communist groups across Europe with their ideal were most effective, giving communism a boost in many postwar Western countries. In the East, the partisan war reached barbaric levels, which was understandable given the behaviour of Nazi forces in that part of Europe.

After Stalingrad, the more Germans realised it was for them a war of defence, but still prepared an attack at Kursk with the largest tank battle known in history, but it confirmed Soviet Russia's ascendency. The Anglo-Americans controlled the seas and skies, but the Russian army (The Red Army until Stalin asserted his authority by suddenly and significantly changing the name to the Soviet Army in 1944) remained the decisive factor. However, it was American resources and the British overseas dominions which added strength against the failing Nazi military led by Hitler. The Nazi leaders attempted to bolster confidence with propaganda nonsense of wonder-weapons (*Wunderwaffen*). Most of it was sheer nonsense but did result in a jetfighter and the infamous V1s and V2s hitting London from June 1944. More significantly the Germans had looked at nuclear weapons, but the Americans with a group of international scientists had made serious developments in the Manhattan Project. Nevertheless, the Germans made the modern rocket, which was of interest to the Americans as Germany collapsed, and their technology helped America be the first on the moon.

The relationship between Soviet Russia, America, and Britain was never straightforward, often with clashes over strategy. The Americans were facing the Japanese conflict as were the British but with limited resources, and Russia ignored Japan while Hitler remained alive. It was clear to some, especially Churchill, that Stalin wanted Eastern Europe within the Soviet Bloc, now returning to a form of expansionist nationalism.

It was a time of political powerplay as Stalin had promised the Western Allies that he would hold elections to keep them quiet, while Churchill managed by manipulation with Stalin to keep Greece under Western influence. Many countries and their leaders were treated like pawns in the end game of chess.

Poland, over whom Britain and France had gone to war in the first place, was to suffer in this end game. Later when Warsaw (1 August 1944) fought back Stalin deliberately kept his army stationed away from the conflict, while the Germans reduced the Polish capital to rubble. Stalin was never going to allow Poland to return to republican status. It was the start when the three powers of Russia, America, and Britain planned the shape of Europe without reference to the peoples involved. The Russians held the upper hand in Europe, the Americans were powerful, and Britain although the weakest was undefeated, and not as frail as France awaiting liberation.

The Russian army proved unstoppable, with Berlin as their major target. They moved towards the Dnieper, in 1944 the Vistula, turning south to the Balkans and the Danube, and finally the Oder onwards towards Berlin. For many the Russian advance was as terrifying as the Wehrmacht, with people shot out of hand and women raped, and it became even more gross as the Russians entered Prussia. Romania changed sides, Hungary was occupied by the Germans to stop a repeat process, while in Yugoslavia Tito joined forces with the Soviet troops. In Bulgaria the royal house was toppled and only Greece (and Albania) remained free from Soviet invasion but had their own civil wars.

On 6 June 1944, the Anglo-Americans started Normandy D-Day with Mulberry Harbours and the Pluto fuel pipeline on the seabed. The Allies had cunningly misled the Germans into the whereabouts of the attack as 73,000 Americans and 83,000 British and Canadians landed on their designated beeches. The logistics were excellent, but as in any battle it did not progress as the plans anticipated. Once the Germans realised it was a major invasion the fighting became intense, but the sheer logistical might and especially airpower led to Allied success.

In Germany occurred the famous but failed 20 July Plot to kill Hitler there was brave resistance to Hitler by some Germans at all levels and age groups, but it was never successful because of Gestapo suppression. Paris rose in rebellion on 19 August and was occupied by the Allies despite Hitler's directive to treat it like Warsaw. On the Western Front an operation organised by Montgomery called *Market Garden* intended to cross the Rhine, was a serious failure, and had to wait until the Bridge at Remagen was found intact. The Germans tried the Ardennes route as a last-ditch attempt, popularly known as the Battle of the Bulge, but the Americans held on with their paratroopers and weather improved, enabling the Allies with their overwhelming airpower to destroy this last-ditch German effort. The Germans were in total disarray and the Volkssturm was formed for defence with personnel ranging from children to grandparents and invalided soldiers, and these last-minute defenders had no chance against Zhukov's army advancing towards Berlin. Zhukov poured troops in to ensure he was there before others, but it is claimed that 'he was probably to lose more men in this one operation than the US army lost in the whole of the war'.[30] If this assessment is correct, which it probably was, it indicated the lack of Soviet care for its soldiers, the fanaticism of the German defenders, and the fear of Stalin who was demanding this success at any cost. Hitler and his new wife committed suicide and the war staggered to its conclusion with a series of retreats by the second week of May. The war continued in the Far East as Stalin with his nationalistic ambition for territory and influence turned his head in that direction at the last moment. On 6 August 1945, the Americans dropped the atomic bomb on Hiroshima, and a few days later on Nagasaki. In the European and Far Eastern conflicts, it was a vicious and bitter war, with Germans in Berlin and the Japanese in the Pacific Islands fighting to its very end.

Immediate Postwar Years

In Britain Churchill was replaced by Clement Attlee, which surprised the outside world more than it did the British. Later the public voted for Churchill as the greatest British leader ever in recent popular votes. However, in 1945 the population had not forgotten nor forgiven the political leadership after the First World War for the impoverished state of the country. Reforms of living standards, free education, and health were demanded by the majority, and after the years of suffering this was almost a natural consequence. Churchill's departure amazed Stalin who had always suppressed his population, and he executed and imprisoned his own soldiers who had been obliged to surrender. There was always a safe opportunity for revisionist nationalism in a democracy, but not in a totalitarian state, which communist Russia had long become.

During these immediate postwar years, Europe was awash with millions of refugees, and it would take decades for normal stability to be restored. National matters were settled with Alsace-Lorraine returned to France, Czechoslovakia had the Sudetenland restored, and Poland's boundaries were fixed with no choice. The victors divided Germany into four occupation zones between the USSR, America, Britain, and France was added because Churchill argued for their entry to increase Western influence. Meanwhile Stalin's Russia now dominated most of Eastern Europe, more than any Tsar had dared hope for in their wildest dreams.

Many wanted the Nazi leaders executed, but it was agreed to hold a disciplined legal trial at Nuremberg, which was prepared for November 1945. It was at these trials that the well-known terms of 'war crimes, crimes against humanity and genocide' (genocide later in the proceedings) became common legal statements. It all gave the impression of a form of international moral guardianship.

Nevertheless, the Nuremberg Trials retained all the failed characteristics of nationalism. Stalin's Katyń massacres, his invasion of Finland, and Poland with Hitler, were politely ignored to keep the international balance safe. The Anglo-American carpet bombing (strategic) was not raised, and the U-boat warfare was condemned even though Western naval policies were similar. The argument of *tu quoque* (you did the same thing) was banned. Vichy France had deported Jews, both Laval and Admiral Darlan had sought a partnership with fascist Germany. Dubost a French prosecutor at Nuremberg, noted that the Nazi State 'forgot that all men are born free and equal before the law, that the essential action of a state has for its purpose the deeper penetration of a respect for spiritual liberty and fraternal solidarity in social relations...it allowed itself to be robbed of its conscience and its very soul'; this indicted only the Germans, not Stalin and his cohorts.[31] When Solzhenitsyn's work was published in the 1960s it became more known that Stalin's immoral behaviour matched that of Hitler, and indicated that there had been a great deal of nationalistic cunning by those who knew about these issues at the time of the trial. As the American prosecutor Telford Taylor wrote, 'These outrages were not the work of faceless or anonymous men or agencies', and he could have added they were the work of men who freely chose to opt for this course of action and based on an aggressive form of nationalism.[32]

The trials later came under heavy criticism, frequently referring to Göring's claim that 'the victor will always be the judge and the vanquished the accused', while others worried it might create Nazi martyrs, but this could never happen because the trial exposed not just appalling barbaric behaviour but the extermination camps. The Americans had anticipated the process would be an educative device for the Germans and followed with a de-Nazification programme. It was only at this stage that the word 'nationalism' became a dirty word and for many its intentions were regarded as immoral, though neglecting that nationalism has many shades. The aggressive side of nationalism was at the fore of postwar thinking, understandably, as this had caused the war which destroyed the old Europe. It has remained an issue since, not least because it continued through the postwar years with resentment against Germans, Japanese, and tainting Italy, and to a lesser extent Spain because of its leadership. Distrust of other countries was prevalent, and the Cold War tensions did little to abate the situation.

After the Second World War

The war had finished, but official and unofficial revenge and retribution continued, and refugees and PoWs became an international problem. Accounts in many countries were settled, with William Joyce (Lord Haw-Haw) executed in Britain, Vichy Prime Minister Pierre Laval in France, (Pétain was imprisoned for life), Quisling in Norway, and Father Tišo of the Slovak Republic also executed. These were the leaders, but there were countless other recriminations in the streets and avenues, many were innocent as personal revenge also surfaced.

In a few years after Hitler's death, the wartime Grand Alliance disintegrated, and only one Peace Conference was held in Paris in 1946 (July-October), which was meant to decide the fate of the smaller defeated states. Italy lost her so-called African Empire, the Danube was declared an international waterway despite protests from Russia, Trieste was declared an independent port. With a view to not repeating the errors of the Treaty of Versailles the Western Allies asked no more, but the Soviets plundered their new areas not just for money but industries. A UN Relief Agency was established, but there were still emigrant and immigrant problems into the early 1950s, with some never resolved. Many of the Polish ex-military found homes in Britain as they had no wish to live in Soviet occupied Poland.

Prisoners of war created many complex moral issues. In trying to co-operate with the Soviet Union the Allies returned many prisoners, including the Cossacks knowing they would face execution or the Siberian prison workcamps, and many of them committed suicide. Not all the PoWs held by the Allies were treated in a civilised way and there were many cover-ups in some cases. In Eastern Europe populations were moved, and there was considerable vengeance against German speakers as they were driven out of Czechoslovakia and Poland, estimated at some nine million people. There were reprisals against collaborators, some imprisoned and many were shot. In Belgium 634,000 were detained and 57,000 sentenced. As is widely known many women who were suspected of having German soldier friends were publicly humiliated, by having their hair shaved off in various market squares. The aftermath of this total war often led to personal vengeance, and many of the so-called trials indicated they often lacked legal integrity, while in Italy and France the ex-resistance and partisans ignored the law and lynching was widespread. People were killed or driven from their homes because they were foreigners, spoke a different language or had a different ethnicity, these ingredients of aggressive nationalism flourished, because it was a time of revenge. 'They are not one of us' was born of nationalism which has tainted the world to this day.

In central Europe the Anschluss was reversed, Germany lost Prussia to the Soviet Union, and the name Prussia was banned. The whole of Germany was a picture of rubble with no infrastructure and controlled by the four powers. Walter Ulbricht (1893–1973) arrived from Moscow and took control as the Communist leader in the German Soviet sector, other German political parties

(SPD) led by Dr Kurt Schumacher, the (CDU) Christian Democratic Union under Dr Konrad Adenauer, and the Free Democratic Union were only able to function in the Western zones.

In Poland it was a straightforward communist takeover, facilitated by the Western Allies who had given Stalin that country, neglecting the fact they had gone to war in 1939 to preserve its political integrity. An NKVD officer called Bolesław Bierut pretended he was a non-Party man and became the leader. There were fixed elections, giving the populations no choice. In Czechoslovakia it first appeared that the promised system might work, with Beneš and Masaryk heading affairs alongside the communists. This only lasted until the Communist coup in Prague 25 February 1948, when an organised communist revolt led to Masaryk being thrown to his death from a window, and the communists took control. Hungary, Bulgaria, Romania, Albania, now rid of their Germanic connected monarchs, all allegedly became republics.

Communism was popular in France, Italy, and Belgium because the communist resistance in these countries had been the most effective, with their propaganda announcing the Communist Soviet Union had crushed the Nazis. There was also in all three countries, a dissatisfaction with their previous governments. While Stalin was still held in a degree of affection by many in the West because of Russia's input in the war, he divided Western opinion with some regarding him as no threat, while others predicted a struggle against so-called communism which was also emerging triumphantly in China. The fear of communism soon spread, and Churchill pleaded for money to stop the civil war in Greece which was heading in the communist direction. President Truman's response was a pledge to help free peoples to resist subjugation, which became known as the Truman Doctrine, indicating American intention to lead the Free World. Europe was no longer the important continent. It was the same year when the Marshall Plan to help European recovery was announced. Stalin, however, believed it was an American ruse to spread its influence and was critical of the aid. The division between Eastern and Western Europe was already exposing itself as the Western countries were economically recovering faster than those in the East.

In West Germany the Church leaders held a Christian Conference (October 1945) at Stuttgart led by Martin Niemöller. It announced and published a confession of national guilt, indicating a new Germany rather than the image which had been demonstrated at the Nuremberg Trial. Even some intelligentsia were talking about the possibility of a Federal Europe, which had been discussed by some of the resistant groups in Nazi Germany. It was hoped it would stop future wars and improve economics. In Britain, the much-loved Churchill recovering from his political defeat at the polls, referred to the communist expansion, spreading concern that Stalin was encouraging the spread of communism. The danger was real in many people's minds, but for Stalin it was his nationalistic passion to spread the power of the Soviet empire and influence. Churchill considered a European Federation given the danger of atomic weapons. He looked at the wider global relationships between a European unity, with America and the British Colonies, and foresaw Britain as the vital link. He and others made their views clear at a Congress of Europe privately organised at the Hague in May 1948. It was an enthusiastic congress with ideas of a United Europe Movement, a European Assembly, and a Court of Human Rights, much needed after the devastation of war. The discussed concepts appeared far-seeing because a Federal Europe would not deny patriotism, but it could possibly eliminate some of the worse aspects of nationalism, which had created so much suffering. Nevertheless, during these postwar years Europe remained unstable, suspicious, with the emergence of the Cold War causing a high degree of friction and instability. It was Goebbels who had first used the expression of the 'Iron Curtain', but Churchill made the expression famous. Stalin, more suspicious of his previous war allies, organised in Poland the Communist Information Bureau (Cominform) which to Western observers appeared like Comintern to convince other communities of communist ideology. The Benelux Treaty (March 1948) was signed by Britain and France with the Benelux group (a collective name for Belgium, the Netherlands and Luxembourg) seeking economic and military unity. When it was decided in Germany to revise the currency to the new Deutschmark the Soviets objected and implemented the well-known Berlin blockade, often pinpointed as the first act of the Cold War which had been simmering for a long time. Many in Western Europe were seeking some form of unity, and the major alliances would soon be NATO and the EEC.

One major feature of the postwar period was the ending of the traditional imperial colonies. Ownership of territory prevailed, and as the British public had rejected the conservatives and Churchill because social change was needed, the same impetus was happening in many of the colonies. In terms of secessionist nationalism, they were justified in their demand to be independent, and the successful outcome of political stability depended on the way it was granted. Not all wanted to grant independence to their colonies, Churchill was angry that India was given the right of self-government by Attlee, and the French, humiliated in the war, appeared to reassert themselves in their colonies. The war had weakened the links between Europe and its so-called possessions and led to conflicts in many places. Britain had the largest empire, but all its 'white' dominions had been given full independence since 1931, and other claimants were being explored. The subcontinent of India with four hundred million people were led by the world-famous pacifist Gandhi. On 15 August 1947,

Mountbatten the last Viceroy, attempted to organise the independence of the subcontinent of India, but it was followed by a massive and appalling slaughter between Hindus and Muslims, which many believe could have been avoided had Mountbatten listened to appropriate advice, taken his time, and given more consideration to the problems. There was mayhem and disruption in many places when independence was granted. In May 1948 Britain returned the mandate of Palestine to the UN, in Malaya the communist insurgency lasted from 1948 to 1957, in Cyprus the EOKA conflict stretched from 1950 to 1960, there was the Mau-Mau conflict in Kenya (1952–57), the Egyptian struggle resulted in the Suez crisis, and there was a serious conflict in Southern Rhodesia now Zimbabwe. Others such as Ghana (1957), Nigeria (1960) and Malta (1964) proved more peaceful and most of the colonies joined together in the voluntary and peaceful British Commonwealth, except for South Africa and Pakistan. Why the British should hold Gibraltar and the Falkland Islands has often been raised, but referendums in both areas made it clear that the populations were overwhelmingly in favour of British oversight. Popular nationalist movements were often active, attempting to rid themselves off European colonial domination.

The Dutch lost their East Indies colonies to the Japanese and accepted this loss to the indigenous population, and Indonesia became a republic in 1950. The French tried to reassert their rights, but by 1951 Tunisia and Morocco were free, and the mandates on Syria and Lebanon were withdrawn. However, they fought in Indochina against the Vietcong resulting in the massive disaster of Dien Bien Phu in May 1954, a precursor of the American Vietcong conflict. Charles de Gaulle changed his mind and granted Algeria independence in May 1962, signalling the end of the Fourth French Republic. The Belgium Empire collapsed in 1960 with war in Congo, the Portuguese colony of Angola found freedom in 1975, and Hong Kong by a long-term agreement reverted to China in 1997.

Many colonial inhabitants saw Britain as a better place to live, arriving to help in reconstructing buildings destroyed during the war, and as in France the population expanded with colonial labour. The intake of this labour had unpleasant reactions by some small-minded racists, and as late as 2018 the scandal called 'Windrush' continued with some reverberations at the time of writing, with journalistic headlines exposing individual injustices. It was the ongoing and seemingly unstoppable racial problem of an ethnic minority resented by the current inhabitants.

As Europe was in the process of returning their colonies to the rightful inhabitants, the perceived threat of Stalin and the communist fear did not cease after the Berlin blockade failed, with a plane landing every minute at Tempelhof Airport. NATO was established with its HQ in Brussels, starting with the Anglo-American alliance which soon included Italy, Portugal, Denmark, Iceland, Norway and expanded to Greece and Turkey in 1952, West Germany in 1955, and Spain in 1982 once Franco was safely dead, and increasing with each generation to this day.

A new German Federal Government was planned and in August 1949, the new government was centred in Bonn under the federal chancellorship of Konrad Adenauer. The Soviet Union responded with the creation of the German Democratic Republic (DDR) but the word democratic was seen by everyone as a façade. There had been hopes of a united Germany, but it would take many decades.

Chapter Six

The Modern Era

Survey of European Postwar Politics

French politics had always fluctuated before the war, and this continued postwar with the Fourth Republic (1946–58) being replaced by the Fifth Republic. The main political personage in the postwar years was Charles de Gaulle who retained a sense of French dignity during the war years but was not much loved by the Anglo-Americans. De Gaulle fought France's corner with nationalistic fervour, but they were confusing times with their problems in the Indo-China War, then Algeria and the Suez crisis. As always, the French took to the streets, in 1968 with serious riots, but it lessened under de Gaulle's successors, Pompidou then Giscard d'Estaing, and Mitterrand managed a degree of stability and economic advancement. In 1966 France withdrew from NATO and De Gaulle made an effort to align France with Germany (Élysée Treaty January 1963, between de Gaulle and the German Chancellor Adenauer) to resolve centuries of Germanic-Franco conflict, which was an achievement for European unity, offering a sense of peace to this day.

In Italy the political situation tended to remain tenuous. The monarchy was abolished in 1946 with a determination to avoid any form of fascism, mainly led by the Christian Democrats. As usual Italy had its regional conflicts, mainly based on the differences between its industrial north and rural south, the latter too often controlled by the Mafia and other criminal organisations. The various cabinets were often unstable, with moments of violence as experienced by the Red Brigades who in 1978 kidnapped then murdered a former Prime Minister, Aldo Moro. The economic recovery of Italy took longer but made remarkable progress within the EEC, and like Spain gleaned much from the tourist industry.

West Germany found political stability under Adenauer, followed by Willy Brandt, Helmut Schmidt and Dr Helmut Kohl. They rearmed after joining NATO, and made an economic progress often described as miraculous. West Germany recovered from the devastation which amazed everyone, and gained sovereign status in 1952, joined NATO three years later, the EEC in 1956, and was given membership of the UN in 1973. Reunification had to wait until 1990, but postwar, West Germany's recovery and progress was exceptional, and its political stability appeared reliable.

Britain tended to retain its old identity with the economy fluctuating under the traditional two-party system. The immediate postwar Labour government of Attlee produced a welfare state including a national health service and free secondary education. The Conservatives and Labour Parties were sometimes disturbed with a lurking third party such as Social Democrats in the 1980s, and the more long-lasting Liberal Democrats who united with the Conservatives in 2010 to form a government, after which they suffered a decline in the polls. The time of Margaret Thatcher (1979–90) was a monetarist period and highly authoritarian with the trade unions almost suppressed. The Welsh and Scottish sought independence but fell at the referendums which were at least permitted. However, the virtual civil war and disturbances in Ireland with British troops on the streets led to appalling conduct by both sides. It was generated by a nationalistic passion linked with Catholic and Protestant flag waving unwanted by the religious centres of Rome and Canterbury. In January 1972 it led to the infamous Bloody Sunday, or Bogside Massacre when British soldiers shot 28 unarmed civilians during a protest march. The effects are still felt today and in March 2019 it was decided that one soldier (known as soldier F) would be prosecuted for murder. By April of 1998, the Good Friday Agreement was signed, and at long last a sense of peace arrived, but remains fragile because of extremists on both sides, more so because of border issues following the Brexit campaign. When Ted Heath the Prime Minister of the day managed Britain's entry, he had to hold a referendum, and many then and later opposed this policy. 'British diehards feared the United Kingdom might lose its soul; their critics argued that internal problems could only be solved in the European context', and the truth of these claims and counterclaims remains uncertain, but there is a growing apprehension by some British that Brexit was more like shooting oneself in the foot.[1]

Some smaller countries had established local alliances, notably Belgium, the Netherlands and Luxemburg (Benelux), while in Scandinavia the Nordic Council was formed in 1953. On the Iberian Peninsula Franco's fascist leadership left Spain a pariah state until his death, when King Juan Carlos took to the throne, helping that country escape its feudalistic and fascist past. Spain joined the EEC in 1983 having joined NATO the year before. Spain became a tourist industry, and its manufacturing and economic prospects improved. The support for Franco had dwindled, but to this day he has his supporters. There were revolts in the Basque region seeking autonomy, and Catalonia's tradition of seeking independence continues to this day. There was a revolt in Greece between 1967 and 1974 known as the time of the Colonels, when a military junta took power, leaving Europe bewildered. To this day, nationalism in its varying shades remains part of each country's political and emotional landscape.

In Europe's previous history religion frequently influenced State leadership, it was used in conflict, often created internal strife and war, gripping individual minds with fear of hellfire. The threat of excommunication had been considered far too deadly to challenge, but these attitudes changed because humankind had created its own 'hell fire and brimstone' here and now and not post-death in some projected galaxy, Church attendance was in decline to this day. The Ecumenical movement (1948) had grown, possibly in response to the decline, but chiefly because modern Christians questioned the stupidity of the divisions. The Catholic Church tended to stay isolationist, but following a series of enlightened and more open-minded Popes and the famous Vatican II Council made the conservative Catholic faith more open. Sadly, the rise of extreme para-military Islam amongst a few activists still disturbs the world of religious faith, causing many to question the nature of religion. Nevertheless, Christianity with its proclamation of love and compassion, and the Islamic discipline of worship makes religion significant in today's world; even in Russia during recent years (since 1990) the Russian Orthodox Church has regained some national popularity, but how far this is politically driven remains something of an enigma.

A Unified Europe

The economic growth in the postwar years raised the question of a possible European unity, not just for economic reasons but some form of political cohesion. These two factors, for the more astute, made sense to not only heal the wounds of the past but stop the endless rounds of war. It had long been a concept for many thinkers, including, as mentioned previously, even in the minds of some German anti-Nazi resistance groups. In the late 1940s political thinkers such as Jean Monnet (1888–1979) and others had thought of this possibility. As early as August 1949 the Council of Europe met at Strasburg to promote the idea of unity, from which developed the Schuman Plan. This concept was the base of the Franco-German reconciliation and gave birth to the European Coal and Steel Community (1951) with its President Jean Monnet, sometimes regarded as the 'Father of Europe'. It brought together France, Germany, Italy, and the Benelux countries with Britain standing insular in its islands. The 1955 Messina Conference helped make economic progress possible through a plan for integration with its political ambitions for unity. There were developments with the Council of Ministers, an Executive Commission in Brussels, the European Court of Justice, and above all a European Parliament. The Common Agricultural Policy (1962) brought welcome relief, and the introduction of the Value Added Tax (1967) raised money to help deprived areas, and there was little question that the economics of the day improved. In 1958 the European Free Trade Area was established, which included Britain who had not been party to the Treaty of Rome with the original six, but its interests were confined to commerce.

Britain tended to remain apart probably because 'the inhibitions were both psychological and practical. Not having suffered the sobering humiliation of national defeat, many Britons still harboured illusions of sovereignty and self-sufficiency'.[2] British interests leaned towards its Commonwealth, America, and its membership of NATO. Perhaps it was no surprise that when in 1961 and 1967 Britain tried to join the EEC they were vetoed by de Gaulle. Britain remained isolated until de Gaulle's death, and in 1973 under Prime Minister Edward Heath Britain was admitted on its third attempt, with Ireland and Denmark. A referendum in Britain was held in 1975 which confirmed this move. In the 1980s Greece, then Spain and Portugal were admitted, and twelve nations appeared united.

When later some poorer economic partners wanted to join it was indicated that 'the main criteria for entry, apart from being European was that applicants should have shed the nationalistic, imperialist, and totalitarian traditions', which had been the hallmark of Europe's history.[3] For many thinking people this was clearly the way to create a sense of harmony in Europe which for centuries had been at war on nationalistic and thereby ethnic issues. The major Western nations of France, Germany, Italy, and Britain were binding themselves together with a sense of genuine security and peace. After centuries of war and division there was now an opportunity for European peace for the first time.

Some countries which had been neutral in the war tended to stand apart. Switzerland had retained neutrality during the fraught war years and remains so today. It had prospered from its banking and wealthy neighbours, avoiding the Council of Europe until 1963 and then limited itself to a free-trade deal in 1972. Sweden had benefitted from neutrality in the war and maintained this position ignoring both the EEC and NATO. Sweden had taken the lead in welfare issues, refugees, and environmental concerns, but with President Putin's aggressive attitudes eventually joined NATO on 7 March 2024. The two Iberian neutral countries of Spain and Portugal were admitted into the European picture once they had lost totalitarian rule.

Finland, having been invaded by the Russians, joined the Germans to attack their oppressor, and postwar were forced to stay neutral. Once Finland became independent of Soviet oversight Helsinki became a popular place to visit. For the same reasons as Sweden with its fear of Putin's nationalistic expansion policies it was admitted into NATO on 4 April 2023. Austria during the Cold War's earlier years alleged it had been the victim of Nazi oppression, as it was divided by the four occupying powers, but regained full sovereignty in 1955 so long as it maintained strict neutrality, and as with Switzerland, benefitted in terms of economic prosperity. Austria eventually joined the EU (1995) and in the second half of 1998 and the first six months of 2006 held the EU Presidency.

Western Europe was holding hands in economic and military terms. However, impulse for European unity found its main momentum in the economic benefits, but for most thinkers there was more to this unity than money. Governed by the same laws, a European parliament, a common currency, the same passport, freedom of movement offered the sense of a continent without armed borders. It was hoped that this should minimise nationalistic fervour which had wrought such destruction. To be able to travel from Germany through the Low countries into France and cross to the United Kingdom without serious border checks, gave a feeling of community in which nationality and ethnicity were not relevant. There may be and there often are disputes over economics and bureaucracy, but for the first time in hundreds of years, as noted above, it would be unbelievable to wake up to the news that Germany, or France or the United Kingdom were massing troops and on red alert against another Western European country. The future of the European Union was cast into doubt when on 31 January 2022 Britain following the Brexit campaign and vote, left the European Union which held 27 states, the vast majority of Europe, leaving the British Isles (apart from the Republic of Ireland) isolated across the channel waters. Economic experts have since noted that this exit has not benefitted Britain (nor Europe) and will have lasting economic effects. Few mention the sense of international peace the union was able to establish, reminding this writer of Marx's belief that money is the driving force in history.

Eastern Europe

Once Europe faced the internal threat of Nazi domination, after the Second World War it faced the menace of Soviet Russia, which had formed its own fabric of an enforced union, called the Warsaw Pact in retaliatory terms to NATO. The map of Eastern Europe after the war was in a state of flux. Inside the Soviet Union with it postwar acquired territories times had drastically changed, and during Stalin's final years it seemed precarious as there was no political opposition, just one dictatorial dictator with no one daring to suggest who would replace him. In China Mao Zedong had triumphed, and to the West it seemed as if communism covered much of the earth's political areas. In America there was a frantic anti-communist movement of McCarthyism (1950–54), which created paranoia, but Mao Zedong was never subservient to Stalin, and both Stalin and the Chinese version of communism had little to do with Marx and Engels, both were a ruse for totalitarian forms of government.

In 1949, because of Lavrenty Beria's (head of the NKVD, later KGB) foreign agents in America seeking scientific and military information, along with Russian scientific ability, the Soviets exploded an atom bomb in 1949, and a hydrogen bomb in 1953 increasing international tension. Stalin died in the same year in bizarre circumstances, as the assistant warden of Stalin's dacha had found him motionless on the floor and 'Malenkov and Beria, who were the first to be informed, arrived at 3.00 am on 2 March, followed by Khrushchev at 7.30 am, and a group of doctors an hour later'.[4] When the astonished daughter of Stalin was brought to the scene she wrote that she saw only the attendant doctors because the 'Academician V. N. Vinogradov, who had looked after my father for many years, was now in jail – were making a tremendous fuss, applying leeches to his neck and the back of his head', producing a bizarre scene.[5] It was a state of sheer panic underlining the nature of the totalitarian ruler of a so-called communist state. The doctors who arrived were terrified of the prostrate body of the leader and the presence of the others, especially Beria.* The dentist called to remove Stalin's false teeth dropped them on the floor in his state of nervousness, and his shaking hands could hardly undo Stalin's shirt.[6] These strange details are outlined to convey the sense of fear during this Stalin period.

Malenkov was anticipated as the new leader but there were rumours of a group leadership, most feared Lavrenty Beria's rise to power, but he was executed by pistol following a secret trial, and Khrushchev made his appearance as the prime leader. This led to what is often called the de-Stalinisation era and the supposed end of the totalitarian rule, but the Soviet system set by Stalin with one prominent leader remained, namely Khrushchev who for a time had a better image than Stalin, and he became almost popular when filmed banging his shoe on the desk at the UN. He was not the hoped-for success with the repression of the Hungarian uprising (1956), and more to the point he held the same aggressive nationalistic views as Stalin. He and the American President Kennedy led the world close to nuclear disaster in the Cuban Missile Crisis, split with China, and was removed from power in October 1964 in a typical Kremlin Byzantine-type coup, but at least he was able to live in retirement, unlike Stalin's days.

He was followed by Leonid Brezhnev from the Ukraine who is generally recalled as following neo-Stalinism, thereby inadvertently allowing the Soviet Union to start its disintegration. Many regarded him as an astute politician, who, coming from the Ukraine, was familiar with the dangers of national assertions

---

* 'Leeches were preferred for bloodletting, because the sharp fluctuations in blood pressure that would have resulted from bloodletting were considered undesirable'. See Brent, J. and Naumov, V., *Stalin's Last Crime: The Plot against the Jewish Doctors, 1948–1953* (New York, Harper Collins, 2003), p.318.

of independence, namely secessionist nationalism, and he had no intention of changing the Soviet system of government. He suffered in his final years from an illness which slowed him down making him the butt of personal jokes. He was followed by Yuri Andropov (1982–3) and although a one-time KGB man he was seeking reform but died of cancer. He is often regarded as the man who prepared the way for Mikhail Gorbachev.

The Soviet Union during this period never changed in any substantial way despite propaganda, the secret police force remained, the Gulag camps were used as forced labour, censorship was still imposed, with the Eastern European block retaining the image of an armed fortress. The Party controlled every aspect of life from sport to military. The current author travelled through Russia in Leonid Brezhnev's time as a Komsomol guest and can still recall the endless lists of advice as well as having to be cautious with whom one spoke. There was one significant change during Brezhnev's time, when it was announced that the non-Russian republics could run themselves under their own Party bosses. However, the pervasive KGB was working from resolving petty crime up to international conspiracy, and as in Stalin's day the bureaucratic elite lived in comfort with their dachas and cars, none of which were available to the public.

However, despite the high living of the Party leaders, the Soviet Bloc was not doing well economically and far behind the standards in the West, mainly caused by the huge amount spent on their military advancements. The general population suffered in terms of living conditions, food, and common consumer items available were a rarity in Russia and the Eastern bloc. The poverty of ordinary Russians was concealed, but the nuclear reactor disaster at Chernobyl in the Ukraine in 1986 underlined the dangers of financial shortcuts. It appeared to many as a long period of ongoing oppression.

Nationalism was prevalent for the Soviet leaders in keeping secure the communist bloc, not because of ideological ideals of communism but holding onto and increasing their territorial gains as in the days of the Tsars. Some of its satellite countries had not lost their nationalistic hope, but secessionist nationalism raised its head in Hungary and Czechoslovakia with their respective revolts and subsequent repressions, but from the Baltic to the Ukraine the sense of national identity although repressed, quietly fermented.

The various countries incorporated into the Soviet Union reflected what was happening in Russia from Stalin to Khrushchev to Brezhnev and onwards, differing from one another in various policies and attitudes. They were tied to the Soviet Union and may have been called republics, but it was known to be a mendacious façade. Many of them were ruled by a 'mini-Stalin' with notorious names such as Ulbricht, Hoxha and Bierut. Only Josip Broz Tito in Yugoslavia dared ignore Stalin, who days before he died, was still planning the assassination of Tito with his agent Sudoplatov.[7] Yugoslavia as a Federated People's Republic had come into being in 1945 and differed from the Soviet Union, not least rejecting the infamous Soviet policy of collective agriculture and was consequently excluded from the Soviet Union in 1948, living under the continuous threat of retribution. A vague agreement of peace was made in 1955 during Khrushchev's time, but Yugoslavia never joined the Warsaw Pact.

Within the Soviet Bloc the DDR (East Germany) came into being on 7 October 1949. There were the usual problems over Stalin's insistence on agricultural collectivisation which Khrushchev also pursued, causing unrest with many seeking refuge in the West. The loss of farmers was so serious the Soviets promised their farms would be given back if they returned. The population was declining rapidly which made the DDR singularly unusual at this time. There were populist clashes with the authorities and in 1953 the Soviets deployed tanks to quell riots. Stalin never anticipated arming his satellite possessions, but with the appearance of NATO the process started with the Warsaw Pact (14 May 1955). When Stalin had died the policy leaned towards the development of 'national communism' seeking some cohesion. It was never a relationship of equals, but a gesture for a national pride and necessary from the military perspective. The DDR developed the infamous Stasi and conformed rigidly to Soviet ideology, with the infamous Wall of division appearing in 1961 on the West-East German border.

In 1956, when Khrushchev at the 20th Congress attacked Stalin's policies, Poland hoped for some form of independence, and when Khrushchev arrived in Poland, he found Polish soldiers supporting the anticipated change. Khrushchev stepped back and allowed Gomułka recently elected a General Secretary to retain his position. Gomułka was probably Poland's only supported communist leader by the independently minded Poles.

Poland, the largest of the Soviet satellites had a degree of self-assertion, and it was strongly supported by the Catholic Church and worker protests in the Baltic ports. The well-known Solidarity Trade Union attracted international interest and ignored the sub-servient communist unions. The protests were led by Lech Wałęsa and avoided violence. Moscow was nervous but using Polish troops thousands of Solidarity's members were arrested on 13 December 1981. Martial law blocked any further progress, but the Polish protest was part of a movement for change. The Russian term for restructuring, *perestroika*, would soon become internationally famous. A sense of nationalistic self-identity was re-emerging and was made easier because the Soviet satellite countries had distinct memories of national independence in their history.

In Hungary, when their revolt had happened with that country in 1956 withdrawing from the Warsaw Pact, there had been a different response. The

Soviets appeared to withdraw then returned with tanks and crushed the effort for independence. An estimated 2,000 people were shot, and thousands of Hungarians fled across Europe, two Hungarian refugees finding temporary refuge in the paternal home of this writer. The Soviet reaction lost considerable favour with those overseas who had some sympathy with their ideology, and it increased the strains of the Cold War. This was quickly followed with the Russian split with the Chinese in 1960 and Albania (with no direct border with the Soviets) and close by the Soviet-estranged Yugoslavia deliberately looked towards China as its political supporter.

Romania remained subdued and there was no rupture with the Soviets. The country was led by the notorious Nicolae Ceauşescu who was made the General Secretary of the Romanian Communists in 1965, and he copied the Stalin cult of the leadership. His security was like the DDR Stasi and the KGB, and he remained in power until his execution in 1989. It was similar in Bulgaria which took time to develop any industrial output and remained in poverty. The Party leader was Todor Žhivkov who followed Moscow's every demand and held power from 1954 until 1989 when he stepped down, avoiding execution.

Czechoslovakia resisted the de-Stalinisation under the leader Antonin Novotny, but he was thrown out by the Slovak Politburo and replaced by the popular Dubček. This new leader set about planning reforms, including more freedom for the press which unnerved the traditionalists. Brezhnev was concerned, and some sinister Warsaw Pact military manoeuvres took place near the Czech borders. Brezhnev and Dubček met, and all seemed peaceful until August 1968, when Warsaw Pact soldiers poured into Czechoslovakia. Dubček was taken to Moscow where he was not shot, as in Stalin's day, but he was obliged to work in the forestry industry. Despite being the post-Stalin era, it was clear under Brezhnev that the Soviet status quo was not changing.

The Cold War

It was about 1948 that the term Cold War started to bring to light the deepening political clash between the so-called Communist bloc and the Liberal Democracies. The Cold War (described by one French commentator as the Hot Peace) dominated a generation, and its tensions exist to this day. It led to many proxy wars, and dangerous stand-offs as in the Cuban Missile Crisis, but sheer fear of global suicide maintained a peace still holding to this day, with concerns over the current attack (2024) on the Ukraine and the fear it could lead to nuclear war. Europe was no longer the supreme power and the Soviet Bloc reached from central Europe to the Far East with territory taken by Stalin's late entry in the conflict against Japan. The ICBMs led to the *Pax atomica*, but proxy wars were fought in Korea, in Indochina (Vietnam War) which included the Chinese form of communism adding another dangerous possibility of another major world war.

The space age became a space-race with nationalistic leanings claiming one side was more progressive than the other. The expense of these grandiose experiments and the military stockpiling was immense, and the tussle for supremacy was a form of empire nationalism, one side seeing itself as superior to the other regarding its competitor as the enemy. Europe was militarily critical because of American missile bases there, but politically unimportant as the superpowers of America, Russia, with emerging China, were growing and the tensions increasing, making Europe less militarily significant. The word MAD standing for 'mutually assured destruction' was used by the CND in the hope that neither side would press the button. There were near dangerous incidents, some contained accidents (one in Spain), and the Cuban Missile Crisis of 1962 which left the entire planet at risk. The Cuban Missile Crisis was caused by Soviet missiles on America's doorstep, and the public were led to believe that Khrushchev had stepped down, but it was resolved by the Americans agreeing to remove their rockets from the Turkish borders. There was also a growing fear of bio-chemical weapon development, which all underlined that humankind had reached a justifiable stage of nervousness about its future as it worried about WMD, namely weapons of mass destruction.

This global concern about an uncertain future resulted in the Strategic Arms Limitation Talks (SALT) in Vienna, leading to the Helsinki Final Act of 1975. Although the world felt slightly safer the tensions remained. The Soviets invaded Afghanistan in 1979 (and their Olympics were boycotted), martial law was declared in Poland, and with the advance of technology sophisticated bugging devices were searched for in the most secure embassies. Soon computers and cyberspace communications would be checked and re-checked as suspicions about other nations never diminished.

The Helsinki Agreement 1975 made little progress, and the disarmament talks continued until 1980 when the Americans suddenly blocked them. There were talks on MBFR (Mutual Balance Force Reduction) which was commonsense because both sides had enough nuclear weapons to destroy the globe many times over. As early as 1957 Poland (with Soviet agreement) asked the UN to consider a nuclear free zone, this was a curious suggestion and was only taken up by some London boroughs who claimed to be Nuclear Free Zones. The nature of nuclear fallout meant nowhere was safe, but it hinted at some hope in a world divided by nationalistic suspicion and distrust.

In Europe, the German Chancellor Willy Brandt in 1969 launched the 'Eastern Policy' (*Ostpolitik*) hoping for a united Germany. It was not to happen for another 20 years, but he produced a German-Soviet Treaty of Co-operation (1970), and a German-Polish Treaty the same year, and in 1973 a treaty of mutual recognition with the DDR. Brandt was outstanding in his efforts, working for a better future in a world still tense with nationalistic friction.

When America, through President Richard Nixon met Mao Zedong there was new friction as it caused a rift between China and the Soviet Union, and the tensions between the superpowers have risen and fallen ever since. It was, and remains, a time of perpetual uneasiness. This was more than apparent when President Reagan mentioned the 'Stars War' project casting doubts on Soviet missiles ever reaching their target. Reagan and the new promising Chairman of the Soviet Bloc, Mikhail Gorbachev met, and to Reagan's astonishment the Soviet leader proposed a 50 per cent cut in nuclear weapons. Gorbachev's arrival took the world by surprise in offering hope, and in December 1989 President Bush and Gorbachev announced the Cold War had ended. There was a genuine relief across the world but only for a brief time.

1989–91 Significant Change in Soviet Russia

The Americans covered much of Europe with their military sites and influence, but changes were happening. During this era Western Europe was attempting to create a political and economic union, whereas the Eastern Bloc signalled a degree of disintegration. Gorbachev, more valued in the West than at home recognised Soviet military expenditure was creating an impoverished population, and their satellite countries were expensive and difficult to control in the changing postwar world. Gorbachev had virtually ended the Cold War, but the Soviet internal problems were increasing. Gorbachev made popular the terms *Perestroika* and *Glasnost*, the latter simply meant publicity but was used in the new sense of 'openness'. Gorbachev was a communist and he appeared to keep the fabric of the Soviet system the same as ever, and never offered elections, while satellite countries felt a glimmer of hope for an independent future. There have been many explanations produced for the collapse of the traditional Soviet system, from economic causes to the absurdity of life under communist rule, but as Norman Davies wrote 'it may be that equal attention should be paid to the everyday lives of ordinary people'.[8]

The demand for change first developed in Poland where strikes were proliferating, so the Soviet regime allowed the hitherto repressed Solidarity Movement to contest for parliamentary seats, and Lech Wałęsa with his party were immediate successful. Meanwhile this did nothing to lessen the fear of communism as in 1989 the brutal demonstration of communist suppression was witnessed in Tiananmen Square, China. In Poland they were able to form their own government with Solidarity under the state presidency of Tadeusz Mazowiecki. This was an indicator of the disintegration of the old Soviet Bloc, and there were more stirrings of unrest in Hungary and East Germany. In October 1989 in Hungary, the Peoples Republic was abolished and the communists, as in Poland, allowed the opposition into their parliament. In November, the world was amazed watching television broadcasts of East German guards casually smoking as protestors dismantled the Berlin Wall. In Prague, Dubček with Havel suddenly appeared together in Wenceslas Square, and then at Christmas the disliked and feared Nicolae Ceauşescu was executed following a revolt in Bucharest. Europe and the whole world were bewildered by the speed of these changes, especially by the almost seeming acceptance by Moscow, which was unlike the usual response of the Soviets in previous years. The following year of 1990 saw the CMEA (The Council for Mutual Economic Assistance, founded in 1949), and the Warsaw Pact stop functioning. It was an astonishing period with unanticipated changes happening at a staggering pace and in various shapes in the Eastern Bloc countries. Above all, East Germany with its iconic wall dismantled raised hopes in West Germany for a unified country. Chancellor Kohl, recently elected, organised a campaign for uniting the two halves of Germany, and in historical terms the ex-DDR soon became a member of the European Community.

In Yugoslavia, the individual states demanded their own autonomy, as in the Baltic States while Chechnya with Ukraine wanted to follow the same pattern. 'The pulverisation of the Yugoslav Federation was especially vicious. Democratic elections had brought militant nationalists to the fore both in Serbia and in Croatia'.[9] It soon led to a ferocious civil war with genocidal consequences and crimes against humanity exposing the worse side of nationalism once again. Poland, always focused on its rights as an independent nation seemed slow, and in Romania there was resistance to de-communisation, but Czechoslovakia was rapid with its Verification Law which excluded corrupt officials.

The European map was suddenly taking a different shape, as the East was becoming once again an area of different nations, while the West with its hope for unity was not concerned about its hitherto strict border controls. The Maastricht agreement was signed (with Britain opting out of the monetary clauses and the social chapter), NATO formed a Joint Co-operation Council looking towards the former Warsaw Pact countries, and the European Union looked towards Poland and Hungary and encouraging the use of the West European starred flag.

In Russia there was a mixture of hope and concern, as their satellite national republics were changing at speed to their own governments. The RSFSR (Russian Soviet Federative Socialist Republic) elected a democratic President,

Boris Yeltsin, but he was faced with an abortive coup during August 1991 to protect the Communist Party. The coup faded without violence, and Gorbachev resigned as General Secretary before 5 September 1991 as the Party dissolved. On 24 October 1991 Gorbachev signed the last decree handing over all powers to the republics while he remained President of the original Russia.

In December 1991 a vote in the Ukraine indicated that over 90 per cent had voted for independence, which made that Republic the second largest tract of territory in Europe, and today is fighting for survival under the current Russian President Putin who has held that post for a quarter of a century (2024, the time of writing). The war is not about the ideology of communism, but aggressive nationalism dressed up as an irredentist right, as Putin attempts to increase Russian territory and world power.

Unresolved Aggressive Nationalism

In the Balkans and South-Eastern Europe communist dominated countries went through their various changes moving from the tightly restrictive Stalin era, through lesser domination to a sense of freedom which had been lost for decades. One of the adverse consequences was the nationalistic aggression which erupted in places. It shook both the West and East of Europe managing to live in some peace throughout the Cold War, despite the many moments of tension. The original Marxist and Lenin's communist ideal had been the classic class-struggle with nationalism regarded as a diversion and a feature of past years, but nationalism had persisted during the Stalin era and afterwards. However, following the end of the USSR, nationalism in places increased with unrepressed violence, and 'It has been said of south-eastern Europe since 1989 that it produced more nationally saturated history per square metre than it could possibly digest'.[10] Countries such as Albania, Romania, Bulgaria had suffered years of restriction and economic poverty and the change to a national independence was not a healing miracle, because the dark sides of nationalism remained central, with the re-founded countries watching their neighbours with suspicion.

The smaller states encompassed in Yugoslavia under Josip Tito (1892–1980) was a federal state and the future even looked promising in terms of peace and development. There were nationalistic rumblings in Croatia and Serbia before Tito died, and by 1990 it was becoming clear that the small states had powerful nationalistic views making war more likely.

The ensuing war resulted in over a 100,000 dead, millions of displaced refugees, genocide, and crimes against humanity. The Bosnian genocide was the first declared publicly since the last world war, and it all reflected aggressive nationalism and cynically dubbed the New World Disorder. It was related to ethnic and religious conflicts, wars of independence, driven by aggressive nationalism. There were those who demanded expansionist nationalism by demanding a 'Greater Serbia', there were irredentist nationalist claims, and nearly every form of nationalism raised its head during this conflict.

The war started in 1991 with the Ten-Day war after the secession of Slovenia when the JNA (Yugoslav People's Army) tried to secure the borders, but after some fighting it was resolved through negotiations at Brioni in July 1991. However, there was conflict in Croatia when resident Serbs opposed Croatian independence. Croatia declared independence in June 1991 and left Yugoslavia. By the summer of 1991 it was an all-out war, but mainly composed of Serbs and Montenegrins as they opposed Croatian independence. The UN in January 1992 made some attempts to bring peace to the erupting brutal conflict. The Croatian military, Generals Ante Gotovina and Lladen Markač, were to be found guilty of war crimes but were acquitted in 2012.

In 1992 the war spread through Bosnia and Herzegovina and the self-proclaimed Herzeg-Bosnia was supported by Croatia and Serbia seeking a partition of Bosnia. What could have been a secessionist form of nationalism had become aggressive and expansionist in the search for more territory. The Siege of Sarajevo came to represent the war in Bosnia which had turned extremely brutal and violent. In 1994 the USA managed peace arrangements between the Croatian forces and the Bosnian Army in the Washington Agreement. However, it was the NATO air strikes on the Bosnian Serbs which brought the Serbs to negotiations. The war ended with the signing of the Dayton Agreement on 14 December 1995.

The Kosovo War (1998–99) originated when Kosovar Albanians began their insurgency against Belgrade (the Kosovo Liberation Army was founded in 1996), with a war resulting in the deaths of thousands of civilians. There was an insurgency in the Preševo Valley (1999–2001) with an armed conflict between the Federal Republic of Yugoslavia and ethnic Albanian insurgents, and in 2001 another insurgency in the Republic of Macedonia, when the ethnic Albanian National Liberation Army attacked the security forces of Macedonia, which ended with the Ohrid Agreement. The principle had been to offer some autonomy to the Albanian minority, but all these nationalistic demands of race, religion, territory had risen in the Balkans with appalling devastation and innumerable deaths. Belgrade had been unable to offer any control of the situation and the Western world was in a dilemma. The EU had recognised Slovenia and Croatia (January 1992) and the United Nations Mission became a presence, but Zagreb unbelievably indulged in ethnic cleansing against Serbs in western Slovenia. In Bosnia and Herzegovina where some of the fiercest fighting took place, fuelled by three different ethnic parties.

Again, the appeal of nationalism was the main ingredient, 'more than any other ideology, nationalism successfully mobilises feelings of belonging'.[11] With the weak political structure during this period of change, nationalism had appeared to offer security, identity, and continuity, but the age-old ingredients of race, language, culture, and religious belief were always present in aggressive nationalism, resulting in catastrophic suffering and mayhem.

The Holocaust and brutal massacres during the Second World War had left a sense of guilt across many nations, especially in their attitudes towards Jewish refugees in the late 1930s. It provided a major motivation in the new humanitarian concern when ethnic groups were subject to genocide. In 1945 George Orwell had written 'if one looks back over the past quarter of a century, one finds that there was hardly a single year when atrocity stories were not being reported from some part of the world, and yet in not one single case were these atrocities, in Spain, Russia, China, Hungary, Mexico, Amritsar, Smyrna, believed in and disapproved of by the English intelligentsia'.[12] After the brutality of the Second World War the international conscience appeared more alert about what was happening in other countries, but political demands and hypocrisy did not help resolve these ongoing issues.

However, with the development of the Cold War, a degree of restraint was applied to the corporate conscience to avoid conflict and nuclear disaster. Had the Yugoslavian problems of assertive nationalism within its structure started in the 1950s or 1960s, it would have been unlikely that the West (or the United Nations where the veto system worked) would have intervened. One of the earliest examples of intervention was 1964 Cyprus when UN peacekeeping forces were deployed to avoid further fighting between the Greek and Turkish elements, but there were no Soviet interests involved. After the remarkable changes in Russia in 1989–90 this element lessened.

During the Cold War there was a belated recognition that in nationalistic disputes humanitarian laws had been ignored. The 'Secretary General Kofi Annan could claim – this time without exaggeration – that state sovereignty was being "redefined" such that the state was now widely understood to be the servant of its people, and not vice versa'.[13] When intervention took place there was always the danger that such action had different political motivations.

The world was aware of this danger, and the UN preventative force sent to Macedonia in December 1992, was only intended to monitor, reporting on the situation. When there was next to no reaction to the barbarities in Rwanda between Tutsis and Hutus, it was hardly news because of its geopolitical irrelevance. The Balkan region was different, and in Bosnia-Herzegovina, organisations such as ICG (International Crisis Group) and NGO (Non-Governmental Organisations) mobilised major political figures to assist. It led to trying to calm down nationalistic clashes, especially concerning refugees who had become a humanitarian issue, for example, the treatment of Muslims in Myanmar. The delivery of aid and trying to bring the attention of the world to their plight had been helped by the increased global news coverage, leading to 'Safety-zones', in areas such as Rwanda and Bosnia-Herzegovina. The UN became involved in trying to provide aid and repatriation when it might help. The third factor was resolving the conflict, which was more difficult in nationalistic conflicts, when a people were demanding their own sovereignty. In the Yugoslavian conflict this was especially daunting because the conflict was intense and when efforts 'proved fruitless the EC member states chose to recognise the republics as independent states', which could be interpreted as accepting the inevitable, but could be seen as an effort to influence areas out of their reach.[14] The EU adopted this position with the conflict in Kosovo. International intervention occurred in legal tribunals for prosecuting those guilty of genocide and crimes against humanity, even involving the head of state, notably the Yugoslavian President Slobodan Milošević. Human rights emphasised that the protection of ethnic minority rights was the only way to maintain peace. The Bosnian Serb wartime leader, Radovan Karadžić appealed after a forty-year sentence given in 2016, only to have it extended to life on 20 March 2019. This epitomised nationalistic wars and their horror. To resolve this conflict there was military intervention by air-strikes which meant war was used to stop war, humankind's unresolved problem.

Holding the Peace

Another method of maintaining peace without having to use military force was 'power sharing', ensuring decisions were shared by all parties in a potential conflict. This happened in Belgium with the Flemings and Walloons, as well as Ireland with its Protestant and Catholic conflict, though this still remains tenuous. It has also been used with a degree of success in the old Yugoslavian area, but it has never been uncluttered. In past years, as noted, peace attempts were made by population movements or exchanges as between Turkey and Greece in 1923, but the nature of this policy was often barbaric. Partition was used in Ireland (1920), in India with Pakistan (1947) in the hope of peace, but always led to many deaths and violence.

Military intervention, as noted earlier, often uses humanitarian claims when it conceals other motives of a more political nature. The Bush administration in America, with the support of the British Prime Minister Tony Blair in 2003, claimed the attack on Iraq was based on humanitarian grounds, the danger of further crimes, and the search for weapons of mass destruction, (WMD). It was a controversial decision meeting wide criticism and because no WMD were found, the critics appear justified. Interventions in Libya and Syria have also raised similar issues. Gaddafi was killed, the country was bombed, civil war ensued and to this day the future of these areas remains uncertain.

Peace keeping in a hostile environment is always risky, both militarily and politically, and even if the peacekeepers are to hold the mandate in question, it often demands force, if only to defend themselves. Experience has shown that the peacekeepers are often bound by their mandate, therefore suffering a lack of firepower, and with the sheer local pressure they face difficult and at times impossible situations. In Rwanda and Bosnia, there were criticisms that peacekeepers needed more effective weapons, as well as freedom of action because they often needed to react in a military way to stop violence. This has often resulted in aerial attacks which is safer and less demanding.

Other bodies apart from the UN have become involved, with NATO and the EU taking a direct interest in Yugoslavia. Since the Cold War ended there has been a rise in nationalist disputes with growing intervention, and the geopolitical international landscape has shifted, as can be observed in Syria. There have been some successes in intervention, but it remains a delicate if not dubious situation to this day. The major problem is always the aggressive form of nationalism in which the ethnic minorities with some religious belief groups suffering. A small nationalistic uprising has potential for global conflicts, but perhaps the most significant element is the humanitarian drive to stop the slaughter of ethnic minorities. When in October 2023, Hamas (a Palestinian Islamic movement started in 1987 seeking a Palestinian state) carried out an outrageous terrorist attack on a Jewish music festival, it aroused a powerful nationalistic fervour in the Israeli government. It exposed the ongoing hatred between the Jew and the Arab and is raging as these notes are being written. It has resulted in a horrendous number of Palestinian civilian deaths in Gaza, a loss of sympathy and support for the Israeli government, with a realistic fear the war could soon involve much of the Middle East with potential global ramifications. It reflects the general acceptance that aggressive nationalism based on ethnic grounds is not only morally wrong but could lead to potential disaster.

Not all nationalistic needs for self-government have led to violence. The historian Montserrat Guibernau wrote an article on democratic nationalism, where small countries have sought their independence without necessarily wishing to be secessionist.[15] He selected three countries namely Catalonia, Scotland and Quebec which did not see themselves as regions. They tend to identify themselves as a singular unity based on their culture, history, territorial and political backgrounds giving them a sense of nationhood. 'The state is a political institution. According to Max Weber the state is a human community that (successfully) claims the monopoly of the legitimate use of physical force within a given territory', but there are other factors.[16] It is a socio-political thrust demanding the right for communities to be able to decide their own political future. They are often seen as peoples who wish to avoid cultural homogenisation by retaining their own identity based on their history. The same impulse can be identified in the Basque areas, in Belgium, and Wales. They are not necessarily seeking secessionism but demanding a recognition seeking their particular nationhood within the larger state based on their cultural and linguistic identity. They tend to hold in common a history in which they once stood as independent countries.

Catalonia until the eighteenth century had retained considerable autonomy, challenged during the centuries but maintaining its singular identity. Its problems increased when Catalonia became an industrialised component on the Spanish scene. There were struggles but Catalonia held to its claim of some self-government and autonomy, but it was blocked by the dictatorship of Primo de Rivera (1923), and in the time of Franco was crushed, and during his lifetime (died 1975) he ensured that Catalonia and Barcelona were simply parts of Spain. When Franco died Catalonia recovered a degree of autonomy in 1977 with its *Generalitat* form of government, and it was confirmed in 1979 by a new statute. The demands for some form of independence persist to this day, with the current government of Spain in Madrid regarding such action and street protests as treasonable, and punishable by long prison sentences. 'This strife was still ripe in 2017 when Madrid imprisoned separation politicians while others fled for sanctuary to Belgium. The undercurrent of the conflict between Madrid and Catalonia persists to this day, and in 2018 three Separatist Parties were still trying to unite in their common purpose, and Madrid was still threatening to imprison the fugitive Catalonian leader should he return'.[17] The leader, Carles Puigdemont had to fight against extradition papers in Germany to avoid a lengthy prison sentence. It was observed that 'officials in Schleswig Holstein will not let Spain give medals to the police who arrested Carles Puigdemont under the European warrant'.[18] The situation with Catalonia was not improving, and the reporter John Carlin in 2019 wrote that 'in Spain you raise the Catalan question at your peril, even with people whose sanity and intelligence you admire. A year ago, I was observing to one such person that all sides ought to accept their share of blame for the mess the country had got itself into over Catalonia. He reacted furiously: 'The Catalan independence leaders are like the Nazis of the thirties and forties!' he cried'".[19] During the Covid outbreak the 2021 voting was limited but the pro-independence parties won over 50 per cent of the votes.

In the same year nine activists who had been imprisoned were pardoned by King Felipe VI on the advice of the Spanish prime minister, and in 2024 there was a vote in favour of an amnesty, it was vetoed by the Senate but at the time of writing it is still anticipated being successful. In March 2024 there was an unexpected election, and the separatist parties lost their majority, falling short of making a government. At least the issue is less violent, but suggestive that the ghost of the Civil War continues with democratic and authoritarian views still clashing over the question of nationalism.

Scotland remained independent with its proud history of nationhood until the Act of Union in 1707. However, Scottish independence was always simmering, and in 1853 the Association of Scottish Rights was founded. Their ideal was to preserve Scottish identity with its sense of nationalism within the power structure of British politics. A Secretary for Scotland was appointed in 1885, but only found a cabinet place in 1892, and there was no full Secretary until 1926. There were further signs of progress when in 1934 the National Party of Scotland amalgamated with the Scottish Party, and in 1967 Winnie Ewing won the Hamilton by-election, this started the time of continuous parliamentary representation in Westminster. The Scottish National Party (SNP) became the second largest party in the devolved Scottish Parliament in 1999. The SNP gained power at the 2007 Scottish Parliament election, won the 2011 election but was reduced to a minority government in 2016. The 2014 referendum on independence was a closely fought debate with the objectors just losing as 45 per cent voted yes. The then leader Nicola Sturgeon took over the leadership from Alex Salmond, and Scotland voted to stay within the EU during the Brexit vote. Today (May 2024) the Scottish National Party remains but suffering from its own internal political problems. The fact that Scotland and Catalonia had once both been independent was significant, and both had long periods with degrees of autonomy. Both Scotland and Catalonia shared democratic means in trying to achieve their end-results with no serious violence.

Wales has leaned towards independence but acknowledges that it is reliant upon English economics. It furthers its sense of nationalism by cultural means, the Eisteddfod, having Welsh television, their language acknowledged and accepted, and currently appears content that its cultural national identity is recognised. Democracy in such areas has remained dominant and the demands sought for political autonomy through the ballot box. The political autonomy is sought by devolving some powers which appears more acceptable in Westminster than in Madrid. So far, it could be claimed so good, but the future cannot be predicted. In Spain Catalonia is important to the national economics, in Scotland there is a dependency on the British economy, but democracy seems to have worked. However, 'currently it is not clear whether the Belgian federation will withstand mounting nationalist pressure of finally breaking up'.[20] Generally, democratic nationalism has proved reliable by upholding different cultural communities, allowing regional politics, and dual identities, and by fostering an integral development of nationhood.

Chapter Seven

Observations on Recent Years

When history becomes a subject, it could be defined as yesterday, but 'yesterday' really belongs to current affairs because it lacks the benefit of studied hindsight and revealed evidence. As such, even ten years ago it is likely to be less objective because historical analysis will be missing, and it may reflect the writer's own views and possible bigotries. However, the issues raised by nationalism are still having a major impact on the daily lives of humankind, and with the pace of current development it is critical to explore recent years to understand the renewed fervour of nationalism, even if the reader holds different views.

Today, Europe is less significant in terms of world history because the superpowers have emerged as holding global controls. After the Second World War the political states and ideologies changed patterns with new hopes and fears. The world is faced by climate change and its future as a viable planet for living in has been thrown into doubt, but despite the catastrophe predicted by scientists, the world since the second half of the last century is still immersed and totally preoccupied by political pressures, wars, the threat of more wars and all the features of the various shades of nationalism still dominate.

Over the last fifty years the Middle East and Gulf regions have once again become a region of serious conflict, not helped by outside intervention, and to this day there is serious war which may expand beyond the Israeli-Gaza conflict started in 2023. The superpowers of America, Russia, and China have varying interests in the region, and they are always seeking influence through economics and the supply of weapons. There are many areas of tension and potential nationalistic conflict prevalent in the news, such as China's demands on Taiwan and the belligerence of North Korea, forever demonstrating its latest missiles with unveiled threats. Superiority of one power over another is often based on economics, resources, influence, but aggressive nationalism remains the critical feature, based on territory, power, and at times still involving religious belief, race, and ideologies. There is even the use of history with such arguments as irredentist nationalism, the excuse used at this moment in time by President Putin to invade Ukraine. Friction and tension are now global and not confined to the nation states of Europe, which as a result of the tragedies of the twentieth century, has sought unity, mainly in the European Union. However, the difficulties of the relationships between the European nations continues to be fraught, not least when Britain withdrew from the Union, and hovering questions about the internal political machinations of some of the member states.

On the global front this fear persists today as Russia has reappeared as a reflection of Tsarist days of expansionism and even Stalin's era of dominating Eastern Europe. The Western press often points out that Putin was for 16 years a KGB foreign intelligence officer, hinting he wants a return to the Stalinist empire or federation of previous years. China and America rise and fall in terms of sound mutual relationships. One crisis tends to arise after the next, with examples such as the 2008 financial collapse having long-term effects, including President Trump signing out of the Paris Agreement, with his tendency to revert to the old American isolationism.

Other issues such as populism in politics has revived, and there is the frightening issue of AI (artificial intelligence) which some see as the Fourth Industrial Revolution, but which raises questions about man's future as a thinking individual. There has even been frightening newspaper gossip that AI may be used in a potential nuclear conflict. Because of developing communication systems, the world has been described as a global village. It is now possible to fly from Berlin to America and back in the same day. The mobile phone means decisions can be made at anytime and anywhere in the world. Computers can hold complex national agreements which can be transmitted in micro-seconds, but are open to cyber interference. Europe no longer dominates the globe but needs to interact with other countries both commercially and politically. Perhaps one of the greatest fears is another war with the development of many types of weapons of mass destruction held by superpowers and smaller states, especially if by accident or design they fall into the hands of terrorists.

Bearing these issues in mind it is necessary to review some of the developments over recent years. As mentioned above the Middle East, probably more than anywhere else in the world has been a focus for friction and continuing tensions, despite being the birthplace of three major religions of Judaism, Christianity and Islam, all monotheistic faiths. Just over thirty years ago there was a major war in Iraq involving European and mainly American military. Saddam Hussein held command of the Ba'ath Party and Iraq, with seeming dictatorial powers, and in the West, there were serious suspicions about his intentions. The problems with oil-producing deserts with ancient names on maps once drawn-up by British Civil Servants, were always fermenting. The nationalistic State of Israel was not the only source of division, because Islam is divided between the Shia and Sunnis, and there is constant rivalry between Iran and Saudi Arabia.

The Iraqi crisis was brought to international disaster levels when Saddam Hussein with nationalistic aggression invaded Kuwait, based on dubious irredentist claims it belonged to Iraq. Saddam Hussein was forced out by the American led First Gulf War in February 1991, but it was the beginning of a crisis which effected the entire globe. The rumours spread that Hussein was hiding weapons of mass destruction (WMD) mainly chemical (especially nerve agents) or biological, and in 1998 President Clinton bombed Iraq over four days seeking to destroy this hidden arsenal. It was an unpleasant period not just in the Middle East, but this was the time of ethnic cleansing and genocide in the Balkans, Sudan, and the appalling massacres in Rwanda.

In 2001 with the Al-Qaeda Twin Towers terror attacks (known as 9/11) occurred, and President Bush was not the sharpest of American Presidents held Hussein to be responsible, probably because of past-grievances, denouncing Iraq, Iran, and North Korea in one breath. President Bush launched the Gulf War supported by the British Prime Minister Tony Blair. It shook other European leaders such as Chirac and Schröder, who believed the world should be moving away from rampant nationalism. When the war finished Iraq was in a state of anarchy, and no WMD were ever found. The Russians invaded Afghanistan (1979–1989), which the British had done on several occasions in colonial days. Later Anglo-American troops moved in to track down the dreaded terrorists in Operation *Freedom* which lasted from 2001 to 2014. That country is now in the hands of the religious extremists the Taliban after President Biden unexpectedly announced the withdrawal of troops.

Back in the Middle East the mutual hostility between Saudi Arabia and Iran continued, with the theocratic leader Khomeini denouncing King Fahd as a traitor to Allah. Saudi Arabia purchased Western weaponry to the delight of Western suppliers, ignoring the corruption of the Kingdom, the lack of human rights (especially for women), and knowing that the Kingdom was a source for the training of Muslim fundamentalists. The war in Yemen was a humanitarian catastrophe committed by Saudi Arabia. The Yemen conflict has led to rampant starvation levels, spreading diseases, leaving a turbulent area attacking shipping approaching the Suez Canal (2023–4).

These difficulties in the Middle East involved the financial concerns of other powers, especially America and many European countries who hold invested commercial interests in this fraught geo-political area. Iran has sounded out Putin, had allies in Hezbollah in Lebanon, and the Assad regime in Syria. The Americans, under President Trump, changed their minds over the so-called Iranian deal regarding nuclear development, and managed to turn Iran into a pariah state. Many of the European countries were unhappy over the American move because there had been opportunities of commerce in that area. As recently as 8 April 2019 President Trump designated Iran's elite Revolutionary Guard Corps as a foreign terrorist organisation, the first time the USA had labelled another nation's military as terrorists.

Saudi Arabia's position at times appeared to be deteriorating, but the Saudis are given space by the West for financial reasons even though it is religiously puritanical, corrupt as mentioned, and the home for the fundamentalist fanatic. In Saudi, the tribal loyalties are considered more important than the nation itself, which is governed by the older autocratic families. The religious danger is not just Sharia Law, but they spread their religious bigotry overseas through fanatical adherents. Saudi Arabia is a repressive country as even their own families frequently discover. Ironically 'the Kingdom is the world's seventh greatest online consumer of porn (position number one goes to Pakistan), perhaps because even pictures of women's legs on imported cornflake packets are covered with black stickers'.[1]

There was, some anticipated, the possibility that the Saudi Arabian type of rule would end, but the rulers were astute enough to recognise the dangers of collapsing states and watched the Arab Spring with vigilance, but their main enemy remained the old Persia, renamed Iran in 1935. Iran is for Saudi Arabia a heretical state since most of the Iranian population are Shia.* During the Shah's time (he ruled until April 1979) there was a constant westernising influence which met the opposition of Ayatollah Ruhollah Khomeini (1902–1989) hidden in France. Since the Shah's overthrow Iran has become a strict and puritanical theocracy which can be brutal in punishing misdemeanours, including homosexuality and drug-dealers, hanging them as a public spectacle. The 1979–80 American Embassy hostage situation strained relations with the USA, and it has been a downhill relationship since.

Iran offered its sympathy to America following the 9/11 attack and offered to help, but President Bush ignored this offer. The Iranians have excellent technology causing concern over nuclear development and are able to block any outside internet. Their car industry is vast, and the French have managed to open markets there. In Iran there remains an intense hatred of the USA, which they refer to as the Great Satan while they are fostering a relationship with Russia. Because of the American animosity Iran has developed relationships with China which is financially rewarding for that superpower. Before President Trump blocked the nuclear deal it had been anticipated that Iran might be a stabilising force in the area, but Trump's decision prompted their growing

---

* The Sunni hold to the belief that the Prophet's successor should be chosen on competence rather than family relationship. Shia adherents reject the three early Caliphs and start with Ali Mohammed's cousin and son-in-law whose son was slain in 680 at the Battle of Karbala.

closeness to China and Russia. Had the West reacted more diplomatically perhaps Iran and Saudi Arabia could have been regional counterbalances rather than the perpetual pursuit of influence and domination in this fraught area.

The global issues appear to centre on these vast desert and mountainous regions, and the once powerful Europe has to sit on the sidelines waiting to see what happens between the three global superpowers in this volatile area. It is not the only concern that Europe feels in the Middle East as the rise of ISIS and their terror threat has often dominated the headlines in recent years. ISIS, the Islamic State of Iraq and Syria, has many titles, but the world has been all too aware of its potential threats. ISIS carried out public beheadings of hostages using computer technology to expose their anger on a global basis, making it more grotesque than the medieval executions. In October 2006, the Islamic State of Iraq was announced, and Iraq was plunged into more battlefield conflict, with suicidal bombings. They equipped themselves with captured American military weapons and Maliki (Prime Minister 2006–14) ignored murderous activities of the Shia militias, in what was essentially another religious war. It was clearly nationalistic, and aggressive because of religious differences. It proved to be barbaric and different from the old Islamic world which tended to be more tolerant of other faiths, using that characteristic division of 'them and us'. Iraq cannot claim any form of stability since its war with America and Britain. Europe on the doorstep has been faced by many confrontations with global ramifications, as foreign fighters poured across the borders to support this movement, ranging from schoolgirls to doctors. The war took its turn when in June 2014 a small ISIS group successfully poured into Mosul, a major city in northern Iraq. ISIS was becoming more than a religious dream. They imposed their medieval views, looting and destroying world famous antiquities.

It faced a degree of competition from Al-Qaeda in Mali and formed a tentative alliance with the savage figure of Boko Haram in Nigeria, and spread its tentacles into the Russian Caucasus, where some Al-Qaeda switched sides. The Chechens were divided, and President Putin soon regarded the ISIS problem as a national threat. Their brutal retribution and punishments were broadcast to a shocked world, thereby helping to encourage religious fanatics to their side. They were of the fundamentalist school of Wahhabis (an Islamic doctrine and religious Salafi movement) strong in Saudi Arabia, which preached the eschatological concept that the end days were approaching. As a matter of curiosity this morbid approach has been exposed in fanatical right-wing evangelicals in America, depicting a traditional picture of Jesus Christ, but holding a submachine gun. Their message is one of Armageddon hoping that if the Israeli-Gaza war results in a global nuclear war of annihilation, the second coming of Christ will occur, and they will be saved at the expense of the enemies of Christ. To this day, for some people, religious belief remains a point of serious contention and strife and a source for conflict.

In Syria their internal strife grew in brutality, not helped by the fact that some states such as Saudi Arabia, Turkey and Qatar wanted the Assad regime, now intensely unpopular in the West, destroyed. President Obama was reluctant to intervene, and Turkey was accused of not assuring its border crossings were secure against foreigners joining the conflict. From August 2014 a coalition of local states started air-strikes in northern Iraq and Syria, and with American airpower. ISIS eventually lost a third of its holdings in Syria and 50 per cent of its Iraqi territory. However, ISIS continued, reaching out towards Afghanistan and Pakistan, and in June 2017 launched terror attacks deep inside Iran. They tried to infiltrate Libya where Western intervention had produced a failed state. Such was their fanaticism there was no hope of negotiations. The Russians have assisted President Assad, and this has caused friction on the international scene, especially with America, who claim that innocent citizens are being killed. By early 2019 the news announced that ISIS areas were almost eliminated, but as one BBC reporter expressed it, the 'main fear was that the broken state was still a state of mind' and ISIS was not finished.

Another ongoing major issue to this day was fleeing refugees and economic immigrants causing problems on Europe's shoreline. Greece, one of the poorest of the EU states became the focus for this surge of incoming humanity. Italy also felt the pressure, causing tensions inside the EU with the financial implications, and increasing international concerns over border control. The sudden influx of peoples has not suited extreme right-wing nationalists who reject multicultural societies as they 'are not like us'. Germany was more tolerant causing right-wing dissent, and some of the new members from the old Eastern Bloc expressed the same views. In February 2019 it was rumoured the EU were paying other Middle Eastern and North African states to halt the refugees leaving, which led to barbarities. Today it is a major issue in Britain where the government has paid the French to stop them crossing the channel with little success, and the previous Conservative government intended to send them packing to Rwanda which was hotly contested in the national courts. This fraught issue clearly defines some of the baser ingredients of rampant nationalism, seeing the migrants as of a different race, their religious beliefs regarded as a perpetual threat, and not speaking the same language, rather than seeing fellow human beings as in serious trouble risking their family lives for somewhere to exist. It seems extraordinary that religious belief still continues as a barrier between people. China, interested in the financial ramifications was exposed for incarcerating Muslims. The Middle East and Gulf regions were never part of traditional Europe, but in the new globalisation they are next-door neighbours and have stoked the fires of nationalism. In the twenty-first century there are distinctive signs of anti-immigration, suspicions of the people next door, and the desire to retain a country's culture free from Islamic influence.

In July 2016 there was a failed coup against Turkey's President Erdoğan (previously Prime Minister 2003–14), which made European neighbours uncomfortably suspicious that the problems of the Middle East were closer to home than believed. Turkey had secularised itself and demanded entry into the EU, but there was the fear that under Erdoğan there was the possibility of a return to an Islamic theocracy. Turkey had a history of military intervention in its political drive to maintain it as a secular state (in 1960, 1971, 1980, 1993, and a peaceful intervention in 1997) but in 2016 there was no unified action by the senior military. President Erdoğan's reaction was to put his opponents into prison. Through a declared state of emergency President Erdoğan gained his executive presidency, enabling him to pass laws without parliament, in the same way Hitler had made himself the Führer. The EEC had signed an association agreement with Turkey in 1963 but full entry has proved contentious, and despite repeated attempts the issue keeps stalling, mainly because of democratic back-sliding. Turkey has constantly been at odds while sometimes flirting with the Kurds, who in their northern Iraqi regions hold oil and gas possibilities, whereas Turkey has next to none. At one time it was rumoured that Erdoğan by his efforts with the Kurds was in line for a Nobel Peace prize, but the Kurds became angry with his seeming compliant support of ISIS, and Erdoğan increased the tension playing on the possibility that the nationalistic side of his supporters would support him at election time. There were tensions with Israel when Erdoğan was criticised at one time for protesting against that country's treatment of the Palestinians. In the Syrian conflict Erdoğan opposed Assad's brutality and there was a time when Turkey looked to Russia, but Erdoğan had backed the Crimean Tatars, and in 2015 a Russian jet strayed into Turkish airspace only to be shot down.

The EU wanted to keep Turkey on side, but they were concerned about the climate of populism, the nationalistic tendencies connected with Islam, and the relationship with NATO appeared to be deteriorating. Turkish relations with Russia have improved, despite the assassination of the Russian Ambassador in December 2016. Erdoğan made an agreement with Russia in 2016 on the Syrian issues, but there were problems with Turkish interest in the Kurds, who are the largest ethnic minority within Turkey. The main European Union members have watched with curiosity as Turkey appeared to have become an authoritarian Islamic state, a seismic shift from the European perspective.

As Erdoğan has used religion in Turkey, in Russia Putin appeared as a devout member of the Russian Orthodox Church, of 'Holy Russia' which remained highly nationalistic. Putin came to the leadership after Yeltsin and despite much publicised elections, it is apparent that Russia is again an authoritarian state. 'Russia's obsession with espionage and security is in the blood' and it is no surprise that Putin was a one-time KGB officer (Lieutenant Colonel until August 1991).[2]

There were some who saw him not as a geopolitical mastermind, but as 'the boss of a mafia state, the centre of a personality cult and the apostle of a new form of ethno-nationalist ideology with mystical overtones and a global outreach'.[3] There was no doubt that for a time he slowed the country's economic disintegration, and it was probably the longest stretch of economic growth inside Russia. Pictures of him fishing, contesting in Judo fights, and riding horses are seen everywhere, indicating that he understands the propaganda for image-building.

Many KGB and others resented the collapse of the USSR, developing a revanchist attitude. Putin in subduing the Chechen problem ended with him as President from 2000 to 2008, followed by a brief interval as Prime Minister, then in 2012 he was once again President, a position he still retained in the 2024 elections. Putin's religious side seems less important at this juncture, but in the Ukraine at the end of 2018 and beginning of 2019 the Orthodox Church of the Ukraine gained independence, marking a historic split with the Russian Church to the 'annoyance' of Russia. The Ecumenical Patriarch Bartholomew the head of the global Orthodox Church signed the necessary documents in Istanbul, but while for many this held no significance, it had major ramifications in the Ukraine where religious belief is still part of their nationalistic impetus.

The Ukrainian crisis led to a ban on the free movement which richer citizens had now taken for granted, and the question of their private wealth became an issue. It was claimed Russia attempted to stir up nationalism in the West which stirred resentment. 'The rise of the populist right throughout Europe helps Russia accentuate Europe's instability while Islamic terror attacks confirm Europe's weakness', as Russia claimed to be a rock of stability.[4]

It is in this climate that Russia's massive natural resources have become a weapon of some significance in the Russian arsenal, most especially the supply of gas. The Russian influence can almost be traced through its international supply of gas lines and pipes. Putin showed considerable interest in the Turkish supply route across the Black Sea to Turkey and into Greece and onwards to the Balkans. It is Russia's resources, with a projected image of a proud people's history of resistance to the invader, which provides their sense of their right on the world stage. They had been the country which halted the unstoppable Napoleon and saved Europe and possibly the world from Nazi domination.

It was easier for Russian chiefs like Putin to deal with single leaders rather than the nebulous shifting democracies. Maintaining his own position in Russia as the authoritarian leader has been easy for Putin with some suspected murders of his opposition (Boris Nemtsov a liberal-minded politician and Putin critic was murdered near the Kremlin in February 2015), which caused much cynicism in the West. Nevertheless, it appears that Putin remains popular with many, with clever propaganda he has used the populist vote in his favour, though most in the West suspect the integrity of the Russian elections.

Putin had been aware that Western agencies like the CIA had encouraged the growth of trade unions in the East during the Cold War, and the same subversive activities using the latest cyberspace techniques to interfere in each other's affairs, and in the post-Soviet Union era a huge amount of mutual distrust exists based on nationalistic motivation. The main Russian problem as they perceived it, and projected by the Tsars and the Communists is Russia being surrounded by potential enemies, and it has not left the Russian mentality, but this time on a larger scale. Hemmed in by the highly populated and economically powerful China, the other side Europe backed by America. Europe's wooing of Eastern European countries into the EU and especially into NATO made the situation obvious to many Russians.

The Tsars had been criticised before the Great War for not encouraging nationalism or even patriotism, and Lenin and Stalin needed it subdued in their projected polyglot empire, but today Russia's need for nationalism has been re-kindled, seeing the West as the enemy. During the 1990s Russia had been humiliated, criticised, and looked down on by the West during the downward years of Yeltsin. However, Putin's strong-man persona has probably reaped its rewards amongst some Russians, especially of the old school.

Putin warned the West in 2008 that if NATO worked its way into the old Soviet Union, he would retake Crimea which took only nineteen days to achieve. This was virtually ignored, perhaps seen by some as necessary irredentist nationalism. The warfare against the West took place by subtle interference inside Western Europe and America by encouraging discontent, stoking nationalism, and often using cyberspace as the means, dubbed 'hybrid warfare'. While the Russians are not the only ones, they are portrayed as the masters of the game.

In the diplomatic tensions which were building up over recent years it was no surprise that the pariah state of Iran (in American eyes) is friendly with Russia and busy selling them anti-aircraft missile batteries. Russia also cleverly consorted with the Kurds probably to drive a wedge between the Americans and Turks. Putin's powerful persona has elevated him in many minds, and many Middle Eastern and Gulf States are looking towards Russia.

Russia under Putin may have economic problems but has huge natural resources and remains powerful at a stage when America appears less adept in international situations. On 24 February 2022 Putin ordered the invasion of Ukraine, a war still raging as this book is being written. The Ukraine managed to find military resources from the West, and it is weakening but still resisting the Russian onslaught. The Israeli-Gaza war has retained more worldwide concern than the Ukraine for whom Western military support appeared to lessen, and the general feeling is that Russia will eventually win this conflict. For Putin it is a case of irredentist nationalism, claiming back Russian soil as he had done in the Crimea. In reality it is rampant aggressive nationalism in search of territorial expansion and greater domination. There is little doubt that this has all stirred nationalistic feelings on a global scale, and within Russia under Putin nationalism is growing as elsewhere, and continues to be divisive, even in Europe despite the efforts of the EU. Russia's impact on European history remains ongoing today, but in this current age with the planet seeming smaller with the communication systems mentioned earlier, China also carries considerable influence.

An ancient country once highly civilised, China is emerging from the era it calls the Century of Shame and Humiliation. It was a time in which China was entangled by civil and foreign wars. As in Russia, China is currently under an authoritarian leader in President Xi Jinping who is somewhat different from his predecessors Jiang Zemin and Hu Jintao.

Mao Zedong is another totalitarian leader, known for his brutality: during his time in office an estimated seventy million people died from war, starvation, and execution, more than Hitler and Stalin had managed. He died in 1976 and many international attitudes toward China still tend to focus on his days as a general image. China has spread its influence through its banks, investments, industries, advanced information technology, and is now the world's second largest economy. Political fears exist in this area, and the Chinese Huawei firm dealing with telecommunications and consumer electronics was recently accused as a potential security risk by the USA. The suspicion of latent nationalism amongst neighbours persists, and probably with some justification, and in 2019 Chinese motivations were raised in the Western World, believing Chinese financial investments are preparations for political interference.

The claim of China as being communist is flawed, like Stalin's Russia in its times, far removed from the ideals of Marx. The 3,000 strong National People's Congress is full of billionaires, and on a visit to China some ten years ago the current writer heard that corruption is considered a major problem. Nevertheless, Shanghai, looking like any city in the capitalistic world, is 80 per cent publicly owned. Those people living in cities have a better lifestyle than those who exist in the rural communities, which is not a feature of just Chinese life, but people migrating to the urban complexes to escape poverty is common in China. Small towns have become major cities and Shenzhen in 1980 had a population of 30–35,000 people, today Shenzhen has twelve million. China unquestionably is emerging as a recognised figurehead of global proportions, with many commentators predicting that the twenty-first century will be known as belonging to the Chinese.

Tiananmen Square when opposition protests in 1989 were put down with brutality, and Muslims were being locked away caused Western criticism, but it appears that for the average Chinese person life has improved, however, China executes more people than the rest of the world. Chinese economic success has enabled the growth of a welfare system, and children must attend school, unlike India and other areas where child labour is a cause of concern.

The so-called democracy of China, its authoritarian leadership, the treatment of internal opponents, its growing wealthy classes, with inbuilt corruption have caused many criticisms, but China remains an economic powerhouse. It is so commercially powerful that Europe takes it seriously for economic survival. It is unlikely that China will become democratic, and it will speculatively maintain its current course. President Xi Jinping holds absolute power, human rights are ignored, but obliged by economic needs, the West most of the time turns a blind eye.

Economics is China's driving force, but for many the financial influence is sometimes as pervasive as a military threat. There are concerns about borders in maritime lanes for shipping, with China from time to time making belligerent stands. When the China Shipping and China Ocean Shipping Groups merged it created the world's largest container-shipping line, and accounts for up to one fifth of the world's container traffic and responsible for 40 per cent of the world's commercial tonnage. This money helps the Chinese in creating influence in the Middle East and Africa. Chinese loans come with strings attached, giving them influence in many countries around the globe. The long battle over Taiwan (once known as Formosa) to this day still causes concern on a worldwide basis, especially in America, and the West nervously waits to see if China will take this offshore island by force. The threats over occupying Taiwan are almost daily, and after the Tawain elections on 22 May 2024 the Chinese government carried out a three-day military exercise over and around the island, a sheer threat and reminder of their intentions.

As noted above, the maritime borders have become potentially contentious, not helped by China creating coral islands as Chinese bases, causing issues with fishing rights and military communication routes. This is dubbed the Nine-Dash Line and has become a cause of concern for America and other nations.

President Xi Jinping has promised that China has no intention of territorial expansion beyond its borders. The Americans know that Chinese investment in America is massive, and if withdrawn could lead to serious devaluation. Even on 10 May 2019 it was announced that new economic talks were projected between China and America, but a BBC business reporter, Ana Nicolaci da Costa, noted that even if a US-China deal happened, it would be unlikely to end the rivalry between the two economic giants. The enormity of these two economies means there could be damaging consequences for the global economy if it goes wrong. However, most observers know the dispute goes beyond trade issues, and represents a power-struggle between two very different world views, with the ever-present nationalism lurking more prominently each year, both from the Chinese and American points of view.

Following the collapse of the Soviet Union the USA saw itself as the major superpower, and the world's policeman for liberal style democracy. Its military strength was so great there was the danger that it could act with impunity, dictating or covertly organising affairs in other countries. From the European perspective, America was often regarded as a benign helper with some justification following the two world wars, and the Marshall Plan. During the Cold War it had provided defence and NATO with vital backup. Western Europe with its liberal democracies saw a partner across the Atlantic with nations such as Britain, France and others claiming a special relationship with America. In the American way of thinking, and for many in the West, democracy is the only legitimate way to govern. Some American politicians have almost been too evangelistic in this outlook.

The military and economic power of America is widely accepted, as is the American President's right to declare war without consulting Congress, which seems a strange trait in a much-celebrated democracy. America has a history of sending troops into potential trouble spots, and President Clinton referred to it as humanitarian intervention when American troops entered Somalia, Haiti, Bosnia, and Kosovo. The Americans trod with care, because following the Vietnam disaster they were not prepared to bring back too many American casualties. Vietnam had left unpleasant memories in America. There is a history of atrocities in Vietnam by both sides, and technically under past agreements, the United Nations should be the policeman, but America had the money and the military which the UN lacks.

When George Bush assumed power, his response to 9/11 was an over-reaction as the world's policeman, because Iraq which was not the perpetrator of 9/11 and did not have WMD. It was the same situation in Afghanistan where American and British troops eventually left on 11 September 2021 on the twentieth anniversary of the 9/11 attack.

Loyalties in the Middle East faltered with America except for Israel, another with a 'special relationship', especially after the Arab Spring. Obama tried to settle the problems, but the interventionist policy created many problems for the American reputation. President Obama called time in Iraq in 2011 but the damage had been done, and Iraq has yet to recover. One of the problems was often American politicians were unaware of the countries and their historical background. Relationships with powers like Russia and China were not always as simple as they could have been. The USA continuously made it clear that it was the world's policeman and guardian, increasingly so, because the 9/11 attack left a scar on the American landscape unused to a direct attack since Pearl Harbor.

There was a growth of right-wing nationalism in America which found its focus in Trump's 2016 election, who had promised to build a wall between Mexico and the USA and make the Mexicans pay. This anti-immigrant stance had already been applied to a list of Islamic countries, to withdrawals from international agreements, and to all appearances President Trump's call 'to make America Great again' was leading to a period of nationalistic isolationism as experienced in the difficult 1930s. Trump also attacked NATO partners for not paying their share, meddled in the EU problems (making much of Nigel Farage during the Brexit debate) and making it clear that he was chief on the international stage. There was more than a touch of nationalism indicating its characteristic themes in the anti-globalisation, anti-free trade with evident signs of racism. Trump's brutal treatment of immigrant families crossing the Mexican border by separating children from their families, and his battle call that they were 'being invaded' was popular in some quarters but ridiculed him in the eyes of thinking people. President Trump used the feelings of an angry portion of the American population, who had felt ignored, by his characteristic tweets on social media to gain support, which elicited a degree of cynicism from others. He also used religious faith turning to the widespread right-wing evangelical church, often known as the Bible-belt.

Trump had many supporters, while others questioned whether his behaviour was denigrating the status of his Office and America's reputation. His insults were simply unbelievable as when he accused the ex-PoW of the Vietnam War, John McCain as being a 'loser', and some newspapers happily retaliated by pointing out that Trump had evaded the Vietnam draft. He also referred to some African countries as 'shitholes', ignoring the dignity of his office. For many people, President Trump became a mockery, claiming he has never read a book, yet read the scriptures daily, but this is probably an elective device for the powerful American Bible belt, the popular evangelical wing, mentioned above.

Trump alienated American allies, not least with his rejection of the Paris Agreement over climate change, rejecting science with an eye to his electoral standing amongst the masses. He abruptly abandoned the Trans-Pacific Trade Pact, which was a gift to China, but unsettled relationships with that country, forgetting that China has $1.115 trillion of US Treasuries.

President Trump abruptly parted from his European Allies by replacing the Iranian nuclear deal, which came as a total surprise as it involved no consultation. He announced the American Embassy would move to Jerusalem thereby making himself a hero to Netanyahu, and creating more problems in that vexed area, clashing with his allies over this issue. In April 2019 he suddenly announced that the USA would end support for the global arms pact known as the Arms Trade Treaty, which again illustrated his aversion to international agreements, stating that 'we will never allow foreign bureaucrats to trample on your Second Amendment freedom', when addressing the Rifle Association's annual meeting in Indianapolis. He threw the pen to sign the withdrawal into the cheering crowd. These moves were meant to appeal to the populist vote, but he risked alienating America's traditional allies. His attitude toward the EU were at the best patronising and his treatment of their politicians was one of contempt, noted in the widely broadcast television shot when he barged a national European leader sideways in order to be at the front of the cameras. His ignorance of other countries, thinking Belgium was a city, which led to clashes between him and his diplomats, while his appreciation for strong men like Putin and Xi Jinping was noticed.

President Trump almost became a caricature with his use of 'tweeting', and he has been described as a 'pathological narcissist'.[5] The fraught question of whether *Pax Americana* was finished created a sense of international anxiety. His rallying cry of 'make America Great again' used widely during the electoral campaign and since, is a characteristic hallmark of rampant nationalism. His attitude towards other nations and immigrants indicated that feature of aggressive nationalism stimulating the 'them and us' situation, placing suspicions on neighbouring nations. When he lost the election against President Biden, he encouraged his outraged followers to attack Congress, and as this is being written, having stood trial on sexual and financial matters he was found guilty on all counts. Such is his right-wing populist nationalistic support he has recently (2025) been re-elected to the Presidency, leaving many to wonder what will happen next.

Europe, no longer the power-centre of the globe still struggles to find a sense of unity with the nations of Russia and Turkey remaining a cause of concern with their authoritarian leadership. The Middle East and Gulf states remain unstable, Iran is viewed as a potential danger and the Israeli-Gaza conflict casts doubts on the Israeli government's behaviour and intentions with the danger of the war expanding in the region. There is the vexed question of Putin's attack on the Ukraine with the West supplying support to the Ukrainians, which is a concern that it may be a flashpoint for a greater conflict. China's appearance as a world leader is of interest and concern to most European nations. There is a great dependency on China's economy and commerce with issues in Britain over the Chinese constructing nuclear power stations on UK soil, reflecting the usual suspicions about those of a different political creed. The world was hit by Covid with insinuations it had its origins in China. It seems that humankind's propensity for being suspicious of other nations is a characteristic which has dogged tribes and nations since the beginning of human existence.

The centre of Europe has through history centred on Paris, Berlin, Vienna, or London, but today it is Brussels as it contains the EU Commission, the European Parliament, and the centre for NATO. As a country Belgium was itself divided and in 2010 and 2011 found it impossible to form a government, and the division between the Flemings and Walloons continues as a problem. The EU in trying to unite Europe has financial and immigration fears, watching the increasing divisions within its ranks, not least the British Brexit vote in 2016. It had been anticipated that the belligerence of nationalism brought about by nation states vying for power at the expense of a neighbour was outdated, but the populist vote of recent years appears to be putting the brakes on this hope.

The Union increased with some old Eastern bloc countries joining, with some economically better off and better prepared than others. In 2016 plans for Turkey and the Ukraine went askew, and since the days of Margaret Thatcher most knew that the UK was not a whole-hearted member. Britain and Europe have never had an easy relationship, not helped by Britain with its insular attitudes mainly caused by being offshore Atlantic islands. The political writer Tony Wright summarised the issue when he wrote that 'When the countries of Europe emerged from the Second World War with the belief that the nation state had failed, requiring new pan-European political institutions to be built, Britain believed instead that it had triumphed. It was the nation's 'finest hour,' when Britain 'stood alone.' It is impossible to understand the subsequent history of Britain's troubled relationship with 'Europe' without also understanding the force of these different historical (and geographical) trajectories; it explains why the Euroscepticism has been much stronger in Britain than in the rest of the EU; and why Britain has acquired its 'awkward partner' status.[6] This had been written long before the troubled years of Brexit.

The freedom of the 'people movement policy' was emphasised when Poland, Latvia, Romania, and Bulgaria joined, with large numbers of mobile labourers prepared to work at minimal pay. During the Brexit debate, few understood the importance of incoming cheap labour, foreign expertise in the health, education and research fields. It was often based on the fear of immigrants with the nationalistic cry of 'our country', and the 'them and us' typical of aggressive nationalism. Brexit arose from a form of nationalism and will remain a point of contention in the future.

Nationalism's ingredients can clearly be identified in the underlying force in the attitude towards refugees, most of whom are fleeing for their lives by seeking a living space away from war-torn areas, bigotry, and sheer poverty. The situation has led to many television pictures of people drowning in the Mediterranean and the English Channel, and the growth of criminal activity in people smuggling. The 1999 Treaty of Amsterdam had abolished Europe's borders, just as some countries started to build border fences, Hungary doing it with determination. In Britain on 1 March 2012, HM Customs and Excise took on a new para-military role as the Border Force, and to this day migrants are at the top of the political electoral debating issues.

It has become a common complaint that so-called host countries are losing out on welfare, health, and all the mainline services, with no return in taxes, which has gripped many of the major political parties with a view for the popular vote. Some countries more than others have immersed themselves in this problem, and in France, traditionally a safe haven, there has always existed the extreme right-wing with its National Front founded in 1972, which is clearly xenophobic. In France the right-wing came close to victory but were eventually faced-off by Emmanuel Macron in May 2017. Even more virulent and disturbing are the right-wing forces in Hungary, where the fans waved the flag last used by the Arrow Cross fascists, who had helped the Nazis round up the helpless Jews.

In the United Kingdom, the right-wing UKIP growth during Brexit attracted many right-wing nationalists. The UKIP led by Nigel Farage played a key role in Brexit, and during the highly publicised debate lavish promises were made, and misleading information given. There has never been a time in modern British politics when the country has been so divided down the centre, verging on a political civil war. In April 2019 a Paul Vallely writing in the Church Times quoted John Denham, a former Labour minister, who suggested Brexit, 'with its talk about sovereignty, borders, and taking back control, was an expression of a revived English nationalism'.[7] At the time of writing the British are holding their 2024 general election, and the extreme right-wing Farage is leading the Reform Party which he claims is the new Conservative Party. Although he claimed he was not standing for parliament himself, he changed his mind on 3 June 2024, and in a recent television broadcast he was also supporting Trump's bid for the presidency and claiming that the immigration problems were an invasion, calling it 'D-Day in reverse', making an appeal for the popular vote.

The common expression which gathered strength during the second decade of the twenty-first century was 'right-wing populism', claiming to be a political ideology, speaking for the common people. Extreme right-wing populism has at its impetus a form of neo-nationalism, encompassing anti-globalisation, protectionism, anti-immigration, and even elements opposed to the welfare state. Despite the warnings of the Second World War it appears to be resurging in Europe. In January 2019 Pope Francis announced to his diplomatic corps in his annual address of the New Year the warning that 'the nationalistic tendencies that led to the Second World War have returned and are threatening the peace-keeping work of humanitarian organisations'.[8] His observations contained the warning that humanitarian efforts were being hampered, but the possible dangers of nationalistic tendencies are so serious it is equally a threat to peace. 'Judging from the resurgence of the populist right (and a neo-Nazi subculture and the American 'alt-right'), decades of academic work on these subjects has not served us well if its aims were immunisation'.[9]

The term populist is best expressed as appealing to ordinary people ensuring them their concerns and views are important. This point became clear when analysists of the Brexit campaign noted that the pro-Brexit areas were the poorer regions. Both European and American populism are frequently associated with the global upsurge in migrants, as being a drain on the country's resources. This soon became associated with the issue of the natural and therefore rightful inhabitants (often migrants from previous generations) a feature which could often be described as racial. There is also a growing tendency against Islamic adherents, re-introducing the ugly spectre of religious friction. The nationalistic element dwells in this British impulse to stand apart from the EU and its anticipated Federalism. The right-wing is not just Britain and France but currently sweeps across Europe.

In 1955 the Austrian Freedom Party (FPÖ) was established, and in 1999 gathered 27 per cent of the votes in the Federal Elections making it the second strongest party in Austria. In 2016 the candidate Norbert Hofer made it as far as the run-off in the Presidential elections, and the FPÖ after the 2017 Legislative elections formed a government coalition in the Austrian People's Party.

Since 2013 in Germany right-wing parties have emerged, the first known as Alternative for Germany (AfD) which finished third in the German Federal election of 2017, making it the first right-wing party to enter the Bundestag since the rise of the dictator Adolf Hitler, and it continues to grow in strength. Others have come into existence by attracting sporadic attention such as Pro NRW, Citizens in Rage, and in 2005 the nationwide Pro Germany Citizens' Movement was founded in Cologne. Their policy was anti-Islam and therefore against Muslim immigrants, denying the policy of a multi-ethnic society. Since then, the German Freedom Party (2010) appeared, all with similar policies, and based on a sense of nationalism, and the AfD is now the largest opposition Party in the Bundestag with 89 seats. In January 2024 it was reported that members of the AfD had met Austrian far-right parties to discuss a 'remigration' for deporting immigrants, including naturalised Germans. Officials of the AfD Party claimed it was only a few of their members had been there and stood back as it was roundly condemned by many German politicians.

After the end of the Second World War, neo-fascist type politicians were ignored in Italy, but in 1994 the then prime minister Silvio Berlusconi in 1994 made them part of his coalition which gave them a sense of legitimacy, with some such as prime minister Giorgia Meloni claiming that Mussolini was a sound politician doing all he could for Italy, even though it led that country into a major war and defeat. There are distinct signs in Italy that fascism persists. Italy has a variety of right-wing parties, but the most prominent is Lega Nord (LN) from 1991, claiming to reject the right-wing label but is more of a regional movement and at times secessionist. It basically wants Italy to become a federal state with regional autonomy, opposes the centralisation of power in Rome, and demands separation from southern Italy, regarding the rural south as lazy, and governed by criminals. This LN Party has similar traits in criticising immigrant influx and aid and is basically Euro-sceptic. During the 2018 elections they emerged as the third largest party in Italy. There are many other right-wing parties in Italy's many-party system, including in the south the Italian Social Movement, heirs of a neo-fascist party.

In Belgium the Vlaams Blok party was established in 1978 with anti-immigration policies aimed at Islamic incomers, also demanding the secession of the Flanders region, which consistently raises it head as regions demand their own autonomy. They demanded a rewording of the policy adopting the position that new immigrants would have to accept Flemish culture, and this policy was undeniable based on its local form of nationalism.

In the 1970s the Progress Party in Denmark was the strongest right-wing party in Europe, but support faded until the 1990s, when the Danish People's Party emerged and became the second largest in Denmark by 2015. This movement also demanded a reduction in immigration and is opposed to becoming multi-cultural. In 2015 the New Right Party emerged.

In 1995 Finland, the Finns Party was the right-wing populist party and second largest in that country. In 2017 the party split (19/37) and some MPs produced a new Party called Blue Reform. On 14 April 2019, following a parliamentary election with over 97 per cent of votes, the Social Democrats took 17.8 per cent, with the Finns Party on 17.6 per cent. The anti-immigration right-wing party soared into second place and the situation still remains complex and confusing.

During the 2018 election in Hungary there was a victory for the Fidesz-KDNP alliance which kept Viktor Orbán as Prime Minister; he has retained that position since 2010. He is widely known for his opposition to immigration.

His dominant position in Hungarian politics is seen as important for the right-wing nationalistic populist movement with critics claiming Hungary is only a democracy in name.

In Greece the Independent Greeks (ANEL) were smaller in number than the more extreme Golden Dawn Party, but after the January 2015 legislative elections, ANEL formed a government coalition with the left-wing Radical Left (SYRIZA). As a direct consequence the Golden Dawn Party has grown in numbers, and their right-wing policies contain the usual anti-immigrant theme, as well as the rather frightening concept of taking Albanian and Turkish territory. This form of nationalism is potentially dangerous even if it is mere political bluster.

In 1982 in the Netherlands the right-wing Centre Party won a single seat, but later a splinter group called the Central Democrats was marginally more successful. It was not until 2002 that a more right-wing populist vote became more prominent, when the Pim Fortuyn List won twenty-six seats and formed a coalition with the CDA, the Christian Democratic Appeal along with VVD, the People's Party for Freedom and Democracy. Its policy was anti-immigration and anti-Islam, but Fortuyn himself was assassinated in May 2002. When in 2006 the PVV, Party of Freedom came to power through coalition, it had similar policies and tended to be Euro-sceptic, opposing Turkey's entry into the Union, and demanding that immigrants be assimilated into Dutch culture. The coalition failed and the PVV was reduced to fifteen seats, but they rose to twenty in the 2017 election headed by Geert Wilders, making it the second largest party. In the same year, the Forum for Democracy was established which is another right-wing party.

The Law and Justice Party in Poland holds the Presidency and a governing majority in the Sejm (Lower House of Polish Parliament), which is best described as social conservatism. As a Party it is highly critical of immigration, and supportive of NATO and interventionist economic policies. In more recent years the Congress of the New Right (2015–17) was headed by Michał Marusik who demanded radical tax deductions, abolishing social security and public health care, he died in 2020 and there is no evidence of a defined party manifesto.

Spain from the 1930s has constantly been divided between the left and right-wings. In the April elections of 2019, the Socialists improved their support and managed to hold Spain's upper house of parliament, but they lacked a reliable majority for straightforward governance. On the other hand, the right-wing national party called Vox drew support from those who believed the previous government had failed to manage the Catalonia situation appropriately. Vox had promised to 'make Spain great again', to be tough on Islam, immigrants, but failed to convince workers who normally voted left, but it was the first time since Franco's death in 1975 a far right-wing party had reached parliament.

Sweden known for their liberal attitudes, now has an anti-immigrant party. The right-wing Sweden Democrats polled 20 per cent, which was a surprise given that in 2008, they polled around 4 per cent, and it was not until 2010 they won their first seats in parliament. In 2014 the seven mainstream parties won 13 per cent and gained forty-nine seats, and the right-wing appears to be taking a grip in a country traditionally world-famous for its hospitality to immigrants and its liberal attitudes.

In Switzerland the SVP (Swiss Peoples Party) reached a record in 2015 with 29 per cent of the vote, which was an all-time high for the Swiss party system. They are regarded as the Right-wing populist party with Ulrich Schlüer leading a New Right study group. It grew to be the largest party during the 1990s.

The right-wing of politics does not necessarily lead to fascism any more than the left-wing to communism. However, the fear of the 1930s is not a distant memory because of its impact, and historical evidence indicates that either political wing when becoming extremist and gathering popular support can be dangerous for any democracy. In the period following the First World War, the fascist growth found support at all social levels and especially from the traditional right-wing, whereas poverty and dominance by the wealthy led to communism. During the second decade of this current century there are distinct signals of extreme nationalism which could be identified, with racism and ethnicity remaining as prominent as they did in tribal days. This was experienced with the British policy of 'hostile environment' when a web of immigration controls was enforced. Employers in all sectors were to check a person's immigration status, and prospective landlords were obliged to check would-be tenants. In February 2019 this was challenged in the High Court as 'the hostile environment is by its very nature discriminatory, so it comes as no surprise that it encourages discriminatory – even racist – behaviour'.[10] This policy was prepared by Theresa May as Home Secretary, and 'doctors, social workers and teachers were forced to act as border guards. Every job application and health emergency could end in arrest, detention, or summary deportation. [Newly arrived immigrants were obliged to pass a Citizen's Test which in its administration is prone to corruption]. Under the hostile environment, fear and penury are systematically imposed on undocumented migrants, legal EU and non-EU migrants and Britons of colour, in an attempt to make Britain as cruel and unwelcoming as possible to those who do not belong here. Post-Brexit, the hostile environment is spreading, jeopardising even those middle-class migrants who previously thought themselves safe'.[11] It was all rather reflective of Enoch

Powell's infamous speech dubbed *Rivers of Blood* given in 1968 in Birmingham, which also led to deep social unrest and division.

However, although many saw these political demands as warning signs of aggressive nationalism, the right-wing in the UK appears mild when compared to the right-wing in France and Hungary. Enoch Powell had lost support from his colleagues and his hitherto good reputation was tarnished, and today the Windrush crisis has been highlighted in parliament because of the public outcry as the facts emerged, with major efforts to repair the situation. Each country has its variations and divisions, but the Papal fears expressed earlier by Pope Francis, who had to tread with care in the political arena, were undoubtedly based on the resurgence of the right-wing which has risen on the wave of anti-immigration issues. It is the appearance of aggressive nationalism which has long created the 'them and us' issue treating other humans outside the nation as ethnically unfit for residence. Nationalism is not necessarily a right-wing phenomenon but its close association with the extreme right-wing is clearly indicated in recent history and current times.

The world has experienced many changes, but some elements have remained part of humankind's makeup. Aggressive nationalism appears as a major factor with nations, despite the lessons of the past, still vying for expansionism, influence, domination, and wealth. Furthermore, the same ingredients of ethnicity or race, language, culture, religious beliefs are used to stir up the emotion required by aggressive nationalism. Totalitarianism in its different guises persists, and extremists in politics and religion increase as does the power of the right-wing which in extreme leads to dictatorship as the extreme left can lead to communism.

Final Thoughts

Speculatively from the time humankind emerged, and certainly from the earliest recorded history it can be taken for granted that most people have built-in propensities or distinctive traits in terms of their attitude towards one another. Although each human has his or her own individuality, and not everyone is dominated by one singular viewpoint, there are some features which are often held in common. It is well known that all wild animals are often suspicious of strangers even of the same breed, it is often based on an instinctive need for self-defence or protecting its resources area. This old trait of suspicion has been a feature of humankind's life on this planet, and it is often triggered by elements which are so powerful and extensive it could, in a cynical way, be described as part of our genetic makeup as it undoubtedly is with so-called wild animals. To recap what has been mentioned in the main text, suspicions often surface when the stranger speaks in a different language making it sound like a code implying dangerous intentions. Another major factor is ethnicity and race, especially if the stranger has different coloured skin, hair, or eyes and for some looks alien. The sense of inbuilt distrust in the newcomer increases over different religious beliefs and cultures. The European history surveyed in this study is inundated with these behavioural traits, from the earliest of times to this day. As animals have their own territories so from the beginning of time with cavemen, humans have designated their own areas, which became their 'home' which was intrinsic to their way of life. This developed the human need to belong to a defined area, from tribal hills to a region, then a country with its own way of life. From the earliest of times man's penchant for coveting a neighbour's possessions can be found in the Old Testament decalogue and read to this day by Christians and Jews.* This has been an ongoing issue throughout history wanting to increase the size of the homeland and seeking better climes. This inclination has often been led by leading individuals seeking to increase their power, prestige, and wealth, be they tribal chieftains, despots, dictators and to this day with modern forms of various forms of government. These factors

---

* 'Thou shalt not covet thy neighbour's house, thou shalt not covet thy neighbour's wife, nor his manservant, nor his maidservant, nor his ox, nor his ass, nor anything that is thy neighbour's'. Exodus Chapter 20; v.17.

are all the propensities of human behaviour and are the ingredients of aggressive nationalism, and they have their roots in man's deepest history.

Nationalism, as argued in the text, is not patriotism, but the two words cause confusion because they can be in some dictionaries uncomfortably close in terms of definition. In general terms nationalism can be seen as reasonable as after the French defeat at Waterloo when it was portrayed as a celebration of courage against overwhelming odds, and as de Gaulle attempted in 1940 to try and maintain a sense of dignity in the country. The British did the same with the rallying cry after Dunkirk. In this sense this type of nationalism can hold countries together in fraught times, but in reality, this vague use of the word nationalism is closer to patriotism.

As noted in the main text, nationalism as a term needs a number of adjectives to verify precisely what is meant, and it can have positive and negative elements making nationalism a word controlled by these essential adjectives. This book has focused on the term aggressive nationalism, which invariably surfaces in every generation because of humankind's incessant need to expand territory and power, so aggressive and expansionist often fall under the same heading. Irredentist nationalism is about reclaiming homeland taken by a victor, or it becomes secessionist nationalism if it means chasing an occupier out of one's own homeland. This is generally found to be more acceptable in terms of human history, but it often carries some inherent weaknesses which can lead to expansionism. Unification nationalism is typified by related regions forming a single state, and isolationist nationalism when a country behaves like a tortoise, wanting nothing to do by withdrawing into its shell ignoring the neighbours. Cultural, sometimes called Romantic or Revisionist nationalism is when the past is explored for a sense of self-identity, which can create a sense of unity or be used for assertion with its natural dangers of fermenting aggression and a sense of superiority.

The main text of the book refers to the many shades of meaning, but it has focused on the dangerous aggressive nationalism as this element has made humankind's existence one of continuous wars, suffering, creating our own hell, making wild animal life look more civilised. Aggressive nationalism demands a reaction of support from the masses, the overall population. In early days, the battle cry of the tribal warriors would stir up their people, later it would be monarchs and their dynasties, and they shared in common what this book has called the necessary ingredients to bring fervour to a boiling point. These ingredients mentioned above, race, ethnicity, language, religious belief, culture, and tradition have always been and remain powerful factors within humankind. The survey of European history has shown this aspect to be a consistent factor throughout history in every country. When this nationalistic impulse embroiled religion or race and the other ingredients the results were always brutal and horrific. In trying to understand the extreme violence of the twentieth century Niall Ferguson summarised them as 'ethnic conflict, economic volatility and empires in decline' are prevalent.[1] These factors are all part and parcel of a variety of forms of nationalism, stirred by a mixture of the necessary ingredients.

The aggressive form of nationalism has become a tainted word because it was generally associated with expansionism and the need for power and influence. It was self-evident in the Armenian massacres and many others, but it was the Nazi policy in which it appeared to reach its hellish depths. However, since then it has been experienced yet again in the Balkans, Rwanda, and Myanmar to mention just a few. The propensity of regarding a person's race, ethnicity, or religion as necessary to challenge and eradicate them can only be described as pure evil. It is not without historical irony that *Richt Oder Unrecht – Mein Vaterland* (My Country Right of Wrong) was the notice which was placed by the opening gates of the notorious Buchenwald Concentration Camp.[2]

Aggressive nationalism can be too easily stirred because the propensities and ingredients mentioned above are deep in the human psyche, and once unleashed always lead to war and suffering. There are still ardent cries of a nationalistic nature to this day with, as noted in the final chapter, the upsurge of extreme right-wing nationalistic movements across Europe both in the West and the East, in nearly all the European nations from the more powerful to the smaller nations. The prominence of President Putin's authoritarian regime and his attack on Ukraine are more than significant but nevertheless a red alert. The right-wing government of Israel has stirred up feelings of hatred on racial and religious grounds against the Palestinians which is also another red alert. Even in democratic America President Trump's rallying call to 'Make America Great again' has indicated a high degree of aggressive nationalism, recalling that he has the support of the extreme right-wing of the evangelical Bible Belt. There is nothing wrong with being right-wing, but it becomes dangerous when it reaches extreme levels utilising the ingredients of aggressive nationalism. Within the UK with Brexit's slogan 'I want my country back', were reverberations on the same theme. Other areas around the globe are also making this continuous nationalistic outcry. As noted above, as this book is being finished the 2024 British elections are underway, and a new Party called Reform led by Nigel Farage has appeared with some concerned that this is a new extreme right-wing party emerging on the political landscape.

It is not, as it is nearly always claimed, for historians to pass moral judgement, but when faced with events such as the Holocaust, Rwanda, the Armenian massacres, and many other incidents of mass destruction, all too frequently caused by aggressive nationalism, it is unnecessary to make a moral assessment because it is self-evident. It is a human problem of not being able to accept others of a different ethnicity, culture, or religion as fellow human beings, followed by the demand that they and their lands should be occupied, dominated or annihilated. It only needs a populist leader to take the reins in any country, democratic or otherwise, for some form of nationalism to be used. Such populist leaders are not always the brightest and best, but they too often appeal to the masses with their views. In 1999 a Kruger and Dunning research unit concluded how some people have a strong tendency not to be able to recognise their own incompetence. This happened with Hitler and Stalin, but the horrific warning is that only the more astute can recognise – often too late – when such leaders rise to national power.

In 2019 *The Times* newspaper ran an article entitled 'Emboldened Far-Right has eyes on the prize of Brussels'. It reflected the issues raised at the end of this study regarding the populist right-wing in Europe, suggesting that there is a new populist right-wing across Europe, with the journalist writing that neo-fascists are proudly back on the streets of Italy… 'about 1,000 fascists sympathisers gave stiff-armed salutes and clashed with the riot police in Milan'.[3] The article drew the reader's attention to fascist sympathisers in Milan, a picture of Jean-Marie Le Pen (looking remarkably like Hitler) presiding over a ceremony for Joan of Arc, the nationalistic icon of medieval France, and further pictures of a gathering of far-right tough-looking tattooed extremists protesting in Germany. The traditional centre-left and centre-right parties which have dominated so long appear to now always be in danger of losing their majority, if only because there seems a need to reject the status quo. Many voters are being attracted by the aggressive nationalistic extreme right-wing promising a crackdown on immigration and more power for national parliaments. Hungary's Prime Minister Viktor Orbán, who in December 2023 upset Ukraine and Romania by wearing a 'Greater Hungary' scarf is a typical example, but even strong-minded democratic nations are developing some of these trends. Referring to the 2019 European Parliament *The Times* correspondent Bruno Waterfield wrote that 'there were gains for populist and right-wing nationalists across Europe last night as the EU's traditional centre ground fragmented…with far-right and ultra-nationalists on course for victory in France and Italy', and he could have added the UK as well with the sudden rise of the Brexit Party.[4]

This writer does not believe in cyclic history but there are some punishing memories of the early twentieth century, and history has failed to make the dangers clear. The clarion call which populists nearly always invoke is characterised by summoning aggressive nationalism with all its dangerous undertones. Aggressive nationalism has proved to be dangerously deep with long-rooted impulse of human nature which is too easily harnessed by ignorant bigots to this day. Some people have started to think that 1930s Europe is again showing itself in the current political climate, and they have some justification in this line of thinking.

Aggressive nationalism has its roots in the ingredients of ethnicity, race, language, culture and religious belief from the start of humankind's history, it is a part of human nature and the Christian theme of 'love thy neighbour as thyself' has been ignored at the expense of war and suffering, and furthermore, it is going to continue because of one other unmentioned human problem, the failure to learn from past mistakes by ignoring the lessons of history.

Notes

Chapter 1
1. Orwell, George, *Notes on Nationalism* (London: Penguin Books, 2018, but first written in 1945), p.2.
2. Acton, Lord, 'Nationality' in *Essays on Freedom and Power* (London: 1956), p.169 (to be found in Create Space Independent Publishing Platform, October 2013).
3. Chadwick, H. Munro, *The Nationalities of Europe* (Cambridge: CUO, 1945), p.vii.
4. Ibid.
5. Davies, Norman, *Europe: A History* (London: Pimlico, 1997), p.44.
6. See Orwell, George, *Notes on Nationalism* (London: Penguin Books, 2018).
7. Harari, Yuval Noah, *21 Lessons for the 21st Century* (London: Jonathan Cape, 2018), p.219.
8. Ibid., p.272.
9. Van der Veer, Peter, 'Nationalism and Religion' in Breuilly, John (Ed.), *The Oxford Handbook of the History of Nationalism* (Oxford: OUP, 2016), p.655.
10. Ibid., p.669.
11. Evans, Richard J., *The Pursuit of Power: Europe 1815–1914* (New York: Penguin Books, 2016), p.266.
12. Grosby, Steven, *Nationalism: A Very Short Introduction* (Oxford: OUP, 2005), p.106.
13. O'Brien, W.V., (Freedman, Lawrence, Ed.) *War* (Oxford: OUP, 1994), p.181.
14. Heizer, Robert F., *Languages, Territories, and Names of California Indian Tribes* (Berkeley: University of California, 1966), p.8.
15. Davies, Norman, *Europe: A History*, p.220.
16. Chadwick, H. Munro, *The Nationalities of Europe*, p.113.
17. Genesis Chapter 11.
18. Davies, Norman, *Europe: A History*, p.220.
19. Chadwick, H. Munro, *The Nationalities of Europe*, p.20.
20. Ibid., pp.48–9.
21. Burke, Peter, 'Nationalisms and Vernaculars, 1500–1880' in Breuilly, John (Ed.), *The Oxford Handbook of the History of Nationalism* (Oxford: OUP, 2016), p.29.
22. Ibid., p.3.
23. Ferguson, Niall, *The War of the World: History's Age of Hatred* (London: Allen Lane, 2006) p.liii.
24. Porter, Roy, *England in the Eighteenth Century* (London: The Folio Society, 1998), p.11.
25. Ferguson, Niall, *The War of the World: History's Age of Hatred*, p.76.
26. Ibid., p.77.
27. Ferguson, Niall, *The War of the World: History's Age of Hatred*, p.164.
28. Grosby, Steven, *Nationalism: A Very Short Introduction* (Oxford: OUP, 2005), p.98.
29. Ferguson, Niall, *The War of the World: History's Age of Hatred*, p.32.
30. Ibid., p.249.
31. Quoted in ibid., p.268.
32. Ibid., p.273.

33. Van der Veer, Peter, 'Nationalism and Religion' in Breuilly, John (Ed.), *The Oxford Handbook of the History of Nationalism* (Oxford: OUP, 2106) p.657.
34. Ibid., p.669.
35. Solzhenitsyn, Aleksandr I., *The Gulag Archipelago 1918–1956* (London: The Harvill Press, 1985), p.285.

Chapter 2
1. Fisher, H.A.L., *A History of Europe* (London: Eyre and Spottiswoode, 1949), Preface.
2. Porter, Roy, *England in the Eighteenth Century*, p.47.
3. Hodge, F.W., 'Tribe' in *Handbook of American Indians North of Mexico*, Vol. 2 (Bulletin 30, Smithsonian Institution, Bureau of American Ethnology), p.185.
4. Quoted in Fried, Morton H., *The Notion of Tribe* (London: Publishing Company, 1975), p.9.
5. Chadwick, H. Munro, *The Nationalities of Europe*, p.159.
6. Ibid., p.165.
7. II Samuel Chapter 8, v.12.
8. I Samuel 18, v.25.
9. Bede, *Historia Ecclesiastica*, quoted in Chadwick, H.M., *The Origins of the English Nation* (1907). Now in reprint by Cliveden Press, 1983.
10. Kroeber, A.L., *Anthropology* (New York: Harcourt-Brace, 1948), p.227.
11. Harris, Marvin, *The Rise of Anthropological Theory* (New York: Thomas Y. Crowell, 1968), p.106.
12. Stenton, F.M., *Anglo-Saxon England* (Oxford: Clarendon Press, 1967).
13. Trevelyan, G.M., *History of England* (London: Longman, 1966), p.6.
14. Legum, Colin, 'Tribal Survival in the Modern African Political System' (*Journal of Asian and African Studies*, 5: 102–112, 1970), p.103.
15. Hoebel, E., *Man in the Primitive World 2nd Ed* (New York: McGraw-Hill, 1958), p.661.
16. Heizer, Robert F., *Languages, Territories, and Names of California Indian Tribes*, p.8.
17. Fried, Morton H., *The Notion of Tribe*, p.68.
18. Ibid., p.98.
19. Chadwick, H. Munro, *The Nationalities of Europe*, p.143.
20. Ibid., p.198.
21. Plato, *The Republic* (London: Wordsworth Editions, 1997).
22. Aristotle, *The Nicomachean Ethics* (Oxford: OUP, 2009).
23. Howe, Stephen, *Empire: A Very Short Introduction* (Oxford: OUP, 2002), p.42.
24. Ibid., p.42.
25. Chadwick, H. Munro, *The Nationalities of Europe*, p.51.
26. Ibid., p.53.
27. Ibid., p.99.
28. Hobbes, Thomas, *Leviathan* 4, 47.
29. Davies, Norman, *Europe: A History*, p.364.

Chapter 3
1. Davies, Norman, *Europe: A History*, p.408.
2. Ibid., p.409.
3. Ibid., p.468.
4. Quoted in Davies, Norman, *Europe: A History*, p.596.
5. Porter, Roy, *England in the Eighteenth Century*, p.36.
6. Davies, Norman, *Europe: A History*, p.640.

7. Ibid., p.654
8. Quoted in Davies, Norman, *Europe: A History*, p.516.
9. Howe, Stephen, *Empire: A Very Short Introduction*, p.70.
10. Davies, Norman, *Europe: A History*, p.526.
11. Ibid., p.557.
12. Ibid., p.733.
13. See Rowe, Michael, 'The French Revolution, Napoleon, and Nationalism in Europe' in Breuilly, John (Ed.), *The Oxford Handbook of The History of Nationalism* (Oxford: OUP, 2016), p.133.
14. Quoted in Ibid., p.139.
15. Ibid., p.141.

Chapter 4

1. Evans, Richard J., *The Pursuit of Power: Europe 1815–1914*, p.13.
2. Ibid., p.266.
3. Davies, Norman, *Europe: A History*, p.767.
4. Quoted in Conklin, Alice L., *A Mission to Civilize: Republican Idea of Empire in France and West Africa, 1895–1930* (California: Stanford Press, 1997), p.55.
5. Ferguson, Niall, *The War of the World: History's Age of Hatred*, p.lxviii.
6. Davies, Norman, *Europe: A History*, p.869.
7. Darwin, John, 'Nationalism and Imperialism, c.1880–1940' in Breuilly, John (Ed.), *The Oxford Handbook of the History of Nationalism* (Oxford: OUP, 2016), p.341.
8. Quoted in Hudson, Max (Ed.), *William Russell Special Correspondent of The Times* (London: Folio Society, 1996), p.414.
9. Ibid., p.413.
10. Darwin, John, 'Nationalism and Imperialism, c.1880–1940', p.349.
11. Davies, Norman, *Europe: A History*, p.802.
12. Evans, Richard J., *The Pursuit of Power: Europe 1815–1914*, p.557.
13. Davies, Norman, *Europe: A History*, p.812.
14. Eatwell, Roger, 'Fascism and Racism' in Breuilly, John (Ed.), *The Oxford Handbook of the History of Nationalism* (Oxford: OUP, 2016), p.581.
15. Ibid., p.100.
16. Breuilly, John (Ed.), *The Oxford Handbook of the History of Nationalism* (Oxford: OUP, 2016), p.163.
17. Davies, Norman, *Europe: A History*, p.826.
18. Ibid.
19. Hroch, Miroslav, 'National Movements in the Habsburg and Ottoman Empires' in Breuilly, John (Ed.), *The Oxford Handbook of the History of Nationalism* (Oxford: OUP, 2016), p.179.
20. Ibid., p.186.
21. Weeks, Theodore R., 'Separatist Nationalism in the Romanov and Soviet Empires' in Breuilly, John (Ed.), *The Oxford Handbook of the History of Nationalism* (Oxford: OUP, 2016), p.199.
22. O'Brien, W.V., (Freedman, Lawrence, Ed.) *War*, p.180.
23. See the opening pages of Lockhart, R.H. Bruce, *Memoirs of a British Agent* (London: The Folio Society, 2003)
24. Marx, Karl, *The Eighteenth Brumaire of Louis Bonaparte* (London: Allen and Unwin, 1943)
25. Martin, T. in Suny, Ronald G. (Ed.), *The Structure of Soviet History: Essays and Documents* (Oxford: OUP, 2014), p.99.

26. Timasheff, Nicholas in Suny, Ronald G. (Ed.), *The Structure of Soviet History: Essays and Documents* (Oxford: OUP, 2014), p.209.
27. Lewin, Moshe, *The Soviet Century* (London: Verso, 2016), p.129.
28. Evans, Richard J., *The Pursuit of Power: Europe 1815–1914*, p.480.

Chapter 5
1. Davies, Norman, *Europe: A History*, p.901.
2. Ferguson, Niall, *The War of the World: History's Age of Hatred*, p.80.
3. Ibid., p.103.
4. Ibid., p.lxiii.
5. Ibid., p.lx.
6. Ibid., p.xlvi.
7. *Daily Herald*, Cartoonist Will Dyson, 13 May 1919.
8. Ferguson, Niall, *The War of the World: History's Age of Hatred*, p.236.
9. Rubens, Bernice, *Brothers* (London: Abacus, 2002).
10. Ferguson, Niall, *The War of the World: History's Age of Hatred*, p.166.
11. Ibid., p.167.
12. Ibid., p.325.
13. Davies, Norman, *Europe: A History*, pp.945–8.
14. Hassell, Ulrich von, *The Von Hassell Diaries, 1938–1944: The Story of the Forces Against Hitler Inside Germany* (London: Frontline Books, 2011), p.40.
15. Ferguson, Niall, *The War of the World: History's Age of Hatred*, p.228.
16. Ibid., p.230.
17. Bullard, J. and M. (Eds), *Inside Stalin's Russia: The Diaries of Reader Bullard, 1930–1934* (Oxfordshire: Day Books, 2000), p.118.
18. Harari, Yuval Noah, *21 Lessons for the 21st Century*, p.238.
19. Davies, Norman, *Europe: A History*, p.969.
20. Hassell, Ulrich von, *The Von Hassell Diaries, 1938–1944*, p.44.
21. Zimmer, Oliver, 'Nationalism in Europe, 1918–45' in Breuilly, John (Ed.), *The Oxford Handbook of the History of Nationalism* (Oxford: OUP, 2016), p.415.
22. This theme generally reflects the insights of Oliver Zimmer in Zimmer, Oliver, 'Nationalism in Europe, 1918–45', pp.414–431.
23. Zimmer, Oliver, 'Nationalism in Europe, 1918–45', p.416.
24. Eatwell, Roger, 'Fascism and Racism', p.588.
25. Ibid., p.586.
26. Ibid., p.574.
27. Zimmer, Oliver, 'Nationalism in Europe, 1918–45', p.426.
28. Gellately, Robert, *Stalin's Curse: Battling for Communism in War and Cold War* (Oxford: OUP, 2013).
29. Davies, Norman, *Europe: A History*, p.1013.
30. Ibid., p.1045.
31. Owen, James, *Nuremberg: Evil on Trial* (London: Headline Review, 2007), p.109.
32. Telford, Taylor, *The Anatomy of the Nuremberg Trials* (New York: Alfred A. Knopf, 1992), p.24.

Chapter 6
1. Davies, Norman, *Europe: A History*, p.1075.
2. Ibid., p.1085.
3. Ibid., pp.1086–7.

4. Gorlizki, Yoram & Khlevniuk, Oleg in Suny, Ronald G., *The Structure of Soviet History: Essays and Documents* (Oxford: OUP, 2014), p.322.
5. Alliluyeva, Svetlana, *Twenty Letters to a Friend* (New York: Harper & Row, 1967), pp.6–7.
6. Montefiore, Sebag, *Stalin: The Court of the Red Tsar* (London: Weidenfeld & Nicolson, 2003), p.570.
7. Sudoplatov, Pavel & Anatoli, *Special Tasks: The Memoirs of an Unwanted Witness – A Soviet Spymaster* (London: Little, Brown and Company, 1994), p.339.
8. Davies, Norman, *Europe: A History*, p.1122.
9. Ibid., p.1124.
10. Rutar, Sabine, 'Nationalism in South-Eastern Europe, 1970–2000' in Breuilly, John (Ed.), *The Oxford Handbook of the History of Nationalism* (Oxford: OUP, 2016), p.516.
11. Ibid., p.529
12. Orwell, George, *Notes on Nationalism*, p.14.
13. See Caplan, Richard, 'International Intervention in Nationalistic Disputes' in Breuilly, John (Ed.), *The Oxford Handbook of the History of Nationalism* (Oxford: OUP, 2016), p.560.
14. Ibid., p.563
15. See Guibernau, Montserrat, 'Nationalism without States' in Breuilly, John (Ed.), *The Oxford Handbook of the History of Nationalism* (Oxford: OUP, 2016), pp.592ff.
16. Quoted in Ibid., p.592.
17. Sangster, Andrew, *Probing the Enigma of Franco* (Newcastle: Cambridge Scholars, 2018), pp. 25–6.
18. *The Times*, 28 April 2018.
19. Carlin, John, *The Times*, 16 February 2019, pp.34–5.
20. Guibernau, Montserrat, 'Nationalism without States', p.608.

Chapter 7
1. Burleigh, Michael, *The Best of Times, The Worst of Times: A History of Now* (London: Pan Books, 2017), p.71.
2. Ibid., p.149.
3. Lucas, Edward, 'Cutting Putin Down to Size' in *The Times*, 9 February 2019.
4. Burleigh, Michael, *The Best of Times, The Worst of Times*, p.157.
5. Ibid., p.21.
6. Wright, Tony, *British Politics: A Very Short Introduction* (Oxford: OUP, 2013), p.8.
7. Vallely, Paul, *Church Times*, 18 April 2019.
8. Williams, Hattie, *Church Times*, 11 January 2019.
9. Burleigh, Michael, *The Best of Times, The Worst of Times*, p.41.
10. See Iberty, I. (Ed.) *A Guide to the Hostile Environment* at www.libertyhumanrights.org.uk/sites/default/files/
11. Broomfield, Matt, 'How Theresa May's Hostile Environment Created an Underworld' in the *New Statesman*, 19 December 2017.

Final Thoughts
1. Ferguson, Niall, *The War of the World: History's Age of Hatred*, p.xli.
2. See Dronfield, Jeremy, *The Boy Who Followed His Father into Auschwitz* (London: Michael Joseph imprint of Penguin Books; 2019), p.48.
3. *The Times*, 4 May 2019, pp.36–7.
4. Ibid., 27 May 2019, p.10.

Bibliography

Acton, Lord, 'Nationality' in *Essays on Freedom and Power* (London: 1956) (to be found in Create Space Independent Publishing Platform, October 2013)
Alliluyeva, Svetlana, *Twenty Letters to a Friend* (New York: Harper & Row, 1967)
Aristotle, *The Nicomachean Ethics* (Oxford: OUP, 2009)
Bede, *Historia Ecclesiastica*, quoted in Chadwick, H.M., *The Origins of the English Nation* (1907). Now in reprint by Cliveden Press, 1983.
Brent, Jonathan & Naumov, Vladimir P., *Stalin's Last Crime: The Plot against the Jewish Doctors, 1948–1953* (New York, Harper Collins, 2003)
Breuilly, John (Ed.), *The Oxford Handbook of the History of Nationalism* (Oxford: OUP, 2016)
Bullard, J. and M. (Eds), *Inside Stalin's Russia: The Diaries of Reader Bullard, 1930–1934* (Oxfordshire: Day Books, 2000)
Burke, Peter, 'Nationalisms and Vernaculars, 1500–1880' in Breuilly, John (Ed.), *The Oxford Handbook of the History of Nationalism* (Oxford: OUP, 2016)
Burleigh, Michael, *The Best of Times, The Worst of Times: A History of Now* (London: Pan Books, 2017)
Caplan, Richard, 'International Intervention in Nationalistic Disputes' in Breuilly, John (Ed.), *The Oxford Handbook of the History of Nationalism* (Oxford: OUP, 2016)
Chadwick, H. Munro, *The Nationalities of Europe* (Cambridge: CUO, 1945)
Conklin, Alice L., *A Mission to Civilize: Republican Idea of Empire in France and West Africa, 1895–1930* (California: Stanford Press, 1997)
Darwin, John, 'Nationalism and Imperialism, c.1880–1940' in Breuilly, John (Ed.), *The Oxford Handbook of the History of Nationalism* (Oxford: OUP, 2016)
Davies, Norman, *Europe: A History* (London: Pimlico, 1997)
Dronfield, Jeremy, *The Boy Who Followed His Father into Auschwitz* (London: Michael Joseph imprint of Penguin Books; 2019)
Eatwell, Roger, 'Fascism and Racism' in Breuilly, John (Ed.), *The Oxford Handbook of the History of Nationalism* (Oxford: OUP, 2016)
Evans, Richard J., *The Pursuit of Power: Europe 1815–1914* (New York: Penguin Books, 2016)
Ferguson, Niall, *The War of the World: History's Age of Hatred* (London: Allen Lane, 2006)
Fisher, H.A.L., *A History of Europe* (London: Eyre and Spottiswoode, 1949)
Fried, Morton H., *The Notion of Tribe* (London: Publishing Company, 1975)
Gellately, Robert, *Stalin's Curse: Battling for Communism in War and Cold War* (Oxford: OUP, 2013)
Gorlizki, Yoram & Khlevniuk, Oleg in Suny, Ronald G., *The Structure of Soviet History: Essays and Documents* (Oxford: OUP, 2014)
Grosby, Steven, *Nationalism: A Very Short Introduction* (Oxford: OUP, 2005)
Guibernau, Montserrat, 'Nationalism without States' in Breuilly, John (Ed.), *The Oxford Handbook of the History of Nationalism* (Oxford: OUP, 2016)
Harari, Yuval Noah, *21 Lessons for the 21st Century* (London: Jonathan Cape, 2018)
Harris, Marvin, *The Rise of Anthropological Theory* (New York: Thomas Y. Crowell, 1968)

Hassell, Ulrich von, *The Von Hassell Diaries, 1938–1944: The Story of the Forces Against Hitler Inside Germany* (London: Frontline Books, 2011)
Heizer, Robert F., *Languages, Territories, and Names of California Indian Tribes* (Berkeley: University of California, 1966)
Hobbes, Thomas, *Leviathan*
Hodge, F.W., 'Tribe' in *Handbook of American Indians North of Mexico*, Vol. 2 (Bulletin 30, Smithsonian Institution, Bureau of American Ethnology)
Hoebel, E., *Man in the Primitive World 2nd Ed* (New York: McGraw-Hill, 1958)
Howe, Stephen, *Empire: A Very Short Introduction* (Oxford: OUP, 2002)
Hroch, Miroslav, 'National Movements in the Habsburg and Ottoman Empires' in Breuilly, John (Ed.), *The Oxford Handbook of the History of Nationalism* (Oxford: OUP, 2016)
Hudson, Max (Ed.), *William Russell Special Correspondent of The Times* (London: Folio Society, 1996)
Kroeber, A.L., *Anthropology* (New York: Harcourt-Brace, 1948)
Legum, Colin, 'Tribal Survival in the Modern African Political System' (*Journal of Asian and African Studies*, 5: 102–112, 1970)
Lewin, Moshe, *The Soviet Century* (London: Verso, 2016)
Lockhart, R.H. Bruce, *Memoirs of a British Agent* (London: The Folio Society, 2003)
Martin, T. in Suny, Ronald G. (Ed.), *The Structure of Soviet History: Essays and Documents* (Oxford: OUP, 2014)
Marx, Karl, *The Eighteenth Brumaire of Louis Bonaparte* (London: Allen and Unwin, 1943)
Montefiore, Sebag, *Stalin: The Court of the Red Tsar* (London: Weidenfeld & Nicolson, 2003)
O'Brien, W.V., (Freedman, Lawrence, Ed.) *War* (Oxford: OUP, 1994)
Orwell, George, *Notes on Nationalism* (London: Penguin Books, 2018, but first written in 1945)
Owen, James, *Nuremberg: Evil on Trial* (London: Headline Review, 2007)
Porter, Roy, *England in the Eighteenth Century* (London: The Folio Society, 1998)
Plato, *The Republic* (London: Wordsworth Editions, 1997)
Rowe, Michael, 'The French Revolution, Napoleon, and Nationalism in Europe' in Breuilly, John (Ed.), *The Oxford Handbook of The History of Nationalism* (Oxford: OUP, 2016)
Rutar, Sabine, 'Nationalism in South-Eastern Europe, 1970–2000' in Breuilly, John (Ed.), *The Oxford Handbook of the History of Nationalism* (Oxford: OUP, 2016)
Sangster, Andrew, *Probing the Enigma of Franco* (Newcastle: Cambridge Scholars, 2018)
Solzhenitsyn, Aleksandr I., *The Gulag Archipelago 1918–1956* (London: The Harvill Press, 1985)
Stenton, F.M., *Anglo-Saxon England* (Oxford: Clarendon Press, 1967)
Sudoplatov, Pavel & Anatoli, *Special Tasks: The Memoirs of an Unwanted Witness – A Soviet Spymaster* (London: Little, Brown and Company, 1994)
Telford, Taylor, *The Anatomy of the Nuremberg Trials* (New York: Alfred A. Knopf, 1992)
Timasheff, Nicholas in Suny, Ronald G. (Ed.), *The Structure of Soviet History: Essays and Documents* (Oxford: OUP, 2014)
Trevelyan, G.M., *History of England* (London: Longman, 1966)
Van der Veer, Peter, 'Nationalism and Religion' in Breuilly, John (Ed.), *The Oxford Handbook of the History of Nationalism* (Oxford: OUP, 2016)
Weeks, Theodore R., 'Separatist Nationalism in the Romanov and Soviet Empires' in Breuilly, John (Ed.), *The Oxford Handbook of the History of Nationalism* (Oxford: OUP, 2016)
Wright, Tony, *British Politics: A Very Short Introduction* (Oxford: OUP, 2013)
Zimmer, Oliver, 'Nationalism in Europe, 1918–45' in Breuilly, John (Ed.), *The Oxford Handbook of the History of Nationalism* (Oxford: OUP, 2016)

Index

Absolutism, 53, 67
Adenauer, Konrad, 132, 135–6
Age of Enlightenment, 56, 60
Age of Reason, 52, 53, 57, 60
Albania,
   history, 57, 95, 128, 149
Al-Qaeda, 158, 160
America,
   history, 60, 103, 109, 120, 127, 167–8
   recent times 16, 157, 159–60, 167–9, 179
Ancient Powers of Greece and Rome, 28
Anschluss, 112, 131
Antonescu, General, 117
Armenian massacres, 106, 179
Arrow Cross, Hungarian Movement, 117, 171
Attlee, Clement, 129, 133, 137
Austria,
   history, 58, 62, 81, 89, 90, 140
   recent times, 172

Balance of Power, 54, 70, 74
Balkan Wars (1990s), 148–50
Belgium,
   history, 122, 137
   recent times, 170, 173
Benelux, 133, 137, 138
Benelux Treaty (March 1948), 133
Beria, Lavrenty, 6, 97–8, 141
Berlin blockade 133–4
Biden, President, 158, 169
Bismarck, Herbert von, 75, 80, 85, 88
Black Death, 11, 45
Blair, Tony, 152, 158
Bonaparte, Napoleon, 55, 68–72, 74, 125
Bosnia,
   history, 82, 92, 95, 149
Brandt, Willy, 136, 146
Brexit, xi, 33, 87, 107, 137, 140, 154, 168, 170–2, 175, 179–80
Brezhnev, Leonid, 110, 141–2, 144
Briand-Kellogg Pact, 109
Bulgaria,
   history, 57, 94–5, 128, 144
Bush, President, 146, 152, 158–9, 167
Byzantine Empire, 31, 38, 43, 141

Calvin, John, 17, 51
Catalonia, 137, 153–5, 174
Ceaușescu, Nicolae, 144, 147
Charlemagne, Emperor, 33, 37, 80
Charles VI-VII (Hapsburgs), 57
China,
   history, 24, 30, 165
   recent times, 18, 156–7, 165–6, 169
Churchill, Winston, 112, 120, 124–7, 129, 132–3
Cold War, 100, 124, 130, 133, 139, 144, 146, 148, 150, 152, 164, 167
Concordat of Worms (1122), 40
Congress of Berlin (June–July 1878), 81
Congress of Vienna, 70, 80, 89, 104
Crimean War, 57, 81, 94
Croatia,
   history, 91, 149
Cromwell, Oliver, 56, 64
Cuban Missile Crisis, 141, 144–5
Czechoslovakia,
   history, 90, 115, 144, 147

Denmark,
   history, 35, 64
   recent times, 173
Dynasties Appear, 34–5

EEC, 133, 136–7, 139, 162
Egypt,
   history, 24
Emperor Joseph I Habsburgs, 57, 89
Emperor Justinian, 5, 31
England,
   history, 22, 26, 39, 45, 56, 63, 64, 83, 116, 137, 139
   recent times, 33, 140, 161, 170–1, 175, 179
English Bill of Rights in 1689, 68
Erasmus of Rotterdam, 50
Erdoğan, President, 162
European Unity, 138–40

Farage, Nigel, 168, 171, 179
Feudalism, 37
Feudal System across Europe, 21, 26, 34, 37–8, 40, 94

Finland,
  history, 121, 139
  recent times, 173
First World War, 3, 10, 12, 90–1, 94, 96–7, 100–102, 104, 109, 113–18, 120, 125, 129, 175
France,
  history, 21, 34, 38–9, 44–5, 55, 63, 67–70, 72, 80, 116, 122, 136
  recent times, 14, 171
Franco, Francisco, 55, 108, 110, 116–17, 123–4, 135, 137, 153, 174
  manipulating, 123
  power-seeking, 111, 116
  totalitarian leader, 112
French Revolution, 53, 55, 67–9, 71, 73–5, 83, 85, 87, 93, 97

Garibaldi, Giuseppe, 88, 95
Gaulle, Charles de, 134, 136, 139, 178
Gaza Conflict 2023, 14, 17, 19, 99, 152, 156, 160, 165, 169
Germany,
  history, 39, 44, 52, 58, 65, 72, 80, 88, 101, 106, 110, 118, 132, 136, 143, 147
  recent times, 161, 172
Goebbels, Jospeh, 12, 108, 119, 133
Gorbachev, Mikhail, 142, 146, 148
Göring, Hermann, 122, 125, 130
Greece,
  history, 93, 128, 137
  recent times, 161, 174

Habsburg Dynasty, 5, 34, 44, 46, 48, 57–8, 65, 74–5, 88–93, 102
Hassell, Ulrich von, 86, 108, 112
Heath, Edward, 137, 139
Helsinki Final Act (1975), 145
Herzegovina,
  history, 151
Himmler, Heinrich, 13, 86, 109, 119
Hitler,
  manipulating, 92, 120
  power-seeking, 18, 109
  racist, 115, 119, 121
Hohenzollern Dynasty, 89, 94
Horthy, Admiral, 104, 117
Hungary,
  history, 34, 57, 89, 104, 117, 128, 141, 144
  recent times, 78, 171, 173, 180
Hussein, Saddam, 157–8

Industrial Revolution, 66, 76–7
Intellectual Progress, 28, 47, 49, 54
Iran, 157–9, 161, 164, 169

Iraq, 152, 157–8, 160–1, 167
Ireland,
  history, 51, 56, 137
ISIS, 160–2
Israel,
  history, 24
Italy,
  history, 30, 44, 50, 82, 86–8, 118, 136
  recent times, 173

Jewish Diaspora, 98–9, 114

Kaiser Wilhelm II, 80, 96, 101
Katyń massacres, 121, 130
Khrushchev, Nikta, 141–3, 145
King Carol II of Romania, 117
King Charles I of England, 16, 64
King Charles II of England, 35, 56, 64
King Charles XII of Sweden, 57, 59, 70
King Christian I of Denmark, 35
King Edward I of England, 45
King Edward VIII of England, 112
King Francis I of France, 62
King Frederick William III of Prussia, 72
King George I of England, 35
King Henry II of England, 5, 21, 22, 39, 47
King Henry IV of England, 49
King Henry V of England, 45, 49
King Henry VII of England, 35, 46
King Henry VIII of England 51, 55, 64
King James I of England, 36
King John of England, 22, 39
King Louis IX of France, 46
King Louis XIII of France, 63
King Louis XIV of France, 53–5, 57, 63
King Louis XVI of France, 55, 60, 67–8
King Richard III, 46
King Zog of Albania, 95
Knox, John, 17, 51
Kohl, Helmut, 136, 147

League of Nations, 103, 107, 111
Lenin, Vladimir, 16, 19, 96–8, 101, 103–105, 109, 148, 164
Lithuania,
  history, 43, 65
Locarno Treaty, 107
Luther, Martin, 17, 50, 51
Luxemburg,
  history, 137

Macedonia,
  history, 95, 150
Mao Zedong, 110, 140, 146, 165
Maria Theresa, 58

Marx, Karl, 76, 85, 97, 109, 140–1, 165
Molotov-Ribbentrop Pact, 108, 113
Mongols, 37, 38, 41, 43
Montenegro,
   history, 57, 92
Mosely, Oswald, 116
Mountbatten, Earl, 134
Mussolini,
   power-seeking, 18, 108, 118, 124
Myanmar, 151, 179

Napoleon III, 75
Napoleon, Louis, 87
Nationalism,
   aggressive, viii, xi, 2, 5, 10, 23, 30, 39–40, 42, 44–6, 49, 60–2, 66, 73–5, 79, 82–3, 85, 97, 102, 108, 115, 119, 121, 123, 126, 131, 142, 148, 152, 158, 176, 178–80
   banal, xii, 27, 82, 127
   colonialism issue, xii, 18, 53, 60–1, 78–80
   cultural issues, 14
   defined by a country's laws, 5, 21–2, 32
   democratic, 155
   ethnic-racial issues, 9–13, 18, 106, 109, 113, 115, 134, 151, 161, 170, 175
   in general, xi, 2–3, 29, 36, 71–2, 85, 100, 113
   irredentist, xi, 3, 101, 114, 120
   isolationist, xi, 3, 120, 126
   language issues, 6–9, 26, 74, 89, 90–1, 93–4, 177
   religious issues, 14–17, 31–2, 41, 47, 66, 161, 177
   revisionist, xi, 113
   secessionist, 3, 70, 75, 120, 126, 133–4
   seeking power issues, 18, 28, 132
   suspicious of strangers issue, 20–2, 161, 177
NATO, 91, 133–4, 136–7, 139–40, 143, 147, 149, 152, 162, 164, 167–8, 170, 174
Netherlands,
   history, 5, 63, 137
   recent times, 174
Nuremberg Race Laws, 119
Nuremberg Trials, 129–30, 132

Obama, President, 161, 167
Operation Barbarossa, 72, 124
Ottoman Dynasty, 5, 57, 59, 65–6, 75, 81, 83, 89, 91, 93–5, 102, 105, 114

Paris Agreement (2015), 3, 157, 168
Patriotism, defining, xi, 1–2, 74
Pearl Harbour, 123–4
Peasants' Revolt (1381), 45

Pétain, Marshal, 117, 122, 131
Poland,
   history, 59, 65, 89, 114, 132, 143, 146
   recent times, 174
Political Arena, 84–5, 87, 100, 106–10, 112–13, 127, 132, 137, 156, 175
Pope Alexander VI, 5, 48, 50
Pope Boniface VIII, 44
Pope Francis, 172, 176
Pope Gregory, VII 40
Pope Innocent III, 40
Pope Julius II, 50
Pope Leo XIII, 78
Pope Nicholas II, 39
Pope Pius VII, 68
Pope Pius IX, 87
Pope Pius XI, 110
Pope Urban, II 41
Portugal,
   history, 5, 48, 56
Powell, Enoch, 11, 175, 176
Putin, President Vladimir, 16, 24, 59, 96, 98, 104, 139, 148, 156–8, 160, 162–5, 169, 179

Queen Victoria, 35, 101

Rapallo Treaty (1922), 105
Reformation, the, 49–52
Religious Power Politics, 38, 40, 43–4, 46, 50
Revolts of 1848, 5, 74–5, 87
Right-wing Nationalism, 168, 171–5, 180
Rivera, Primo, 111, 153
Romania,
   history, 30, 94, 114, 117, 128, 144
Romanovs, 5, 35, 59, 65, 67, 96, 102–103, 114
Roosevelt, President, 120
Russia,
   history, 33, 35, 39, 47, 59, 65, 81, 96–8, 110, 140–2, 146, 148
   recent times, 19, 157–8, 162–4

Saudi Arabia, 157–61
Scotland
   history, 45, 56, 154
   recent times, 154
Second World War, 2, 10, 27, 93, 95, 99–100, 116, 119–20, 122, 130, 140, 150, 156, 170, 172–3
Serbi,
   history, 70, 92
Slovakia,
   history, 75
Slovenia,
   history, 91

Spain,
   history, 35, 47–8, 56, 63, 111, 116, 137, 153
   recent times, 154, 174
Stalin,
   manipulating, 120, 126
   power-seeking, 18, 72, 128–9, 133
   the nationalist, 98, 126
   totalitarian leader, 101, 109, 129–30
Stresemann, Gustav, 106
Superpowers, viii, 145–6, 156–7, 160
Sweden,
   history, 57, 64, 139
   recent times, 139, 175
Switzerland,
   history, 116, 139
   recent times, 175
Syria, 24, 29, 134, 152, 158, 160–1

Taiwan Issue, 156, 166
Teutonic knights, 40, 43, 46, 65
Thirty Years War, 52, 55
Tiananmen Square, 147, 166
Tito, Josip, 92, 124, 127–8, 142–3, 148
Treaty of Versailles, 70, 100, 103–106, 112, 117, 126, 131
Treaty of Westphalia, 52
Tribe to Nation, 23–7, 30–1, 33–4, 36
Trotsky, Leon, 103–104, 126
Trump, President, xi, 3, 33, 103, 157–9, 168–9, 179

Tsar Alexander II, 11
Tsar Catherine, 59, 69
Tsar Ivan, III 65
Tsar Nicholas II, 35, 67, 96–7
Tsar Peter I, 59
Turkey,
   history, 105–106
   recent times, 162

Ukraine,
   history, 59, 65, 96, 104, 125, 148
   recent times, 156, 163, 165
Ulbricht, Walter, 131, 142

Vichy France, 98, 117, 122, 127, 130–1
Vietnam War, 145, 167–8

Wales,
   history, 86, 154
Wałęsa, Lech, 143, 146
Warsaw Pact, 140, 143–4, 147
Weimar Republic, 105–107, 118
Wycliffe, John, 44

Yeltsin, Boris, 148
Yemen Conflict, 158

Zwingli, Ulrich, 17, 50

Dear Reader,

We hope you have enjoyed this book, but why not share your views on social media? You can also follow our pages to see more about our other products: facebook.com/penandswordbooks or follow us on X @penswordbooks

You can also view our products at www.pen-and-sword.co.uk (UK and ROW) or www.penandswordbooks.com (North America).

To keep up to date with our latest releases and online catalogues, please sign up to our newsletter at: www.pen-and-sword.co.uk/newsletter

If you would like a printed catalogue with our latest books, then please email: enquiries@pen-and-sword.co.uk or telephone: 01226 734555 (UK and ROW) or email: uspen-and-sword@casematepublishers.com or telephone: (610) 853-9131 (North America).

We respect your privacy and we will only use personal information to send you information about our products.

Thank you!